T3-BNW-216

REASON

A PHILOSOPHICAL ESSAY WITH HISTORICAL ILLUSTRATIONS

LONDON
Cambridge University Press
FETTER LANE

NEW YORK · TORONTO
BOMBAY · CALCUTTA · MADRAS
Macmillan

TOKYO
Maruzen Company Ltd

REASON

A PHILOSOPHICAL ESSAY WITH HISTORICAL ILLUSTRATIONS

(COMTE AND MILL
SCHOPENHAUER, VICO
SPINOZA)

BY

THOMAS WHITTAKER

Author of *The Neo-Platonists*

GREENWOOD PRESS, PUBLISHERS
NEW YORK 1968

First published 1934
Reprinted with the permission of
Cambridge University Press

First Greenwood reprinting, 1968

Library of Congress catalogue card number: 68-19298

PRINTED IN THE UNITED STATES OF AMERICA

NOTE

My thanks are due to the editors of *Mind* for permission to reprint two articles; to Messrs T. and T. Clark and to the representatives of Dr James Hastings for permission to reprint the article on "Reason" from *The Encyclopaedia of Religion and Ethics*; and to Messrs A. Constable and Co. for the similar permission as regards the primers of "Comte and Mill" and "Schopenhauer".

T. W.

July 1934

CONTENTS

CHAPTER I

INTRODUCTION

SINCE the time when the antagonism between the school known in England as "Hegelian" and the traditional English philosophy called Empirical or Experiential died down, there seems to have been no definite attempt to sum up the result. Yet one school has not simply vanquished the other and left no more to be said. A very fair-minded view was expressed by Bosanquet, one of the chiefs of the opposition to the typically "English" philosophy. That phase of thought, he declared, does not rank second to any philosophy except that of the ancient Greeks: but, as a drawback, he finds that it had always an insurgent character in relation to other expressions of the national life. It was a non-academical philosophy. Yet he did not deny that the experiential character of English thought is that by which it has impressed the world. As Croom Robertson, from the other side, has said,[1] thinkers who have held opposing theories—theories of *a priori* type, as they are called—on the foundations of human knowledge, have passed relatively into the shade. This, it must be admitted on all sides, is still true. The Hegelian doctrine in England, for a time academically triumphant, has never succeeded on the Continent in getting its claim to be called "the English Idealism" recognised. That name has been reserved for the empirical idealism which descended from Berkeley through Hume and Mill. And outside their own country the chiefs of the Hegelian school are little known. Mill and Spencer remain still for the world at large the last great English thinkers.

In England itself, however, those names have not retained their pre-eminence. The criticisms adapted for English use from Kant and Hegel made it evident that the principles with which the native empirical philosophy tried to work had shown

[1] See "The English Mind" in *Philosophical Remains*.

themselves inadequate to actual knowledge. And, in turning back historically, it is now easily seen that experience as they understood it never made up the whole content of knowledge for the experiential thinkers themselves. Many *a priori* positions that had come down from antiquity through scholasticism remained part of the form of thought of Bacon, Hobbes, Locke, and Berkeley; and Hume, who with the most conscious purpose aimed at reducing all knowledge to experience, found that he could not rationally explain something so apparently obvious as causation without importing from the human mind elements not, in his view, to be counted among the given facts.[1] Hence Green showed real insight when he devoted himself to minute examination of Hume's most radical work, the *Treatise of Human Nature*, in order to expose the failure of the experiential philosophy traditional in England.

In my own view, set forth in the essay that gives its title to the present volume, the effectiveness of the criticism, within certain limits, is acknowledged: but it is treated as a correction, not as comparable to the revolution by which the great experiential thinkers themselves had at once enlarged and restricted our conceptions of the method of seeking truth. The Greeks had established for ever the appeal to reasoning; but, in spite of some attempts of their own, had failed to give its due place to experience. Many moderns in the new European nations put forth the thought of direct appeal to nature and fact as against dogmatic deductions from principles supposed rational; but English thinkers first, by continuity of effort, had carried the thought as far as it could go. No reversal of this has been possible; but it had to be seen also that, however dominant the element of given fact, or, in psychological language, sensation may be; and however "thin", as compared with what was assumed in the ages of all-embracing deduction, may be the irreducible *a priori* elements in thinking; these nevertheless exist. Induction itself implies deduction behind it; as was easily shown out of Mill's *System of Logic*; and this in the end rests on indispensable principles of know-

[1] See the chapter on "Reason" below.

ledge, not on generalisation from experience. We may then frankly recognise that we owe a very important critical re-examination of the traditional experiential assumptions to what no doubt seemed to many at the time an obscurantist reaction. For on the Continent, as in England, "Experience" and "Enlightenment" had in the end made common cause. Everywhere "the *a priori*" was in name at least banned.

An element both of strength and of weakness in English philosophy has been its special regard for physical or natural science. Apart from continuous pressure, there have been two great periods of the intensive influence of science on philosophy: that of the pre-Socratic schools of Greece, and that of the movement in modern Europe from the Renaissance onward. Yet it cannot be said with truth that at any time philosophy sprang purely and simply out of scientific consideration of nature. It arose at a certain stage in the search of man, from the time when he became man and passed beyond what has been called "animal faith", for a total imaginative interpretation of his own life, conscious as well as active, and of the nature of his dependence on the world which surrounds him. Science, on the other hand, began with the search into particulars of causation aroused by the interests of active life. Even at first, anything that we can call by anticipation science required in its votaries a certain removal from immediate practical preoccupations; but it remained attached to the vaguely discriminated facts of the world of perception, while the effort to imagine the whole proceeded rather from the mythical element in religion. This in its turn proceeded from the animism of the primeval or early thought of man when he was passing to the distinctively human stage and beginning to have words to mark off his internal life from the movements of things around. Yet philosophy, though derived from it, tended to oppose religion by bringing under intellectual and moral criticism the authority of the traditional stories taught by its representatives, the priesthoods. In its intellectual criticism it received the most tangible aid from science; which, in the meantime, had furnished much accurate knowledge of detail that was discordant with the sacred stories elaborated by religion and subservient to its cult of invisible powers. Science, however, dealing primarily with external nature, had no account to give of man as a conscious being. Therefore philosophy, which (as Bacon said of himself) took all knowledge for its province, after turning its criticism, with the aid of science, on religious tradition, turned it at the next stage on current scientific dogmatism, which, in the absence of a criterion either of consistency or of methodical verification, was running more and more into incoherence precisely as it tried to become more general. In virtue of this "subjective" criticism, we get the transition from what has been called Naturalism in philosophy to what has been called Idealism. While science has been successful in exploring details of nature, philosophy has been successful in showing that mere accumulation of these gives no insight into the whole; especially because the "objective" view of all this detail is merely dispersive and leaves out of account what most of all interests feeling and imagination. Again and again the process has repeated itself; and now we are in a marked phase of the conflict—often disguised in its essence by relations to historical religion; which, so far as it concerns empirical fact, is an affair of science and not of philosophy.

To the Hegelian school in England must be conceded, besides what has been already said, the merit of bringing back English thought from a too exclusive belief in the sciences as a preparation for philosophy—viewed sometimes as finding its culmination in a "creed of science"—to a more adequate understanding of its synoptic aim. The Hegelians helped to make it clear that science itself cannot go on effectively without reference to philosophical principles. And, to some extent, the study of Kant and Hegel has given deeper insight. English philosophers have seen the necessity of a revision either in the light of foreign points of view or by going back to the great Greek thinkers who were the ultimate source of philosophical Rationalism in modern times. There is no longer any fear that European thought should forget the lesson of "English Empiricism" and return to unexamined *a priori* maxims. The danger is rather that the ultimate necessity of trusting Reason should be forgotten and that haphazard trial and error under no guide but volition should take its place.

What Hegel has contributed to philosophy is above all the supreme position he assigns to Thought. In Thought he claims to find all the Being of the world; not by conjectures going beyond experience, but by a dialectical process within experience that always carries on the thought without limit. This does not mean that he is an "intellectualist" in any exclusive sense. One of his profound sayings is that nothing great is achieved without passion. "It is only a dead, indeed too often a hypocritical, morality, that inveighs against passion as such."[1] In his mind there was no doubt a hard intellectuality to which the sentimental "appeal to feeling" in religion or ethics was abhorrent; but this does not seem an unfortunate temperament for a philosopher. His own later antiliberal prejudices, which perhaps had some basis in a sentimental reaction against "sentiment", were easily set aside by a considerable portion of his own school, which in its "left wing" even went to revolutionary extremes. And the "dialectic" in which his system was expressed was for the most part ignored by his English disciples. Here, I am inclined to think, the depreciation went too far. It may be allowed that Hegel's Logic did not mark a stage in the theory of deductive or inductive proof, like the logical doctrines of Aristotle and Mill. It did, however, give a clear conception of the actual process in the development of thought; and the way of writing the histories of art, of religion and of philosophy would not have been the same if Hegel had never elaborated his dialectical method. He himself claims for it that it takes account for the first time of the element of negativity in the movement of mind. Progress is to be explained not by a straightforward following of deduction from one accomplished result to the next, but by a gradual revelation of contradic-

[1] *Encyklopädie der philosophischen Wissenschaften im Grundrisse*, § 474, p. 406 (ed. Karl Rosenkranz, Berlin, 1870).

tions in the first position taken, till contradiction is again contradicted and what was true in the primal thought is restored with due qualifications. But this is not achieved once for all. Each new synthesis breaks up in turn, and the restoration through the series of negations is again repeated. Such a generalising notion, I think, though it cannot be made to conform to any preconception of strict syllogistic proof, has shown itself very powerful in grasping the action and reaction by which the everlasting movement of thought goes on.

Here, however, there comes in a correction from the empirical side. Hegel's German disciples and their imitators have been apt, when writing the history of philosophy, to treat his dialectic as determining in advance the position of every thinker in the series. Everything comes at its time; and so, if any philosopher has shown insight not belonging to his assigned phase in terms of a "law of progress", his individual advance must be treated as unjustifiable! And, in spite of Hegel's logical admission that in his view nothing is final, finality is sometimes asserted for his own philosophy of dialectical evolution.

The correction may be made by a term borrowed from biology. Evolution once signified purely inward development from a germ; and it is this sense of evolution that Hegel must have had in his mind when he employed it to expound his philosophy. Biology, however, went on to recognise in the process of development in the embryo not simply an inward unfolding all prefigured, but "epigenesis", or addition of organic determinations that could not have been predicted. So also there have been, and there may be again, developments in thought and experience that could not have been foreseen by the deepest meditation. To give an example: in the early nineteenth century thinkers who were not specialists in physics or biology could foresee as about to establish themselves something like the theories of conservation of energy and transmutation of species. So far there was a kind of applicable dialectic. No one from outside, however, by "taking thought", could have foreseen the new discoveries in radiation or the rise of the modern scientific theory of relativity. For the new doctrine in mathematical physics, whatever points of contact may be found in the terms, did not spring out of the philosophical "relativity" familiar since the time of the Greek sceptics. It is really novel, and has arrived off the line of the expected.

That philosophical thoughts resembling one another can emerge on different lines of reflection is, I think, obvious in the chapters that follow. Comte and Hegel, for example, in spite of the highly synthetic character of the minds of both, are often treated as antitheses. Yet in their classification of the sciences there is a fundamentally important agreement. Here I am able to recognise a distinct value in a portion of Hegel's doctrine—namely, the Philosophy of Nature—about which his own disciples are inclined to say as little as possible. It was always indeed largely unintelligible to readers not living in the atmosphere of the German *Naturphilosophie*; but Comte also shares in the obscurity that comes from allusions to obsolete controversies of the past in rapidly growing sciences. In compensation, it is still noticeable that Hegel was strikingly lucky in some particular hits. His statement on heat might pass now as exactly "up to date",[1] and no one could have pointed out with more clearness that in the case of electricity no intuition as distinguished from abstraction is attainable, so that the reproach often made by scientific specialists against philosophy here completely fails.

To leave questions of detail, however, it needs to be emphasised that the representative of Positivism spontaneously coincided with the supposed representative of Transcendentalism in separating himself from those who regard nature as in its essence mechanical through and through. Hegel and Comte find, quite independently, that chemistry can never be constructed purely and simply from physical principles, nor

[1] See *Encyklopädie*, ed. Rosenkranz, §303, p. 261: "Die Wärme ist das sich Wiederherstellen der Materie in ihre Formlosigkeit, ihre Flüssigkeit, der Triumph ihrer abstrakten Homogeneität über die specifischen Bestimmtheiten".

biology from physics and chemistry. That is, to whatever extent the details of the sciences later in the series can be explained from the earlier, the principles of these can never enable us to understand how the objects of the later sciences came to exist at all. Both philosophers also agree in recognition of "final causes" as characteristic of organisms. Hegel declares[1] that the Aristotelian conception of the inner teleology of organic life had been almost lost till Kant in his manner re-awakened it. This he sets as the right view against external teleology. And Comte, expressly against the mechanicist preconceptions held scientific in his day, asserted teleology as irreducible law manifested in the empirical order of nature known to us phenomenally.

Going beyond the series of what are commonly called natural sciences, and entering upon the study of man, Comte and Hegel agree with their predecessor Vico in recognising teleology in history. With Vico and Hegel this might seem to follow from their Platonic principle that mind or spirit is supreme in the universe. Yet Comte also, carrying forward his empirical method into the most original part of his system, for which he invented the term Sociology, proclaims a thoroughgoing belief in a "human providence". So far did his confidence reach that he claimed to predict the future, at least in the abstract outline which is not incompatible with science. Here it was the empiricist who had most faith in the applicability of his doctrine. His weakness seems to me to lie in his formula "progress the end"; as if we knew what progress is without a philosophical criterion to distinguish between end and means. Vico's cyclical view theoretically excludes indefinite progress, though he makes none but hypothetical predictions. It is sufficient for his teleological doctrine if the causal order in the universe does not permit Humanity to perish. Hegel here in general, though not with particularly happy political applications, reaches the highest point, making freedom the ultimate expression of the spirit immanent in man. For the present, however, the main result is that the

[1] *Encyklopädie*, §360, p. 315.

three great modern founders in the science of man as a social being were all in their different ways teleologists.

Comte and Hegel may both be called in a sense optimists, though certainly not optimists who avert their eyes from the elements of pain and evil in the world; while Schopenhauer was an ostensible pessimist whose "dearest foe" was Hegel. Yet he too has a place for "final cause" in the Aristotelian sense. And it has been said with truth that the universe as conceived by Schopenhauer is by no means "the worst of all possible worlds". Let us remember also that the teleology of organisms was inexpugnable for Voltaire, in spite of his treatment in *Candide* of the optimism of Leibniz. That optimism, besides, furnished to Voltaire little more than a formula that lent itself to ridicule. "The best of all possible worlds" is not necessarily "very good". Leibniz, like Voltaire himself, allowed that there are in the world limiting necessities with which its "final causes" have to contend. Not that his *Théodicée*, which contains little of his distinctive philosophy, goes very deep. His most discerning philosophic admirers, such as Renouvier and Croom Robertson, did not think highly of it. By accepting points from the popular theology of the time, it might seem, in an impartial view, more pessimistic than Schopenhauer's account of the way to deliverance. For Leibniz, while admitting that there is a case for a view like that of Origen, undertakes to reconcile his optimism with the dogma of everlasting punishment. Schopenhauer, on the other hand, has no place for irreparable evil.

As exceptional great men who completely rejected final causes, Schopenhauer names Lucretius and Spinoza. Here, I think, we have a good example of the coming in of individual genius not explicable by the dialectical process of the ages. There remains for historians of philosophy an irreducible empirical element. For some disciples of Hegel, Spinoza became simply a phase in the logical development of the Cartesian philosophy: it was "bound to come" and then bound to give place to the next phase in the history of thought. Spinoza's metaphysical doctrine can, of course, be traced to sources; no known thinker is simply without precursors; but he was, to a certain extent, out of the current of his age. In tendency, his direction was that of Nicholas of Cusa and Giordano Bruno, neither of whom he probably knew. And so he had to undergo a long period of neglect, till his fame was revived after more than a century by those German successors of Kant who were in search of new inspiration.

It may be said of him—perhaps with a touch of paradox—that while his rejection of final causes leaves a gap in his science, he had carried philosophy to a level of contemplation that goes beyond even the most refined reasoning about means and ends. At the height, he passes from volition to acquiescence. This was not due simply to his logical development of the mechanicism imperfectly formulated by Descartes; though the model of grasping all under a mathematical intuition allured him. There were earlier sources of his thought; as I have shown in chapter vi of the present volume. But, with all his synthetic power, his developments from these sources leave an incoherence in his system. In what manner exactly they are to be resolved remains a problem for the future. Hegel may give us some help when he says, in his own technical terms, that Spinoza's Absolute must be conceived no longer as Substance but as Subject.

There is the same latent incoherence in Lucretius, different as was his science. With Lucretius the incongruity is at the beginning; with Spinoza at the end. The invocation of Venus as the symbol of a vital principle in the life of nature can find no explanation in the sweep of atoms through the infinite void; and to explain the "intellectual love of God" from the pleasure evoked by natural knowledge always seemed to me inadequate to such an impassioned emotion. Although Spinoza nominally excludes "passion", the feeling evoked by philosophy both in himself and in Lucretius seems much more akin to religion than to the mere satisfaction of scientific curiosity —which, however, was an element in both their minds. And this to me indicates a true "law of progress". Hegel, it seems to me, rightly places conscious philosophising beyond religious faith as the way in which man disinterestedly contemplates the universe; but as a stage beyond, not as a departure from the effort to grasp the whole. A French critic has called magic "the tactic of animism". The tactic failed because it thought to go straight to the concrete reality of external things and, in virtue of knowing them from within, to modify their responses. The successful tactic was, as Berkeley put it in an anticipatory formula, first to learn the "language" of phenomena. Comte's Positivism may pass for a new formulation of this; erroneous if taken as a final philosophy, but true if taken as meaning that phenomenal science might be called "the tactic of philosophy". If a final philosophy shall come, we may look forward to it as destined to be in the future more unquestionably the queen of the sciences than theology ever succeeded in being in the Middle Ages. This, however, must be entirely by free consent, not by a cunning or violent bending of the will to the purposes either of a select few or of a dominant many.

CHAPTER II

REASON

1. DEFINITION

In the most generalised sense of all, reason might be defined as the relational element in intelligence, in distinction from the element of content, sensational or emotional. Such a definition could justify itself by etymology; both λόγος and *ratio*, from which the word as a philosophical term descends historically, have sometimes the meaning simply of "relation". This, however, is too generalised to be serviceable. We must seek for something more limited.

At the beginning of the search we are met by an ambiguity. Man is defined as the "rational animal"; yet the "reason of animals", at a level below the human, is currently spoken of. The explanation of this ambiguity will point out the definition which we require.

It is true that the lower animals have "reason" as well as "instinct" (which may be defined as the direction, psychical as well as physical, of actions to ends, without knowledge of the end) in the sense that they, in varying degrees, direct their actions intelligently to desired ends; but not even the animals nearest to man have the power of thinking in general terms expressed in language. Man has this; and, in the traditional definition of man, it is this that is distinguished by the name of "reason". The subject may thus be dealt with either psychologically or as "theory of knowledge"—*i.e.*, we may consider the origin and growth of conceptual thought; or we may consider it as actually exercised in the discovery of true propositions. In the present chapter we shall consider reason, not in relation to the classification of the mental powers, and not genetically, but in relation to the philosophical discussions on the validity of scientific knowledge, of moral precepts, and of metaphysical beliefs.

2. THE TERM IN GREEK PHILOSOPHY

(*a*) *The pre-Socratics.* Reason, of course, was used by man long before the use of it was reflected on, and long before it was appealed to as the ground of knowledge or belief. When it is thus appealed to, it comes to be set, along with experience, in antithesis to passively accepted custom or tradition; and then again, more precisely, in antithesis to the particular facts known, as distinguished from the form and the generality of knowledge. The last stage was reached in the early philosophy of Greece—not at the very beginning, but as early as Heraclitus and Parmenides (sixth to fifth century B.C.). For the earlier period of the Hellenic world, as for the pre-Hellenic world generally, the vague Homeric use of such words as νόος, φρένες, πραπίδες, in which reason is not clearly distinguished from sense, or the mental process from the organic process that goes with it physiologically, may be taken as characteristic. Something of this vagueness indeed always remains in literary and even in philosophical usage;[1] but there comes a time when language enables us to distinguish if we choose. The time when generalising thought was consciously recognised, in distinction from the sense or experience in which it is immersed, arrived when the deductive science of mathematics had begun as a new departure of Greek science, marking a step beyond the accumulation of observations and empirical formulae in the science of the ancient East. It was this, though perhaps neither thinker was fully aware of the source of his thought, that caused Heraclitus and Parmenides to begin the series of articulate statements of a philosophical criterion. Earlier thinkers had already started the series of doctrines, but without a definite test of truth.

The balance, as a necessary consequence of the new departure in which the inquiry had its source, inclines at first to reason in its distinctive meaning as against the later-formu-

[1] *E.g.*, some misapprehensions would have been avoided if the "common sense" of the Scottish school had been described as "common reason". Historically it takes its origin from κοινὴ αἴσθησις, but its meaning approximates rather to κοινὸς λόγος.

lated criterion of experience. Heraclitus, indeed, appeals also to experience against tradition[1] in the saying, *ὀφθαλμοὶ τῶν ὤτων ἀκριβέστεροι μάρτυρες* (frag. 15 [Bywater], 101[a] [Diels]); but to reason is given the predominance. The final criterion is the judgment of the soul, not the witness of eyes (experience) or of ears (tradition), though the eyes are more trustworthy than the ears: *κακοὶ μάρτυρες ἀνθρώποισιν ὀφθαλμοὶ καὶ ὦτα βαρβάρους ψυχὰς ἐχόντων* (frag. 4 [B.], 107 [D.]). This, however, is still vague philosophically. Parmenides is more precise, and in his affirmation that reason[2] is the criterion he is more exclusive: we are to "judge by argument" (*κρῖναι λόγῳ* [frag. 1. 36]). Anaxagoras returns to a kind of balance, distinguishing the two modes of knowing as "by rational consideration" (*λόγῳ*) and "by experience" (*ἔργῳ*). This at least seems a fair interpretation of a fragment translated less determinately by Burnet: "So that we cannot know the number of the things that are separated off, either in word or deed", *ὥστε τῶν ἀποκρινομένων μὴ εἰδέναι τὸ πλῆθος μήτε λόγῳ μήτε ἔργῳ* (frag. 7; Burnet, p. 300).[3]

Democritus, not much later, declares outright that true knowledge is not by the senses but by reason. This is the interpretation of Sextus Empiricus; and it is supported by the

[1] See Burnet, *Early Greek Philosophy*², p. 147, n. 2.

[2] The meaning of λόγος in Heraclitus is still disputed; but, when it most approximates to reason, it seems to mean a rational law of things capable of partial appropriation by the mind, rather than a test applied by the mind to its knowledge of things. The Stoics, adopting both the language and the meaning of Heraclitus in the objective sense, also conceived the cosmic law as psychologically "reason". The sayings of Heraclitus never require this last meaning; but certainly "word" in a quasi-prophetic sense is far too obscure to render the λόγος of a Greek thinker.

[3] Diels translates "weder durch die Vernunft noch durch die Wirklichkeit", thus supporting my interpretation, which I at first ventured without consulting his rendering. In frag. 8 Diels seems to me right as against Burnet, who translates *τὰ ἐν τῷ ἑνὶ κόσμῳ* "the things that are in one world" instead of "the things that are in *the* one world"—which would support the opinion (rejected by him) of those ancient authorities who denied that Anaxagoras believed in many worlds like the Ionians generally. Here Diels expands a little, but brings out what seems the obvious meaning: "die in unserem einheitlichen Weltsystem enthaltenen Stoffe".

strong terms in which Democritus rejects the claim of the senses to judge. As Sextus sums up his positions: δυὸ φησὶν εἶναι γνώσεις, τὴν μὲν διὰ τῶν αἰσθήσεων τὴν δὲ διὰ τῆς διανοίας, ὧν τὴν μὲν διὰ τῆς διανοίας γνησίην καλεῖ,... τὴν δὲ διὰ τῶν αἰσθήσεων σκοτίην ὀνομάζει....οὐκοῦν καὶ κατὰ τοῦτον ὁ λόγος ἐστὶ κριτήριον, ὃν γνησίην γνώμην καλεῖ (*adv. Math.* vii. 138 f.).

These positions of the pre-Socratics may not be ultimately compatible with the outlook implied in their tracing of reason as well as other modes of mind to dependence on certain material mixtures in the bodily organs; but complete clearness could not be attained so early; and it is interesting to find that the most decided materialist, Democritus, lays most stress on reason as against the experiences of sense-perception. Perhaps, however, Democritus ought rather to be counted as belonging to the next phase, when attacks on the possibility of knowledge had to be expressly met. In his appeal distinctively to reason he was at one with his constructive contemporaries, however he might differ in his ontology.

(*b*) *Plato and Aristotle.* When, in the Sophistic period, the subjective criticism that examined the mind's own process was turned against the efforts of the early thinkers to arrive at truth in a direct objective way, Socrates, as a preliminary to reconstruction, set himself to examine the nature of the concept. Though by Aristotle induction from particulars (ἐπαγωγή), as well as the search for general definitions, is ascribed to Socrates, it was as a dialectical rather than as an experiential thinker that he became most influential. His central effort, as distinguished from incidental positions that interested eccentric thinkers like Antisthenes and Aristippus, was carried forward by Plato and then by Aristotle. For Plato reason, or coherent thinking, decidedly had the predominance, as a test, over experience of particulars. "Dialectic" was conceived as a more general method than that of deductive mathematics, which implies it when principles are in question, but as a separate study proceeds from untested "hypotheses" (supposed self-evident) of its own. The appeal to reason, in Plato's ideal system of knowledge, thus became part of a whole in which, while experience had a place, dialectic, with deductive mathematics at the next step below, was the model of ultimately valid thought. At a higher stage than that of discursive reason (διάνοια) there was pure intellect, intuitive thought (νοῦς, νόησις) by which true reality is to be grasped; at a lower stage was opinion (δόξα), not properly scientific because not dialectical or mathematical, which deals by more or less conjectural methods with the phenomena presented to sense-perception.[1] On the dialectical side, what had been partially formulated by Plato was definitely formulated by Aristotle, who stated the axioms since known as the "laws of thought", and made them the basis of his codified formal logic. Aristotle, on another side of his mind, was much more of a naturalistic inquirer into detail than Plato; but, in his general view of the test or tests of truth, he remains faithful to the principles of his master.

(*c*) *Epicureans and Stoics.* The next period of Greek thought, occupied as it was with the effort to formulate a rule of life for the individual in a cosmopolitan world for which the bond of the city-State had become a waning tradition, brought on the search for a more tangible reality than that of the metaphysics in which the Platonic and Aristotelian dialectic found its consummation. To arrive at some external reality in the most expeditious way was the theoretical problem. Then, without useless lingering over this, the philosophic learner could go on to the essential thing, which was practice. The great positive schools of this period, the Epicureans and the Stoics, while differing much in detail, solved this problem fundamentally in the same way. Going back to the earlier thinkers, they developed more consistently the naturalistic side of their doctrines. The rudiments could be found in them of theories which, in the explanation of mind, proceeded from the physiological organs and made the senses psychologically fundamental. From these rudiments the new schools, with the long dialectical development of the intervening period behind them, worked out in considerable detail what we may

[1] See *Republic*, end of bk. vi, for an exact account.

call an experiential theory of knowledge. Not rational argument as such was the criterion, but a certain mode of experience. Epicurus, while taking for his ultimate account of reality the atomism of Democritus (with changes that were scientifically for the worse), completely inverted the position of Democritus with regard to the senses. For Epicurus sense-perception is the criterion: things are exactly as they appear. This is formally stated by Sextus Empiricus, who was our authority for the precisely opposite affirmation of Democritus. Epicurus, he says, affirms that sense-perception is trustworthy in its hold of reality throughout: *τὴν αἴσθησιν...διὰ παντός τε ἀληθεύειν καὶ οὕτω τὸ ὂν λαμβάνειν ὡς εἶχε φύσεως αὐτὸ ἐκεῖνο* (*adv. Math.* viii. 9).

The more elaborate doctrine of the Stoics equally adopted for its criterion sense-perception, though not indiscriminately, but only when it was perception of a certain kind. The difference was in effect that Zeno and his successors laid stress on an active element in the grasp of external reality; mere recipiency did not seem to them sufficient. Reality is seized, they said, by the *φαντασία καταληπτική*—a kind of presentation that is known to give a true account by the sense of possession that goes with it and the absence of any opposing presentation. As Sextus puts it, *κριτήριον εἶναι τῆς ἀληθείας τὴν καταληπτικὴν φαντασίαν...μηδὲν ἔχουσαν ἔνστημα* (vii. 253).

The part of *λόγος* in the Stoic system, like that of *νοῦς* for Anaxagoras, is ontological. In one of its meanings *λόγος* is the law that runs through the world; it also means psychologically reason as a mental faculty; but reason as the procedure of the mind in dealing with the general is not for the Stoic theory of knowledge the ultimate test of truth. The ultimate test for the Stoics, as for the Epicureans, is experience.

(*d*) *Sceptics*. The opposition that this doctrine had to meet came from the sceptics, especially those of the New Academy. That the most reasoned scepticism should have proceeded from the Academy reveals its essential nature. For a time the attempt to build a positive system from the points of view developed in Plato's *Dialogues* was abandoned, and his school threw itself into negative criticism. A system of confident dogmatism like that of the Stoics provided it with material exactly to the purpose. Carneades recognised his dependence on his opponents when he said, parodying the verse that made Chrysippus the effective founder of the Stoa, *εἰ μὴ γὰρ ἦν Χρύσιππος οὐκ ἂν ἦν ἐγώ* (substituted for *οὐκ ἂν ἦν Στοά*).[1] The method was to apply to the Epicurean and Stoic tests of truth a stringent dialectic which, after the emergence of idealistic criticism, no naïvely realistic doctrine could bear. Indirectly, therefore, scepticism, earlier and later, was the preparation for the next constructive school, that of the Neo-Platonists, which, arising independently, at length absorbed the Academy.

(*e*) *Neo-Platonists*. With a positive, and no longer a negative, aim, Plotinus revived the Platonic idealism, bringing into it more system through the study of Aristotle, and turning it critically against the Stoic materialism. Even sense-perception, he showed, is inexplicable from the basis of mere physiology; but, for the test of truth, he turned away from sense and insisted on reason as that which judges. Mysticism, though a distinctive feature of his thought, does not furnish the criterion. For the mystical experience, being a state beyond knowledge, seizing upon that which is beyond mind, cannot be explained to one who has not had it. The reasoned system points to it, but does not include it as part of a completely rational process; it is *ἔκστασις*, a standing out of system. The system itself consists of demonstrations, and its criterion is reason. Thus, after a long and fluctuating process, thought had returned to the dialectic and logic of Plato and Aristotle as offering the soundest principles of knowledge yet discovered.

This was, however, more clearly brought out by Proclus (A.D. 410–485) two centuries after Plotinus (204–270). For Plotinus the ideal of reason is an intuitive thought such as Spinoza[2] holds to be the highest order of knowledge. Proclus

[1] The verse parodied by Carneades was no doubt itself parodied from an argument assigned to Theseus in the *Suppliants* of Euripides, to the effect that goods predominate over evils in human life: *εἰ μὴ γὰρ ἦν τόδ', οὐκ ἂν ἦμεν ἐν φάει*.

[2] *Eth.* ii. prop. 40, schol. 2.

does not reject this, as he does not reject the more distinctively mystical experience beyond it; but for the definitive test of truth he selects a more generally applicable criterion. The criteria that the thinker may use for himself in relation to different kinds of subject-matter are many; but the soul is a unity as well as a multiplicity; and there must be some universal criterion for every soul. This he finds to be neither pure intellect (νοῦς) at one extreme nor sense-perception (αἴσθησις) at the other, but discursive reason (λόγος). Here is the process of explicit formulation by which the higher is mediated to the lower and the lower to the higher. The mind may start from the glimpses of intuitive reason and may use sense-perception as material for criticism or confirmation; but, if there is to be a system of knowledge, it must be established by a process of argument. The circumspection which he ascribes to Plato in assigning their proper part in knowledge to all the modes of mind is certainly to be found in the passage where he gives this guarded expression to philosophical rationalism: *εἰ τοίνυν τὸ κρίνειν ψυχῆς ἐστιν—οὐ γάρ που τὸ ἡμέτερον σῶμα κριτικὴν ἔχει δύναμιν—ἡ δὲ ψυχὴ ἕν ἐστι καὶ πλῆθος, καὶ τὸ κριτικὸν ἄρα ἕν ἐστιν ἅμα καὶ πολλά, καὶ μονοειδὴς ἡ κριτικὴ δύναμις καὶ πολυειδής. τίς οὖν ἡ μία δύναμις; φαίη τις ἄν. ὁ λόγος, φήσομεν.* (*Comm. in Tim.*, ed. E. Diehl, Leipzig, 1903, i. 254–255).

As first matter, or mere possibility, below the limit of true knowledge, is seized by a kind of bastard reasoning (*νόθῳ λογισμῷ* in Plato's phrase), so the One, at the other extreme above knowledge, is seized by a kind of bastard intuition (*νόθῳ νῷ*). Thus every test finally has a certain resemblance to the model test of explicit reason. If the other tests are to be regarded as having their own validity, it must be shown by argument how they can have it; though argument, of course, cannot enable us to dispense with direct perceptions whether of intellect or of sense.

For antiquity, therefore, what may be called in the philosophical sense "rationalism" remained finally supreme.

3. MEDIAEVAL AND MODERN USE

(*a*) *Scholasticism.* In the mediaeval schools rationalism became predominant in a narrowed sense. The passage cited above from Proclus might have been taken by the Schoolmen of Western Christendom, without its qualifications, as a text to prove the exclusive value of their characteristic activity. It was long after Proclus, and long after the suppression of the school at Athens of which he was the last great name, that the revival of philosophical thought began in the West; but, when it came, it gave evidence of continuity with the latest thought of antiquity. Its first great movement was an immense development of discursive reason. Precisely because the Middle Ages had lost the freedom with which in classical antiquity ultimate beliefs could be discussed, there was such an elaboration of formal method as had never been known before. The value of this must not be underrated. In a sentence from Sir W. Hamilton's *Discussions in Philosophy* which J. S. Mill prefixed to the first book of his *Logic* it is put thus: "To the schoolmen the vulgar languages are principally indebted for what precision and analytic subtlety they possess". Croom Robertson says: "All the world has heard of scholasticism as an oppressive system of pedantic belief: it has still to be known as a system of rationalism struggling to be" ("The English Mind", *Philosophical Remains*, London, 1894, p. 34). The reverse side of the case remains, of course, that this rationalism was very limited. The Schoolmen made a fine art of formal reasoning; but the habit of accepting traditional authority for facts and data was so fixed that the attempt to bring again into view the claims of experience remained merely sporadic. To get out of the circle of things taken for granted or assumed dialectically, a revolt against the School-philosophy itself became necessary. The controversy about the reality of universals was primarily ontological. By their contention that only particulars are real, and that the genus or species is only a name indicating resemblance between the members of a class, the nominalists might seem nearer to modern experientialism than the realists, for whom class-names indicated a reality like that of the Platonic ideas; but the methods of both were equally dialectical. An aid to the imagination in forming a notion of the time that it took new views about method to emerge is to remember that there is a longer interval between the exhortations of Roger Bacon, to go to experience, and those of Francis Bacon, than between the publication of the *Novum Organum* (1620) and the present date (1934).

Roger Bacon is an isolated figure in the greatest period of Scholasticism, the thirteenth century. Another great English thinker, William of Ockham, in the next century, promoted by his dialectic the disintegration of the imposing dogmatism of St Thomas Aquinas and John Duns Scotus. Then came the beginnings of the new movement of humanism taking the form at first of a more literary interest in the Latin classics. After the revival, in the fifteenth century, of direct knowledge of Greek thought in its original sources, followed by the setting up, in the sixteenth, of older types of thinking, in conscious rivalry with the whole mediaeval scheme of theology and philosophy, the movement against Scholasticism took a more systematic new departure.

(*b*) *Experientialism and rationalism.* This, in the seventeenth century, expressed itself in the effort to establish once for all the right "method" of seeking truth. The new aspiration for firm knowledge, instead of barren disputes about insoluble questions, culminated for the time in the philosophical reforms of Francis Bacon and René Descartes. Bacon not only clothed in the most impressive language the appeal to experience as the test by which every claim to possess real knowledge must be verified, but also developed some genuine outlines of a theory of induction, no longer unsystematic, but rising by stages from particulars to generals, as deduction descends from generals to particulars. Descartes, himself a discoverer in geometry, set against the sterile formalism of mere logic, which could bring out only what had been implicitly asserted, the real deduction of new truth in the mathematical sciences. Thus began the two great movements of philosophy known as English experientialism and Continental rationalism; but it is important to note that these were not so definitely rivals as they had become later when Kant turned his "critical" thought on both at once. The great Continental rationalists, Descartes, Spinoza, and Leibniz, all took occasion to recognise in some way the new departure of the English in their appeal to experience. In all the English thinkers, on the other side, unreduced elements from the rationalism of ancient science and of the Scholastic tradition remain over. It would be easy to show this in the case of Bacon, Hobbes, Locke, and Berkeley. And Hume, who carried farthest the effort to resolve all "principles of reason" into derivatives of pure experience, treated his results not as "dogmatic" but as "sceptical", *i.e.*, as suggesting problems for reconsideration; finally abandoning his first elaborate attempt to explain mathematics as an essentially empirical science. By Kant, while the opposition with him arrived at the most explicit statement, the reconciliation of "reason" and "experience" as constituents of truth was most systematically attempted. Reason, according to Kant, does not merely enable us to arrive at "analytical" judgments implied in what has been already said, but, in mathematics at least, yields genuine new truth in the form of "synthetic judgments *a priori*". Yet, while these are not given in mere experience, they have no valid application beyond all possible experience. All true science consists in carrying reason into the construction of nature so as to make it intelligible to thought. Even those highest principles that seem to go beyond this have value only as furnishing an ideal that the actually working system of science may try to approach and so gradually perfect itself.

(*c*) *The Kantian reaction and the revival of experientialism.* If we were to stop here, it might seem that now, as at the end of ancient thought, the supreme place, though with circumspection, was assigned to reason. Kant, however, did not, even at first, approximately satisfy any considerable group of thinkers. The problem became on the one side to develop him, on the other side to answer him. Hegel has been thought to have carried philosophical rationalism to the highest point. By a new logic, the whole order of the universe, he seemed to promise, was to be shown forth as a manifestation of reason. Yet, curiously, his power appears most in a strong grasp of experience intermittently attained, but unmediated by any method fitted to carry general conviction. The next representatives of experientialism, in contrast, were men of pre-eminently deductive minds, whose strength was in reasoned exposition, and who, in the days of Scholasticism, might have been famous as irrefragable doctors. For the complex period at which we have arrived it is more true than ever, in the phrase borrowed by Hegel himself from Anaxagoras, that things are not "cut in two with a hatchet".

It would have contributed much to a clear issue for the thinkers just alluded to had they known Kant at first hand; but they knew him only indirectly or very imperfectly. Comte, who, like Descartes and Leibniz among modern philosophers, was a mathematician of original power, thought that he could explain even mathematics philosophically as based in generalisations from pure experience. J. S. Mill, who succeeded in founding a valid inductive logic by deducing the actual tests of experimental science from a general principle, "the uniformity of nature", fell back, for the proof of this, on the weakest mode of induction—*viz.*, that "induction by simple enumeration" which the Baconian canons and his own had been devised to supersede. And this, in both cases, without any close consideration of Kant's arguments for the necessity of *a priori* principles in the science of nature as in mathematics. It is not surprising that, both in France and in England, the two countries where the experientialism that took shape from Locke had been strongest, there was a reaction—or a forward movement, as some put it—in the Kantian direction. For the whole of Europe, however, it must be said that the predominant movement in the nineteenth century, through the influence on philosophy of the enormous new developments in the sciences of experiment and observation, was greatly to enlarge the place given to experience as compared with that which it held in antiquity, and to reduce the principles of reason which science finds that it cannot do without to an attenuated form. The elaborate apparatus of Kant was not adopted by men of science; and in Germany the movement which took for its watchword "Back to Kant" signified a return to the experiential side of Kant against the extreme speculative developments of his successors.

There is, however, it has also become clear, an element in scientific knowledge not explicable as a resultant of accumulating experience. The most general principles of logic, whether of formal inference, of mathematical deduction, or of the natural and humanistic sciences, remain more than arbitrary linkings of ideas that can have their validity proved or disproved by their applicability to certain subject-matters. They are not in the end mere "working hypotheses". There is in reason, as Kant with all his over-elaboration proved, an *a priori* factor in virtue of which we distinguish it from pure experience.

4. *A PRIORI*

This term, which is currently used in various senses, calls for a brief discussion in relation to the present subject. Its source was Aristotelian. Aristotle distinguished between that which is first in relation to us and that which is first by nature. In knowledge the experiences of sense-perception are first in relation to us, *i.e.*, in the order of genesis: but, since, in his view as in Plato's, the formal essence (εἶδος), expressed in a concept, is the determining reality of everything, the ideal of knowledge for the philosophically trained mind is to begin with the general and proceed to particulars. Thus the syllogism, into which all formal reasoning can be thrown if we need expressly to test its validity, is "first by nature" and has more in it of true cognition; but induction, which is the procedure from particulars to generals (ἡ ἀπὸ τῶν καθ' ἕκαστον ἐπὶ τὰ καθόλου ἔφοδος), is more persuasive and carries plainer evidence to the ordinary mind.[1] Quite fitly, therefore, the term *a priori* was adopted by Kant as the technical expression for reason in its

[1] See *Top*. i. 12, 105ª 13, and *Anal. Pr*. ii. 23, 68ᵇ 32.

purity, proceeding, whether theoretically or practically, as something necessarily general and not to be derived from experience conceived as a sum of unrelated particulars presented to the mind from outside. Since Kant the expression has become a kind of shorthand, understood without reference to its historical origin or to any distinctive system. Those who use it do not imply that they are reasoning from a formal cause, which has priority in the Aristotelian sense as being the real essence; nor even that they regard their general principles as transcendental in the Kantian sense, *i.e.*, as not derived from experience though having possible application only within experience. Their claim is simply to be in possession of general principles, whatever the source of these, from which they are justified in inferring propositions applicable to groups of particulars. Herbert Spencer, *e.g.*, while he is always classed with the series of the English experientialists, uses the term as freely as Kant, and he was at least as confident an *a priori* reasoner as Aristotle and decidedly less of an observer. The ground of his *a priori*, however, was quite different. For him the order of genesis is the real order of nature; and the *a priori* principles of the mind, though it can now apply them with scientific security, are valid only as the last result of accumulated experiences in the race and the individual. Yet, perhaps, in a very broad sense, a philosophical conception of the *a priori* akin to that of Aristotle or of Kant lurks behind. For experience, according to Spencer, does not simply consist of "feelings", but includes "relations between feelings"; and these are not derivative, but constitute a kind of λόγος, or *ratio*, in which all explicit knowledge had a prior existence. In this extremely general sense of the *a priori*, Spencer also may be classed with the philosophical rationalists.

5. REASON IN ETHICS

Moral conduct may be considered as practically determined either by the notion of an end of action, a final good, or by the notion of a law to which action ought to conform. In whichever way it is considered, both reason and experience must be allowed a part in deciding what actual conduct shall be. For Greek and Roman antiquity moral philosophy was on the whole dominated by the idea of an end or good. This might be derived from experience and treated as something empirical to which the means had to be sought; or it might be determined in relation to some metaphysical reality that was thought to confer on it its ultimate desirability as an end. In the latter case it would naturally be regarded as ascertainable by the direct insight of reason. Plato's idea of the good is conceived as the final object of rational insight, conferring on all ends their desirability as on all modes of being their reality; but he admits that he cannot say what it is.[1] In Plato's and Aristotle's actual treatment of moral problems there is a mixture of points of view, both reason and experience being appealed to. This, however, does not make the philosophers illogical. Their ideal is that the end or the good should be rationally knowable; but they recognise, in the conditions of human nature, the need for much empirical balancing of one thing with another. The conceptions of "pleasure" as the end, interpreted by Epicurus as in its highest degree tranquillity, and of the "life according to nature", selected by the Stoics as their final good, may be considered as experiential, in accordance with the theoretical philosophy of the schools that adopted them. In these schools, however, points of view came decisively forward that led on to the later "ethics of law", which in modern times has tended to become the type of rationalist, as distinguished from experiential, ethics. The Epicureans made considerable use of the notion of keeping contracts, already present in the Aristotelian theory of justice; and the Stoics brought the detail of their ethics under ideas of a natural justice or of a law common to all. This had much influence on the formulation of Roman legal conceptions. Neo-Platonism treated ethics on the whole from the metaphysical point of view, according to which degree of worthiness in ends corresponds to degree of reality in the scale of existences. Christian ethics adapted, for philosophical systematisation,

[1] *Rep.* vi. 506.

Stoic, Platonic, and Aristotelian positions, in this chronological order. Its notion of a divine legislation tended to reinforce the beginnings that already existed of the "ethics of law", moral duties being put in the form of commands. Thus in the Middle Ages ethics took the name of "moral theology". In the early modern period a kind of ethics of law, placed on natural or rational grounds, was formulated by Hobbes. Its precepts might be also divine commands, but they could be known, though not enforced, independently of all positive legislation, human or divine, as declarations by natural reason concerning that which ought to be done. A certain end was fixed, *viz.*, social peace and security as the general condition allowing individuals to seek their personal good, which is no one thing, but consists in a multiplicity of things that present themselves as desirable in the course of experience. The social end being fixed, the "law of nature" in its ethical sense becomes demonstrable. Since, however, all ends are considered as known only empirically, and the law is determined ultimately by relation to these, Hobbes, though in part rationalist in his expressions, has always been classed with the experientialists, in ethics and politics as in general philosophy. His successors and opponents, Cudworth and Clarke, with their appeal to "right reason" and "the fitness of things" as the proper determinants of action apart from command or self-interest, were stringently rationalist in form, but did not disentangle their ethics of law from the metaphysical points of view that they had inherited from Plato and his ancient or Scholastic successors. A new departure was taken by Kant when he insisted that the only generally valid form of ethics is that which expresses itself as the "moral law", obligatory without relation to ends; and that moral obligation is rationally determined by itself without reference either to experience or to any metaphysical propositions about the nature of a reality beyond experience. Ultimate moral judgments, stating what ought to be done, are determined by "pure practical reason", as the ultimate types of assertion about what is or may be real are determined by "pure speculative reason".

This mode of ethical thought has since been developed and modified with most originality by C. Renouvier (*Science de la Morale*, 2 vols., Paris, 1869) and by E. Juvalta (*Il Vecchio e il Nuovo Problema della Morale*, Bologna, 1914).

6. REASON *VERSUS* UNDERSTANDING

An antithesis that has had considerable importance historically is that which was set up by Kant's distinction between reason in an eminent sense (*Vernunft*) and understanding (*Verstand*). Understanding relates one thing to another within experience, but does not go forward to the ideal completion of experience in a total system. Such an ideal completion is wrought by the reason, which rises above the bounds of experience and affirms the three transcendental ideas of the soul as a permanent being (the psychological idea), of the world as a totality (the cosmological idea), and of God as the necessary being who is the cause of the whole (the theological idea). These ideas of the reason, Kant argues, are not theoretically demonstrable; but neither are they theoretically refutable; and we have the intellectual right to assert them as postulates of the moral life. For, while this, being autonomous, is independent of any metaphysical doctrine, it does not simply rest in itself, but claims that it shall find its fulfilment in a universe ordered in relation to its demands. By Kant's idealist successors in Germany the antithesis of reason and understanding was often turned to account—in defiance of Kant's aim at limiting the pretensions of the speculative reason—to claim the warrant of a higher faculty for their own utterances, all detailed criticism being treated as an affair of the "mere abstract understanding". To English readers this procedure became familiar through its use by Coleridge and his disciples to discredit attacks on tradition, political or religious. The reason saw in this a deep meaning, placing it at once beyond the vulgar hostility of crude radicalism and the arid defences of conventional conservatism, both alike bound within the limits of the inferior pedestrian faculty. In Germany Schopenhauer made an attempt to turn the tables by contending that the understanding is always the originative thing: reason, as merely conceptual, being only the means of preserving consistency—*e.g.*, to be reasonable (*vernünftig*) is not necessarily to be moral; it may mean only consistency in pursuing well understood self-interest; true morality implies a sympathetic insight that is not merely rational. Understanding no doubt includes what is below, but it also includes what is above, the process of logically connecting concepts—at once the instincts and perceptions of animals and the perception or "instinct" of genius. This, however, means that Schopenhauer in his own manner continued the old distinction, while inverting the reference of the names. This he could easily do by limiting "reason" to its sense of ratiocination. Whatever the terms used, the distinction in fact remains. A mind so strongly developed on the side of the understanding, or of reason in its sense of ratiocination, as that of J. S. Mill could acknowledge that in some respects Coleridge had deeper insight than Bentham. And Comte, while maintaining the claim of his philosophy to complete "positivity", found that, because it was philosophy and not merely science, the supreme place in it belonged to certain "vues d'ensemble". The problem of a truly philosophical reform must be to make the "esprit d'ensemble" predominate over the "esprit de détail". "Dispersive specialism", when uncontrolled, becomes an aberration of the human mind, relatively justifying that conservative reaction which at least maintains the synthesis of the past. The Coleridgian distinction, it is evident in the light of these testimonies, cannot be dismissed as a mere verbal trick. The problem is to find the right terms. Thus only can we hope to set ourselves free at once from arrogance and from confusion. Now the right terms are ready to our hand in Milton,[1] who puts into the mouth of Raphael the declaration that the soul's being is reason, "discursive, or intuitive", "differing but in degree, of kind the same". Those terms, taken no doubt from a Scholastic source, go back to Plato and Aristotle. Intuitive reason is the *νοῦς* of the Platonic theory of know-

[1] *Par. Lost*, v. 486–490.

ledge; discursive reason is the διάνοια. The former corresponds to the reason of Kantism; the latter to the understanding. These terms, "intuitive" and "discursive" reason, have the advantage of accurately rendering, without arbitrary specialisation of meaning, a difference that really exists and is plain when it is pointed out. No difficult introspection is needed to see that there is a total grasp, a "synoptic" view of things, and that there is also procedure from point to point. But it must always be borne in mind that, if the former is higher, it is unavailable till it has been mediated by the latter. The ideal of philosophic presentation is achieved by those who, like Plato and Berkeley, have both in due balance.

LITERATURE

As the antithesis between reason and experience runs through all the history of philosophy, the following general authorities may first be mentioned:

J. Burnet, *Early Greek Philosophy*[2], London, 1908.
H. Ritter and L. Preller, *Historia Philosophiae Graecae*[8], Gotha, 1898.
F. Ueberweg, *Grundriss der Gesch. der Philosophie*, i.[10] Berlin 1909, ii.[10] 1915, iii.[11] 1914, iv.[11] 1916.

On the impossibility of reducing the supreme principle of inductive logic to "hypothesis":

Carveth Read, *Logic*[4], London, 1914, p. 286 f.

On rational and empirical ethics:

T. Whittaker, *The Theory of Abstract Ethics*, Cambridge, 1916.

On the "synoptic" view to which philosophy returns:

J. T. Merz, *History of European Thought in the Nineteenth Century*, iii, iv, Edinburgh, 1912–1914.

CHAPTER III

COMTE AND MILL

ANTECEDENTS

THE two thinkers who have been brought together as the subjects of this chapter spring out of what is broadly the same movement of modern thought. If within it they are in some respects antithetic, this makes them all the better adapted for simultaneous treatment. Both, on the intellectual side, were adherents of the philosophy called in general experiential; and with both alike the whole effort of thought was inspired by a social aim. The difference is that by the younger of the two the experience regarded as the ground of knowledge was supposed to be explicable by impressions on the individual mind; whereas the elder had transcended "individualism" in this sense, and conceived of knowledge as fundamentally a social product. For Mill, the individual human being is a component of society known prior to the composition. For Comte, he cannot be known as human except in relation to it, and can only be thought of apart from it by abstraction.

This change of view is often said to characterise the advance made by the nineteenth century on the eighteenth. Because Mill had not appreciated this advance, it is sometimes said that he ought to be classed as still belonging in spirit to the eighteenth century. Comte, in this resembling Hegel in spite of his very different general philosophy, was one of those who had most unquestionably made the new point of view their own. At first sight therefore he might appear to have all the advantage over his younger contemporary. This impression, however, would be wrong. The whole value of a philosopher's thought cannot be tested by any single point of view; and there were lines on which Mill, though not so systematic and powerful a thinker all round, went deeper and achieved more than Comte.

There is not space to say much of the biography of either;

but the leading facts must be given. Auguste Comte was born at Montpellier on the 19th January, 1798, and died at Paris on the 5th September, 1857. John Stuart Mill was born at Pentonville, London, on the 20th May, 1806, and died at Avignon on the 8th May, 1873. Comte's systematic training was in mathematical and physical science; first at the Lycée of Montpellier and afterwards at the École Polytechnique in Paris. In youth he also accumulated extensive knowledge of history and literature, and an extremely tenacious memory gave him ever afterwards full command of his material. Henceforth, however, he only elaborated and did not add to the store. His later abstinence from the reading of contemporary literature and journalism he described as "cerebral hygiene". The greater part of his life (1816 to 1851) was more or less absorbed by the private teaching of mathematics and by the duties of posts as public teacher and examiner. What he always regarded as his distinctive work had to be done in the intervals of obligatory tasks; till at length, having been deprived first of one post and then of another through the hostility of scientific specialists whom he had failed to conciliate either for his philosophy or for himself personally, he was supported, in further developing his doctrine, by the subsidies of disciples and sympathisers. In one respect Mill's external circumstances were similar. He too was never a teacher of philosophy, but had duties extrinsic to the purpose of his life as he had been led to conceive it from the first. A severe and elaborate education by his father, James Mill (1773–1836), in ancient literature, in mathematics, and especially in logic, was followed by an official career in the service of the East India Company, which lasted from 1823 to 1858, when the government of India was transferred to the Crown. His education, it may be observed, was in a manner complementary to that of the Polytechnic student. Physical science was a study in which Mill was not directly trained, but in which he eagerly sought information for himself. For his actual work this was not the least important part of his preparation; as, similarly, Comte's historical reading was not the least important part of his.

To Comte the impulse towards the philosophic work of his life came at once from the thinkers who, before the French Revolution, had speculated with conscious regard to the better ordering of society, and from those who, after the Restoration, were aiming at social reconstruction either by a continuance of the revolutionary movement or by a return to the past. The names he has himself selected from his nearest precursors are those of Condorcet and of Joseph de Maistre. From the former he took the idea that the total movement of history is progressive; but, precisely as the consequences of this idea, found him in detail of little value because, with the eighteenth century generally, he had nothing but condemnation for the Middle Ages. From the latter he took the vindication of the mediaeval order and of its culmination in the papacy, but only, as he says, relatively to the stage then reached by the European mind. Condorcet had failed to recognise the "relative" justification of the past. De Maistre, in accordance with the old theological philosophy, held its justification to be "absolute". A sound philosophy, emancipated equally from theological and antitheological prejudices, and regarding every order relatively to its own conditions, and not as absolutely good or bad, will move towards a synthesis under which the provisional value of both views alike can be recognised. This synthesis, to which the most advanced minds are tending, is declared to be itself pre-eminently "relative"; not merely because it too belongs only to one stage—though the final stage—of the human race, but also for reasons that we shall meet with later.

Comte's aim was thus to be a reformer of thought for the sake of action. This was also Mill's aim, directly impressed by his father, who preceded him as a thinker and worker for the cause of political and social reform in England. A disciple of Jeremy Bentham, James Mill indoctrinated his son with the principles of utilitarian ethics and jurisprudence as they were understood in Bentham's school. To these he added a training in the English psychology of Association as developed especially by Hartley. The works of the Scottish school of Common Sense were also read, but with a view to their correction and development on Associationist principles. For the merely verbal explanation of cohesions of feeling in consciousness by "mental faculties", called Memory or Imagination or Reason, different for each kind of product, was to be substituted the explanation of them in common by laws of grouping or "association of ideas", yielding different results according to the nature of the elements associated and their degree of complication. This doctrine James Mill himself worked out, in his *Analysis of the Phenomena of the Human Mind* (1829), to explain the appearance of necessity in mental judgments that present themselves as axioms. The psychological origin of this appearance, he tried to show, is the "inseparable association" of mental states that have been constantly conjoined in past experience. From this theory there resulted, in the view he passed on to his son, an almost unlimited power of education, by modifying the associations formed, to change men's modes of thinking and feeling. Associationist psychology was not a part of Bentham's own doctrine, but was added to it by his disciple. Again, though great in legislation, Bentham was found inadequate in pure politics. For a new starting-point Hobbes was recurred to; but, instead of absolute monarchy, representative democracy was held to be the best form of the State. This position was laid down in James Mill's article on "Government", contributed in 1820 to a supplement of the *Encyclopaedia Britannica*. Beyond the theories of government and legislation, the social science chiefly studied was Political Economy. The most recent authorities here were Ricardo and Malthus. Ricardo was a personal friend of James Mill, who had first encouraged him to express his views in writing. By Malthus' "law of population", J. S. Mill's social theories were afterwards deeply influenced.

He and Comte started in effect equally clear of theology from boyhood. Comte indeed was brought up as a Catholic; but he was thrown at school (from his tenth year) into the intellectual atmosphere of post-revolutionary France; and he himself relates that at thirteen he had rejected all historic religion, including theism. James Mill brought up his son in the conviction that "concerning the origin of things nothing whatever can be known". Christianity, he held with the school of Bentham in general, is not only false but pernicious, the God of orthodoxy being "the most perfect conception of wickedness which the human mind can devise". By Bishop Butler he had been convinced that the attempt to argue from the natural order to a benevolent Creator breaks down, since the moral difficulties of the Christian revelation have their analogy in the ordinary course of nature. But, as J. S. Mill observes, during the period in which he grew up, opinion in England on religion was more compressed that it has been earlier or later. If the Utilitarians were not to throw away all chance of influence, they must observe a rule of strict reticence in public; though as a matter of fact their real opinions were well understood. Comte was more fortunately situated in this respect. Even under the restored monarchy he could speak as he liked in lectures as in writing; and he never left any doubt that he regarded every form of theology, including the Christian, as superseded, to use his own expression, for all minds at the level of their age.

COMTE'S FIRST PHASE

For a very short time Comte classed himself, along with others who aimed at continuing the work of the revolutionists against the reaction, simply as a political liberal. This youthful stage is just perceptible in his earliest correspondence; but it was not long before another side of his mind responded to the influences of the counter-revolution. As in the case of Hegel, personal circumstances had little or nothing to do with this. The conservative element in Hegel's mind is clearly marked in his first great work, written before he occupied any official position. So Comte, making the transition with more precocity from his early revolutionary enthusiasm, expressed to his friend Valat his sense of the relative justification of the party that was content if it could preserve order against anarchy.

The revolutionary party, he found, had no constructive plan. The destructive work of the eighteenth century had now been sufficiently accomplished. A new synthesis must be thought out before any further direct action ought to be undertaken. When this was adequately developed, it would be found to supersede mere "negativism", or revolutionary liberalism and free thought, as well as the old theology, by a programme which the conservative party or its dictators, no longer fearing social dissolution, would see the wisdom of accepting at the hands of "positive" thinkers.

In his quest of constructive ideas Comte thought at first that he had found what he desired in the social projects of Henri de Saint-Simon (1760–1825), with whom he came into contact in 1818. Saint-Simon is a characteristic figure of the transition from the eighteenth century to the nineteenth. A noble of reforming aspirations, he had with varied success devoted himself to finance in order to acquire the means of procuring assistance in elaborating the schemes evolved in his fertile but theoretically untrained mind. Comte, with his encyclopaedic training in the sciences, presented himself as exactly the assistant he required; and the connexion between them lasted for seven years. From Saint-Simon Comte undoubtedly first took up some of the phrases and modes of thought that were his own starting-points. Among these was, for example, the antithesis between "organic" and "critical" periods, the Middle Ages being regarded as organic and the eighteenth century as critical. The general name given by Saint-Simon to his conception of the new social order was "industrialism". Industrial capacity is to hold in modern life the place that military capacity held in the Middle Ages. The practical direction is now to pass from feudal nobles to industrial chiefs. In the new "organic" period there will be a new "spiritual power" corresponding to the mediaeval Church. For the clergy will be substituted men of science, artists, and generally the theoretical as distinguished from the practical class. The spiritual power, however, is to be strictly subsidiary. The aim of society is "production" in its industrial sense, and the practical chiefs are the supreme directors and judges. To them belongs the selection of the doctrines to be taught.

Comte for a time called himself a Saint-Simonian, and worked out the new ideas in papers of which he did not claim the authorship. One of these, dated 1820, and entitled "Sommaire appréciation de l'ensemble du passé moderne", is reprinted in the series of "opuscules" appended to the last volume of the *Système de Politique Positive.* Comte himself, in the preface to the "opuscules", notes two points in this as original: first, the separation of the destructive and reconstructive, or "negative" and "positive", movements that have been the components of the "Occidental revolution" since the eleventh century; and, secondly, the contrast drawn between France and England according as the "central" or the "local" power gained the predominance. The two antithetic movements, he concluded, have been everywhere simultaneous; but in France the old "temporal power" was prepared for final supersession by a provisional predominance of the monarchy in alliance with the commons, while in England the commons allied with the aristocracy reduced the monarchy to a position subordinate to the latter. For the rest, this paper is not otherwise original, being in the main simply a glorification of the joint triumphs achieved or to be achieved by the spontaneous progress of science and industry. Comte had not yet seized his own problem.

The break between the master and the pupil came with the next paper, dated 1822, and now entitled "Plan des travaux scientifiques nécessaires pour réorganiser la société". In that year only a few copies were distributed. The short treatise was not effectively published till 1824, when Saint-Simon repudiated Comte's distinctive views. It then bore the title "Système de Politique Positive", thus anticipating the title, as well as the ideas, of the later great "Treatise on Sociology" now known by that name. The point of difference was that, according to Comte, the work of the theoretical class must come first and give the direction for the new social order; whereas, according to Saint-Simon, "industrial capacity" is in the first line, and all else is to work for its advantage. Also, Saint-Simon found that Comte had not developed the "sentimental and religious" part of his system. This will not seem surprising when we know that the name given to the religious doctrine was "Neo-Christianity". By his successors this was put forward as the consecration of the socialistic side of his teaching, which they carried further. For Saint-Simon, while his practical scheme is essentially a kind of benevolent capitalism, has a place among the precursors of socialism in so far as he proposes to abolish the inheritance and bequest of property, and to substitute a selection of industrial aptitudes by the community or its chiefs. Here it would be easy to find relations with Comte's ideal polity; but Saint-Simon is admittedly incoherent, and his immense projects were never systematically worked out. Now the last thing of which Comte can be accused is incoherence. Even the mechanism of his system is all there to be criticised in detail. It was not strange, though it was regrettable, that he should afterwards repudiate any obligation to Saint-Simon. The connexion, he declared at last, had only fettered the course of his spontaneous meditations.

The early *Politique Positive* is certainly an astonishing work. At the age of twenty-four, Comte appears already as a master, clearly in possession of the central ideas of his system. Here was originally formulated his "law of the three states". Of this his disciple Littré, who became a dissentient from his later doctrine, and thus fulfils the condition of impartiality, has failed to find any trace in Saint-Simon. As a separate thought it is anticipated in a passage he has brought to light from Turgot; but the idea, as he points out, was by Turgot left quite undeveloped. In Comte it is undoubtedly independent, and by him first it was made the basis of sociology conceived as a positive science. The general idea is that the human mind first explains the course of nature by "theological" fictions, in which objects are imagined to be moved by a quasi-human will; these are then reduced to depersonalised abstractions, or "metaphysical" entities; finally, every attempt is renounced to go behind the "positive" or scientific law of the successions and resemblances of phenomena. This formula having been arrived at historically, society itself becomes the subject-matter of a positive science. For the characteristic of social phenomena, in distinction from all others, is the peculiar kind of continuity that unites the historical past with the present and the future; and the formula of this is the law of the three states, now discovered. Social science, as it develops, will, like the other sciences (astronomy, for instance), be made the ground of prevision. The thinkers who work out this new science will be able to show that a certain type of social order is in the future inevitable, as the past stages have been in their time. Its advent can indeed be retarded by want of insight, but that is all. Nothing can prevent its final realisation. By showing this, the insight of theorists may cause many otherwise inevitable revolutionary disturbances to be avoided on the way. The final movement, Comte holds, is towards supersession of a theologico-military by a scientific industrial order. The intermediate system, in which metaphysicians and jurists took the lead as respectively the theoretical and practical directors, is merely transitional. Men of science, when science has been systematised and unified under a positive conception, will form the spiritual power. The temporal power will be that of the industrial directors, by "industry" being understood in general the action of man on nature. This will have taken the place of "conquest", or the effort to reduce other men to subserviency, which was the characteristic activity of militarism.

In the next "opuscule", entitled "Considérations sur les sciences et les savants" (1825), Comte gives an outline of the classification of the sciences afterwards set forth by him in detail in the *Philosophie Positive*. The paper contains some further development of his views on the "spiritual power", but these are more explicitly stated in the "Considérations sur le pouvoir spirituel" (1826). Here he definitely declares for the institution of a scientific or philosophical clergy, separate from the State, and corresponding to the mediaeval Church. This, he maintains now as later, is the only cure for the temporary anarchy brought on by the division of labour and the dispersive specialism that accompany the generally beneficent march of a progressive movement. The theological base of the old "organic" order as it stood having been irrevocably destroyed by criticism, the problem is to find for the new order a positive base that shall be indestructible by criticism because it is perfectly rational.

THE POSITIVE PHILOSOPHY

The result of Comte's development so far was to turn him away for several years from schemes of direct social reconstruction. This he had decided, as against the Saint-Simonians, was premature, till a philosophy, itself scientific, had been founded on the positive sciences. He had already in his mind the scheme of such a new theoretical construction, and was able to draw up the plan of a "Course of Positive Philosophy" in 1826. The "fundamental work" in which it was embodied —the *Cours de Philosophie Positive*, in six volumes—occupied in actual publication the twelve years from 1830 to 1842. At the end of the last volume he declared himself at length ready to set to work on the elaboration of the social doctrine adumbrated in the early treatises. This he completed in the later *Système de Politique Positive*, which must be reserved for another section.

By "positive philosophy" we are to understand a philosophy not only founded on the sciences, but in its whole substance consisting of their higher generalisations. The structure is thus homogeneous, but there is no thought of deducing all scientific laws from some single law or principle. Such a deduction is admitted to be impossible. Each science has methods and laws peculiar to itself. The abstract sciences form a hierarchy, beginning with Mathematics, which is fundamental as method and also as doctrine, being itself one of the sciences of phenomena. Beginning with Calculus (in the most general sense), it proceeds through Geometry to Rational Mechanics. Next come the sciences of inorganic nature—Astronomy, Terrestrial Physics, and Chemistry. Above these are the sciences of the organic group—Biology (ending with Cerebral Physiology) and Sociology. On these six abstract sciences depend the concrete and the applied sciences. Science, Comte recognises, is really one. The laws of its component sciences interact, and it grows as a whole. But, while it is divided only for convenience, the grouping adopted, he contends, is the natural one. That is to say, it has been discovered as something given, not invented and then imposed on the facts. For the series of sciences is determined by a corresponding series of distinguishable phenomena, the more simple, general, and independent preceding the more complicated, special, and dependent. Social phenomena are at the extreme at once of dependence, speciality, and complexity. To deal with the first point, the relation may be traced all through. For social phenomena depend on the nature of the organisms comprising the society; the phenomena of organic life again depend on chemical and physical, and these on astronomical phenomena; and the conditions of investigating astronomical and physical phenomena are furnished by mathematics. This order of successive terms does not exhibit the whole dependence. The phenomena of society are further directly influenced by those investigated under the heads of chemistry, physics, and astronomy. To take the most remote from man: consider the difference that would be made to the human lot by some astronomically very slight change in the solar system. On the other hand, mathematics, directly applicable to astronomy, is somewhat less applicable to physics, and still less to chemistry; and when organic and social phenomena are reached it is almost without efficacy. The scale of the sciences from mathematics onward, Comte observes, is the descending scale of perfection in the sense of quantitative exactitude; but perfection is not to be confounded with certainty. The less perfect sciences are no less certain, though they are less exact, than those that precede them. Since all phenomena without exception are capable of being brought under positive laws or formulae, there can be, when the scale is complete, no difference as regards the positive character of the sciences. Sociology, once formed, will be as positive as mathematics.

The primary reason by which Comte determines his hierarchy is the relation of the several sciences to the "law of the three states", to which we must now return. The sciences, it appears historically, do not all pass simultaneously through the theological, metaphysical, and positive stages. Taken as wholes, those that deal with the simplest and most general phenomena are the first to become positive. The historical order is that of the scale given. The sciences of organic life, in Comte's view, had reached the positive stage only just before his own time. For him it remained to complete the hierarchy by making the science of society positive. This he was able to do by assigning a law of intellectual development with which other social phenomena could be connected, for there is a consensus among all of them. It is enough for the present that one law has been determined. We have in this something quite distinctive of social phenomena. There is nothing even in organic life quite like the linking of each generation of mankind to those that preceded it by the preservation and successive modification of the products of thought. Hence results a unique method, altogether unlike the "introspective" method of the psychologists. His historical law, he insists, has been determined, not by the necessarily illusory method of "self-observation", which is impossible because the observed and the observer are one, but by an examination of the results of man's mental processes as they lie before us in the actual system of objective knowledge.

The only method Comte recognised of investigating the individual mind, prior to social consideration of it, was an attempt, such as had been made in the phrenology of Gall, to connect the different regions of the brain with corresponding mental faculties. It is sufficiently remarkable that, with no more satisfactory position than this to start from, he determined the mode of establishing generalisations in sociology which was adopted by Mill, who had long been in search of it, and confesses that without the aid of Comte he might never have arrived at it. The procedure is this. A law of historical development having been attained by empirical generalisation from experience, it is tested by trying whether it can be deduced from previously known laws of human nature: biological laws, they are called by Comte; by Mill, psychological. Comte, it must be observed, regards his law of the three states as also a law of the individual human mind, in which the historical stages of the general mind are recapitulated. How this is ascertained, or whether it is a happy illustration of the method, we need not discuss. Comte's "historical method" itself stands secure. It has taken its place in Mill's logical doctrine as the "inverse deductive method", in distinction from the "direct deductive method" characteristic of physics. In actual historical work of a generalising kind it may be seen constantly in use, and by Sir Edward Tylor it has been further developed as a method applicable in the special researches of anthropologists.

Comte himself carried his sociological theorising beyond the limits of recorded history. His explanation of the origin of religion ascribes to primitive man a doctrine of universal animation, called by him "fetishism". At the beginning of the theological stage, men spontaneously regarded each particular thing exhibiting active powers as alive. It was thus at first the particular object that was deified. By a process of abstraction and generalisation, classes of objects were brought under the imaginary dominion of a separable deity. The stage of polytheism was thus reached. Further generalisation led to monotheism, the last phase of theology. Through all this process "metaphysical" thought was already at work, reducing by its dissolvent criticism the potency of theological explanations. Finally, it has attenuated even theism to the point where it becomes superfluous. The God of the Deist is equivalent to the metaphysical abstraction Nature, and becomes merely a name that is allowed to furnish no element of detailed explanation, this being left to the growing sciences. When the sciences are mature, the "causes" (more than phenomenal) of the theologian and the metaphysician are alike dismissed; and, as was said, nothing is left but a formulated law. Not till this mode of thinking has successively extended itself through the series of the sciences, and prevailed in Sociology also, can the human mind be considered as having finally reached the positive state.

Already in the *Philosophie Positive* Comte has arrived at his conception of Humanity as the organic unity within which sociological law is manifested. This organism consists of men past, present, and future; excluding, however, from participation its anti-social elements, while, on the other hand, the useful domestic animals are associated with man in a subsidiary relation. Humanity is conceived as having a beginning and an end in time, though Comte does not speculate about origins. It tends as a whole to a final order, which will approach equilibrium but never actually reach it. After this closer and closer approximation to a fixed ideal, there will be an inevitable decadence as the earth ceases to be fit for human habitation, and the problem for man will then be to adapt himself with dignity to the descent. With this, however, sociology need not now concern itself: we are still in the movement of ascent, which is of more interest. The progressive movement with which we are specially concerned is that which has gone on continuously in the West from the period of Asiatic or Egyptian theocracy to the attainment of the positive stage by the most advanced minds of contemporary Europe. To explain historical progress, Comte does not recur to theories about race or climate. These, indeed, are not excluded. They may, it is allowed, furnish minor explanations when the time comes to carry sociology into detail, but the progress now dealt with is held to be a necessary evolution of man as man, not due essentially to the character of some particular race or races. What is at present the most advanced part of humankind will afterwards extend its completed type to the whole, all men as such being capable of assimilating the progress at first achieved only by favoured societies or individuals.

With his law of intellectual evolution Comte seeks to connect a corresponding law of practical evolution. To the theological stage corresponds militarism. This first takes the form of aggressive warfare and systematic conquest. As theology passes into its last or monotheistic phase and becomes attenuated into metaphysics, defensive is substituted for offensive war. Then, as positivity grows, militarism is slowly superseded by industrialism. These, Comte maintains, are necessary phases of human progress, and their treatment belongs to abstract sociology; but in the concrete we find the first realised in different degrees in Asia and Egypt and in classical antiquity, the second in the Middle Ages of Western Europe, and the third in the outlines of a new positive order now appearing in the most advanced nations of the West.

By the Greek States, although their history belongs generally to the theologico-military phase of offensive warfare, this is not typically represented. Since no one State could subjugate the rest, the characteristic movement was checked on the side of activity, and the distinctive development of Greece became intellectual. The last result of this was to reduce polytheism to monotheism, and to prepare for the Catholic type; though Catholicism, in the account it gave of itself, traced its monotheism exclusively to its Jewish predecessors. The Romans successfully carried forward the system of conquest, in which the Greeks had failed; and the stage of offensive war culminated in the Roman Empire. The problem for this, and for the social groups into which it broke up, became henceforth defence. The Middle Ages represent the system of defensive warfare combined with a reduced form of theology. In this period, the greatest advance is the separation of the temporal and the spiritual powers, confused both in the theocratic East and in classical antiquity. This advance was made only by the Catholic West. Byzantine Christianity and Islam—the rival form of reduced theology that shared in the division of the Roman world—alike retained the confusion. The Catholic synthesis reaches its typical form in the twelfth and thirteenth centuries. Ever since, it has been breaking up under the joint action of the critical or revolutionary "metaphysics" and the growing positive sciences, now tending, along with the rising industrial system, to a definitive reconstruction of European life. During the fourteenth and fifteenth centuries the decomposition was spontaneous, and was shared in by all the Western populations. After that it became systematic, first in Protestantism and then in Deism, and brought with it first the break of the Reformation in the sixteenth century, and then the revolutionary crisis at the end of the eighteenth. This crisis can only be terminated when the positive, as distinguished from the negative, movement has furnished the elements of a new and final synthesis.

The practical or "temporal" power of the positive age, dawning in the nineteenth century, will be that of industrial, and no longer of military, chiefs. Its supreme "spiritual" power will consist of philosophers who have undergone an encyclopaedic training in the positive sciences, and are able to view them in their systematic unity. These positive philosophers will be properly a special class of scientific men set apart to deal with generalities, since the specialists in particular branches are clearly incompetent for the work of coordination. The highest social rank will be conceded to them, but they will have no material power. Thus they will take the place of the mediaeval priesthood, which has furnished the ideal pattern of a theoretical class standing apart from practical life, but directing it through the consultative voice it has in affairs and, above all, by its system of education applied to all the other social classes and permeating them from youth with its dominant conceptions.

We can now see how Comte, in his "fundamental work", while moving away for a time from the social problem he had set himself to resolve, was preparing the ideas that were to be brought together in a more concentrated form in the *Politique Positive*. Naturally he found it difficult to understand on what ground disciples and admirers of the *Philosophy* could repudiate the *Polity*, which was to him its necessary sequel. A partial understanding, however, is possible. The chapter of the *Philosophy* vindicating the progressive character of the Catholic Middle Age opens with some pages in which he sets forth a doctrine regarding the separation of the spiritual from the temporal power which liberals like Grote and Mill might think themselves able to accept. The direct dominance of a theoretical class is there described as superficially plausible, since it places intelligence apparently at the summit, but as in reality the most fatally unprogressive of social orders. It renders ineffective the most powerful and original minds of theoretic type, for which an administrative hierarchy has no proper place. By the immediate connexion of the theoretical class with practice, no room is left for speculative research undertaken without reference to material needs. Yet this detachment is of supreme importance for the progressive character of the practical arts themselves. The true form of a spiritual power is one in which the few eminent theoretical minds are protected by the State in freely doing their own work, but do not aim at any place in a governing corporation.

This is, of course, a very singular prelude to a defence of the mediaeval hierarchy, not simply as an institution adapted to its time, but as a model for the future. It may be compared with a paragraph in one of the early "opuscules", where the position of the Catholic clergy in the Middle Ages is declared to be analogous to that of the Greek philosophers in relation to the State as compared with the hierarchs of Asia. The presupposition, however, that European history has been continuously progressive, whence it followed that the Middle Ages must embody a progressive phase, was not peculiar to Comte. Mill was quite willing to accept the whole view so far as the past was concerned; and, in critical articles, commended to English readers the work of French historians by whom what he thought to be Protestant prejudice was controverted. The difference appeared when Comte fully recognised his own affinities, ceased to recur to merely fanciful combinations, and left no doubt that it was of the essence of his own spiritual power to be an authoritative corporation, which he no longer hesitated to treat as analogous to an Egyptian or Chaldean theocracy.

By way of comment it need only be remarked that Comte certainly did not in the end fulfil the condition of impartiality he at first laid down for himself in rebuking the revolutionary hatred of the mediaeval past. The antipathy he has expressed again and again for the "critical" periods of Greece and modern Europe is quite equal to that of any Protestant or revolutionary Deist for the Middle Ages. This apparent necessity to hate the one type and love the other seems to indicate contrasts hard to deal with on any theory of continuous progress. And, indeed, it may be observed that there is a place in Comte's sociological doctrine for pathological phenomena and reversals of progressive movements, though he has given it little theoretical development.

MILL'S LOGIC AND METAPHYSICS

In the preceding section I have dealt only with the generalities of the *Philosophie Positive*, as set forth at the beginning, and with the Sociology contained in the last three volumes. The intermediate part of the work contains the systematisation of the five preparatory sciences, Mathematics, Astronomy, Physics, Chemistry, and Biology. Comte himself did not claim the knowledge of a specialist in any of these except mathematics, nor did he exaggerate the importance of his preliminary work. Perhaps afterwards, when those who had accepted it almost without qualification would follow him no further, he came to underrate it. It had a genuinely emancipating influence, especially in England, where it soon began to draw more attention than it had gained in France.

Among the most enthusiastic readers of the successive volumes was Mill, who in 1841 began a correspondence with Comte which continued till 1846. At first Mill announced himself as a disciple, but he was a disciple who claimed the right to criticise, and thought to exercise as well as to receive influence. Later, what seemed to him the appallingly systematic character of Comte's mind, for which every principle was settled and every detail had the certainty of positive science, showed him that the kind of interchange he had hoped for was impossible. To Mill, as to early friends, Comte frankly declared that he had no use for criticism, except regarding the legitimacy of deductions. That any one who remained at the theological or at the metaphysical stage should not accept the new system was intelligible: but for a mind that had reached full positivity he did not see what attitude was possible but adhesion. At first, however, the correspondence was extremely cordial. Comte read with interest Mill's *System of Logic*, published in 1843, making for it an exception from his rule of not reading contemporary work. He found in it the most advanced position, next to his own, occupied by any European thinker; and this, he perceived, had been independently arrived at. It was Mill's generosity, he declared, that had led him to cite the *Philosophie Positive* so frequently. The development of his thought would have been substantially the same without it.

This is true, as Mill showed himself aware later. Still, in the history of inductive logic Comte ranks as his immediate precursor, his remoter precursors being Bacon and Hume. His direct studies for his work had been mainly in actual science and in contemporary English writers of minor originality. As the essential problem, he fixed at last on the question: What constitutes scientific proof in the experimental investigation of nature? It is here that he himself came to see his distinctive strength as compared with that of Comte, who, he found, had never attained a just conception of the conditions of proof as distinguished from method. The problem of method had of course been specially raised by Bacon, who gave a first sketch of the procedure formulated by Mill in his "canons of induction" as the ground for applying his test of truth. On the question of ultimate truth in science, which was Hume's special problem, Bacon was quite vague. Here Comte and Mill were equally clear in substance, and, by more serious occupation with the actual processes of science, had disentangled the idea of fixed law or order; which, while it had been put forward by Hume, had received from him a sceptical colour. This, he said, is all that there seems to be in science; but, if our scholastic dogmatists are right, there ought to be something more. That the order was really positive or certain,

Comte was assured by the applicability of mathematics to the things of nature. For the power of dealing with them by quantitative measurement implies positive law. With this insight he was content; and here he fell short of Mill. In the proper sense of the term—not in Comte's rather abusive sense—Mill was a metaphysician; that is to say, he was concerned, like Hume, with the first principles of knowledge or science. He could not be content till he had determined on what most general ground we are entitled to assert one fixed order and no other in each particular case.

We may see this even where Mill is thought to have failed. Take Comte's opening mathematical chapters. He starts with a discussion of the end of mathematical science, not indeed its practical end, but its end as pure theory. This he defines as "indirect measurement". Then he applies his immense analytic and synthetic power to determine and classify its methods. The problem, how we know mathematical propositions to be true, is scarcely touched. Essentially he regards mathematics as a natural science of given phenomena. A problem like that raised by Kant does not exist for him. Mill, on the other hand, though not in close contact with Kant's thought, regards the question about the evidence of geometrical axioms as fundamental. Are they "synthetic judgments *a priori*", or are they generalisations from experience? His conclusion that they are generalisations from experience is not now accepted, at least in the form he gave to it; but he dealt with the problem.

Where Mill completely succeeded was in putting the logic of Induction on a firm basis. To begin with, he had been thoroughly trained in the scholastic logic and its Aristotelian original, and knew exactly what it could do and could not do. With a view partly to refuting the indiscriminate prejudice against it that had reigned in scientific quarters since the seventeenth century, and was only now beginning to give way, he first worked out the theory of Syllogism on lines of his own. Only when he had disposed of this did he go on to Induction, by which he was for a long time stopped. The question was,

How can we get, from the result of a particular experiment, a general law which we know to be true? The formal logicians had little to say on this. What they called "perfect induction" was a barren summary of particulars already known, not a process leading to new knowledge. An impression was left that scientific induction—all of it formally "imperfect"—is a kind of mystery, producing conviction no one can say how. This air of mystery Mill at length dissipated. Certain forms of experimental "method", he showed, yield a valid general conclusion because it can be seen that no conclusion but this is compatible with the axiom called the "uniformity of nature". The expression he chose for this uniformity was the "law of causation", which he stated as the proposition that every event has an "invariable and unconditional antecedent", which we call its cause. That is to say, there is some determinate phenomenon or group of phenomena, the existence of which being given, the phenomenon we call the effect will follow. His attempt to assign the ground of our belief in this law itself, like his theory of mathematical axioms, has not found permanent acceptance; but none the less his determination of the valid forms of inductive inference remains definitive. This does not mean that it was incapable of improvement, or even that he left it relatively as perfect as Aristotle left the theory of syllogistic logic. Physical science has been going on ever since, and logicians formulate and justify its methods after they have been invented, not before. It is now generally admitted, for example, that Mill underrated the place of deduction from hypotheses in physical science. He had a theory of rational deduction that was in great part true, but he limited it too much to a tracing of the consequences of known generalisations from experience. There is more place than he cared to allow for conjecture as the starting-point of deduction —of course with a view to verification by facts. But, as far as the process of induction is concerned, the "new organon" that Bacon had called for was at last created. Every induction was shown to imply at once some particular experience, and a deduction from the "law of causation" assumed to be universal.

There can be a system of scientific truths, because nature as seen in the relation of cause and effect is uniform.[1]

With respect to the idea itself of "cause", Mill and Comte differ only in the form of expression. When Comte rejects the use of the word, and prefers to speak only of "law", he means to dismiss ontological causes, supposed realities behind phenomena that have intrinsic power or efficacy to produce certain effects. Mill retains it because he thinks it is most properly regarded simply as a name for the phenomenal antecedents that "invariably and unconditionally" precede their phenomenal consequents. The negative result of Hume's analysis is accepted, implicitly or explicitly, by both. We have no knowledge of any power in the cause to produce this effect rather than that, or of any tie between the cause and the effect. The laws of nature are phenomenal laws, not laws of "things-in-themselves", and our knowledge of them depends wholly on experience.

Nevertheless there is in Comte a negative dogmatism to which Mill did not commit himself, and which he did not hold as a belief. Comte has at bottom no doubt that a real world of mindless objectivity composes the sum of existence prior to the appearance of animal life.[2] On the origin of life, as on the origin of man, he has no theory. His position is distinguished from materialism by the rejection, on principle, of every attempt to derive the higher from the lower. Thus he can take an essentially teleological view both of life and mind. A true providential order, he holds, has been introduced into the world by man. He has no objection to the association of this doctrine historically with a teleological optimism like that of Leibniz. Yet, while he rejects the name of "atheism" (with some asperity, as Mill remarks), the rejection means only that

[1] Bernardino Telesio (1508–1588), whom Bacon most appreciated among the innovators of the preceding age, came nearer than anything in Bacon himself to formulating the principle of the uniformity of nature, "quae, perpetuo sibi ipsi concors, idem semper et eodem agit modo, atque idem semper operatur" (Bacon's *Novum Organum*, Fowler, 2nd ed., Introduction, p. 95).

[2] This was never explicitly stated, though I think it was implied; but there are positions that depart from it in his later phase.

he has no interest in atheistic cosmogonies. His objection to them indeed is that they are in essence a kind of theology or metaphysics, seeking explanation where the human mind can find none. He would not even permit a speculative interest in the physical universe beyond the solar system, because nothing external to this can have any sufficiently direct bearing on the human lot. With the humanistic, as against an attempted cosmic, point of view, Mill had much sympathy; but he was more aware than Comte ever became that the limitations of objective science are narrower than those of the human mind.

Mill's metaphysical positions are to be found partly in the *Logic*, but chiefly in the *Examination of Sir William Hamilton's Philosophy* (1865). This treatise was written, as he has himself explained, with an aim that was ultimately practical. He regarded the kind of philosophising rather vaguely called Intuitionism as the enemy of all reform, because its tendency was to treat mere customary associations of ideas, dissoluble by analysis, as "necessary truths" known prior to experience. Of this philosophy Sir W. Hamilton (1788–1856) seemed to him the best and strongest representative; descending as he did from the Scottish school of Common Sense founded by Reid, but deriving some of his ideas from Kant, and generally impressive by the copiousness of his learning. To Kant and his successors, representing the latest phase of Continental Rationalism (as distinguished from English Experientialism) eclectic thinkers both in France and England had turned under the impression that this was somehow an antidote to the irreligious "philosophy of the eighteenth century" descending from Locke. Hence arose hybrid philosophies like those of Cousin, of Whewell, of Hamilton himself, and of Hamilton's disciple Mansel. The relations to religion on both sides, if we take the complete historical series in England and on the Continent, are rather varied. Mill has noticed the paradox that in his time those who regarded the law of causation as an intuitive truth were understood to allow miracles, and those who derived it only from experience to reject them. The controversy that burst forth over the *Examination of Hamilton* (in which Mansel also was dealt with) may be considered as having closed this particular phase of the opposing philosophies in England. Successors may be found both of the "Intuitionists" and of Mill, but none would now class themselves precisely with either side.

Much of the *Examination of Hamilton* is constructive. In pure philosophy the most effective chapters are those in which Mill has restated and developed Berkeley's idealism as against the "natural realism" or "natural dualism" of the Common Sense school. According to this characteristic doctrine of Reid and Hamilton, consciousness has an immediate intuition of its object in contrast with itself. Matter and mind are directly known as antithetic realities. Against this, Mill worked out on psychological grounds a positive explanation of our belief in the external world, reducing what we come to know of matter wholly to phenomena and their relations. The grounds were furnished partly by Reid's successor, Thomas Brown, who had developed the Scottish philosophy in the direction of Associationism, and partly by Professor Bain, then rising as an original psychologist of the Associationist school. Having defined matter, in a phrase that has become famous, as "permanent possibility of sensation", Mill goes on to investigate the nature of the psychological subject. This he finds more resistant to analysis than the object. If we call mind a "series of feelings", we must add that it is "aware of itself as a series", and this makes it something quite peculiar and not finally explicable. Thus he remains in the end nearer to Berkeley than to Hume (whose *Treatise* perhaps he had not read). Mind is for him ultimately more real than matter.

Against all attempts to establish "necessary truths" on the mere deliverance of consciousness, he urges the law of "inseparable association", recurring here to his father's *Analysis*. He would like to reduce not only arithmetical and geometrical axioms, but the formal laws of thought, to generalisations from experience. Free-will, which Hamilton made the basis of morals, he declines to accept as a deliverance of consciousness; but puts forward a doctrine of his own which, while fundamentally determinist, allows in each person a certain power to modify his own character if he has the desire. From ethical theism, as we can now see in the light of his later work, he is not averse. Indeed he shows himself rather anxious to prove, in opposition to sceptical theologians who would ground theism itself on belief in revelation, that the idea of a God with moral attributes is not irrational. What he will have nothing to do with is an ontology of the Absolute, such as Hamilton and Mansel attempt to combine with personal theism and acceptance of revealed religion. At the point where an ontology of his own, differing from that of his antagonists, might have been expected, his idealistic theory breaks off. It serves merely to limit dogmatic affirmations, without suggesting any doctrine concerning the reality of the universe that goes beyond particular scientific hypotheses. In later sections we shall see more in detail both his likeness and unlikeness here to Comte.

THE RELIGION OF HUMANITY

Between the last volume of the *Philosophie Positive* and the first of the *Politique Positive* there took place what is sometimes regarded as a revolution in Comte's manner of thinking. In definitely returning from the laws of social development to a scheme of social reconstruction, he no longer called himself simply a philosopher, but came forward as the founder of a religion. This has been explained by thorough-going disciples as merely a change in expression. In his earlier works he spoke uniformly as if rejecting everything that was called religion, and made philosophy the highest name. But by "religion", it is said, he then meant only theology. Later he distinguished more exactly, and, while continuing to reject every theology, took religion instead of philosophy for the name of what is highest in his synthesis. This may serve as a partial explanation; but there was also something unforeseen. The germinal ideas of the social reconstruction that afterwards took form are indeed present in the earlier works, but the organised "cult of humanity" is new. The men of science or philosophers who constitute the revived "spiritual power" are now not merely successors of the mediaeval clergy, but are definitely clothed with sacerdotal attributes. The ideal for the future is theocracy minus theology. The sciences are conceived as co-ordinated finally in authorised text-books in a way that was hardly prefigured in the first outlines, where we were left to suppose special theoretical researches still going on in freedom side by side with the work of the class that is to co-ordinate them. And Comte at first had an apparently clearer sense that the work of co-ordination could not be done once for all by any one man. There is in him, after the completion of the *Philosophie Positive*, an undeniable "exaltation", as Littré called it.

The revolution, however, is more apparent than real. A well-known distinctive point in his later system, for example, is the supreme position assigned to the life of the affections. To this, in the ideal order, the intellectual life will be secondary, while practical activity comes third. Mill, in his *Auguste Comte and Positivism*, traced this prescription for mankind in general to the circumstances of Comte's life. With his disposition to organise everything, he would have made the life of feeling supreme for all during the whole of life, because during the short period of his attachment to Madame Clotilde de Vaux (before her death in 1846) he himself had found full satisfaction in it. In an earlier correspondence, however (not published when Mill wrote), Comte had expressed precisely the same view. In fact, a biographical explanation no more applies than in the somewhat similar case of Mill himself, who has pointed out that his advocacy of equal social and political rights for both sexes was not originally due to the influence of his wife. His position that justice absolutely demands equality dated from his youth, when he had maintained it against his father's view, incidentally expressed, that democratic government does not strictly require that women should take part in electing representatives. The mental history of both philosophers, it may be observed, suggests something very like "innate ideas".

An occasion for bringing forward his new conceptions with practical effect seemed to offer itself to Comte in the Revolution of 1848. It was in that year that he published his *Discours sur l'Ensemble du Positivisme*, afterwards incorporated in the first volume of the *Politique Positive*. From the chiefs of revolutions and reactions alike, however, nothing but discouragement was to come to him. We may completely assent to what his disciples say of his heroic persistence in his own course, now as during the rest of his life. At the same time, there came in more and more an element of illusion that was absent from his first period. The new religion, he predicted later, would have received official recognition in Europe at the end of a century from the Revolution of 1789. He himself, if he lived long enough, would be saluted as the High Priest of Humanity. But to say more on this is not worth while, even if there were space. The social reconstruction forms an imaginative synthesis not affected in its real interest by failure, actual or prospective, to realise itself in the expression that Comte gave to it.

His later doctrine is expounded in the *Système de Politique Positive* (4 vols., 1851–1854) and in the *Synthèse Subjective* (1856). The superiority, in some respects, of these works over the earlier ones is admitted even by Mill, who was least in sympathy with them. Their retrograde character is seen chiefly in the growing antipathy, which Mill notes, to intellect as such. But, as an intellectual structure, they themselves rise above the earlier works, both in discrimination and in breadth of view, not to speak of the advance generally allowed as regards imagination and feeling. The superiority may be seen especially in the historical exposition; where it was less to be looked for, since Comte was more preoccupied than he had been formerly with "order" as distinguished from "progress", with what he called "social statics" as distinguished from "dynamics". The religious type of Western Asia is now far more clearly marked off than in the *Philosophy* from that of

Greece and Rome. The highly organised theocracy of the first type is classed as distinctively industrial rather than military. Thus the term "theologico-military", as a general name for the old order, loses its typical value, though it is never quite discarded. "Progressive" took the place of "conservative" polytheism, Comte now finds, precisely through the superior position gained in the West by the military class. This was at most adumbrated in the "fundamental work". In the *Philosophy,* the "revolutionary transition" essentially kept in view consisted only of the five modern centuries from the end of the thirteenth. In the *Polity,* the analogy of the modern West to ancient Greece being more clearly seen, the break-up of the old order is found to occupy (with intermediate reactions) thirty centuries from the Homeric age. If the unfairness to the "critical" periods has become intensified, the insight into their analogies has deepened. There is added further a remarkable speculation on prehistoric man. Before the typical theocracy, Comte places a kind of fetishistic Golden Age, in which man felt himself at one with nature, conceived as universally animated. An interesting suggestion is thrown out that it was at this stage that animals were first domesticated. Man, being then less removed from them in intelligence and sympathy, could put himself with more spontaneity in relation with them. The period of force and dominance came later. Had it been necessary to begin by violent subjugation, no taming could ever have been effected.

These, however, are relatively subordinate developments. Both in method and in doctrine, Comte's later phase is marked by one unquestionable advance of the highest scientific generality. At first Sociology was conceived by him as the supreme science. He held it to be dependent on Biology as the next in order in the hierarchy. From Biology (or a special department of it) sociological laws must be deduced. He had seen, however, from the first, that Sociology is not wholly thus dependent. It has a method and a doctrine of its own: namely, the historical method and the law of the three states. But this brings into relief another aspect of the individual man. By the time he had completed the *Cours de Philosophie Positive,* Comte perceived the necessity of a revision, as he told Mill in their correspondence. Hitherto the individual had not been explicitly considered at all, except as a biological organism. This point of view he now perceived to be even more inadequate than he had thought. Individuality had seemed at first to be a mere biological notion, and then to be effaced under the conception of a social unity. From Comte's later point of view the individual person in the full sense can be restored as an object of science, not indeed as a unit that enters into society, but as determined by sociological laws. There is a true science of man as individual; but it is posterior, not prior, to Sociology. To this science Comte gave the name of Morality, making it the seventh in his hierarchy. Moral science being conceived as supreme, all below must be ordered from its point of view. With this conception there naturally goes (according to his social scheme) the position that the philosophers or priests are, above all, to be moral teachers. Being the educators of the community, they will direct practice from the ethical point of view, to which all intellectual pursuits can now more definitely than ever be subordinated.

Theoretically, it must be noted that Comte's new science is properly not ethics, but psychology of the individual. For such a science, his insight into its true relation to sociology is undoubtedly of immense importance; but he failed to distinguish it from moral philosophy, which is not the same thing. Just as he does not discuss philosophically the criterion of scientific knowledge, but takes it for granted, so he does not discuss the criterion of action, but supposes it to emerge as a matter of course from his theoretical "moral science". He has, indeed, an ethical doctrine, but it is nowhere critically justified.

His ethical principle is Love or Altruism. The supreme precept of his morality is "Live for others". Sympathetic as well as selfish feelings, he finds, are in fact innate in man though they are weaker. In the stages of human history, in spite of this weakness, altruism slowly gets the better of egoism.

Taking the historical view as sufficient, and passing over "critical" questions about the proof for the individual conscience, supposed autonomous, and claiming the right to give or refuse its assent according to the reason of the case, he goes straight to the practical social question. The principle granted, as he thinks it cannot but be, how is it to be brought to bear systematically on every action? His answer is, by a religion—the Religion of Humanity. On Humanity as the highest form of life upon earth, the "Great Being" of the planet, each person depends for all that he is and does. Humanity, we have seen, is an organism in a higher than the biological sense. Its continuity is that of history and not of merely organic life. It is a real providence, in distinction from the imaginary supra-mundane providence of the theologians. Thus it becomes for us the supreme object of devotion. Through the graduated unities of family first, then city or country, the individual rises to the conception of the highest real being known to him, having a life in the past and in the future that far transcends the mere present. Humanity, then, can become the object of a cult, of which the devotion to incarnate gods or goddesses was an adumbration. Of this cult the founder of the religion proceeded to draw up the outlines and a considerable part of the details.

The new religion is the "Religion of Humanity" not only in the sense that its practice issues in the service of man, but also in the sense that it is destined to become finally the religion of the human race. From its beginnings in the central people of Western Europe, where it is directly the heir of Catholic monotheism, it will spread over the rest of the world, aiding the populations that have remained polytheist or fetishist to rise to the stage of positivity without the painful theological and metaphysical transition that has been necessary in the historic past. Agreement having been arrived at intellectually, the religion will aim at the systematic cultivation of the sympathetic feelings by exciting emotions of love and gratitude. The cult, in the definitive order, will be both public and private. Woman as domestic goddess will be the object of the private cult. In its public form, the adoration of Humanity will be organised in a series of feasts dedicated to the constituent elements and stages of man's life impersonally conceived, the private cult being directed rather to personal objects. The well-known Positivist Calendar is intended only to prepare the way for this definitive form of "Sociolatry". The months and weeks and days of the provisional calendar are dedicated to the great names, theoretical and practical, that stand for all the progressive movements from the "initial Theocracy" to the modern "Republic of the West", consisting of the "five advanced populations", French, Italian, Spanish, British, and Germanic. The dating to be brought into use in substitution for the preceding era of Europe is in years of the "great crisis", the opening of the French Revolution in 1789 being taken as the beginning.

I do not propose here to give any account of the hierarchical order to be imposed on the society of the future. As a scheme to be adopted outright, few Positivists now accept it; though, if not taken too literally, others as well as Positivists may find in it suggestions of great value concerning the stages of an encyclopaedic education and the practical ordering of life. I pass on to give a few points from Comte's last work, the *Synthèse Subjective*, which represents in some respects the highest stage of his thought.

No more than the rest of his later writings is it a reversal of his earlier doctrine. It is, as he maintained, a completion of it from the other term of the series. The stages in his hierarchy of the sciences he still holds to be objectively given; but his view all along was that they lead up to man as the end. Everything, then, has to be gone over again from the human point of view when this has at last become positive. The sciences in general, objective though they be, were never supposed to be other than "relative"; and this means finally that they are relative to man. That is to say, no "objective synthesis" is attainable. The only possible synthesis is "subjective". This does not mean that it is merely individual. A subjective synthesis is attainable from the point of view of humanity and not merely of some particular thinker. But no synthesis is objectively universal. The objectivity that exists is only that of abstract science, and carries with it no knowledge of the whole.

This is, I think, a fair representation of Comte's thought. He did not live to work it out in full, but in the only volume published of what was to be a third series of writings (after the *Philosophy* and the *Polity*), he applied it to mathematics, always in his view the fundamental science both as regards method and doctrine. The most remarkable part of this volume is the opening section, in which the Religion of Humanity is extended to the universe—or at least to that portion of it with which man is in effective relation—by what is confessedly poetic fiction. The "fictions" of the theologians, according to Comte, were of course not deliberate. Primeval fetishism, the fundamental form of "theology", by which objects were endowed not only with will and feeling, but with intelligence, was a spontaneous belief. Like later theologies in their degree, it served the purpose of giving to human curiosity a sufficient stimulus till the formulation of positive laws could be substituted for the futile search after "causes". The positive philosopher, however, when the whole series of stages has been traversed, may deliberately restore in the contemplation of nature what he knows to be a purely subjective and human mode of thought. First, the birthplace and home of man may be endowed with sympathy and will for human good. An imaginative extension of this hypothesis makes the Earth the "Great Fetish", as Man is the "Great Being". Further, to abstract laws we may assign as their seat Space, which thus becomes the "Great Medium", imagined not indeed as actively volitional like the Earth, but as benevolent. Space, the Earth, and Man form the Positivist Trinity. The other planets of the solar system may be regarded in like manner as animated, and the Sun and Moon especially may be made the subject of poetic personifications.

Unaware, probably, of the remarkable coincidences between these suggestions and the personifications in the last Act of

Prometheus Unbound, Comte leaves them to the poets of the future. By Shelley, it is worth observing, not only these "fictions", which with the poet were of course no less fictions than with the philosopher, but many of Comte's distinctive theoretic ideas were anticipated. The glorified humanity of the future is conceived not in terms of "atomic individualism", but as the Great Being—Man, not men. To develop this further might seem to the reader fanciful; but the comparison was worth making in order to show how easily the general conception of a Religion of Humanity can be cleared of what is merely personal in it. And, indeed, Comte himself, in this last stage, is visibly getting beyond anything that may appear to us sectional in his choice of models. From the typical mediaeval conception of the world, with its agency of external spirits acting on matter, nothing could be more remote.

MILL'S POLITICS, ECONOMICS, AND ETHICS

It has been mentioned that Mill derived from Comte the Inverse Deductive or Historical Method, which he finally came to regard as the only possible method for the more complex investigations in the science of society. This is set forth in the sixth book of the *Logic* ("On the Logic of the Moral Sciences"). At an earlier stage of his political thinking he had already received an impression from Comte, and had come under the influence of the Saint-Simonians, as may be seen in the letters to his friend Gustave d'Eichthal, who was a member of the group. The contact was one of those that contributed to modify his Benthamism, others being his relations with what may be called generally the counter-revolutionary movement in England. Here, as in France, recognition that errors had in fact been swept away was accompanied in many educated minds by a disposition to find, mainly in the order that had been singled out as the object of revolutionary hate, something more noble and beautiful than that which seemed to be taking its place. The structure of Catholic feudalism and the mediaeval Church attracted not only theological reactionaries, but some who, like Carlyle, saw that the old system of belief was irreparably destroyed. It is noteworthy that Hegel, for all his Prussian conversatism, never took this direction, but sought a true organic base, as against mere anarchism, not essentially in a Church at all, but in the classical or the modern national State. This, as an organic order, had not impressed any of the minds by which Mill was especially influenced. And, as he had never abandoned what Comte called the "revolutionary metaphysics", the effect of the new influences was not one of unqualified attraction. He was willing to find something impressive in the mediaeval past that periods like the eighteenth century had lost, but the critical spirit remained alert. He found already in Comte's early *Politique Positive* an excess of system, and remarked on the special favour he shows to the Middle Ages as contrasted with his unfairness to classical antiquity. Mill himself might come to be over-impressed later by the "rehabilitation of the Middle Ages"; but the large part played by Greek studies in his early education gave him the superiority over Comte in actual knowledge concerning the other term of the contrast. To the Saint-Simonians, with their zeal for industrial "production", he insisted on the disadvantages that accompany its success in England, which they were disposed to envy. A profound egoism of tone, not merely in formed men of the world, but in young men, who in France and Germany are usually full of generous enthusiasm, is what he finds to result from the predominance of the life of commerce. With the aspirations of the Saint-Simonians to a new order of society, and even to a new religion, he was at the same time completely in sympathy, though already afraid of the sectarian spirit which would try to impress on entire communities a single direction to be fixed by the doctrine of a school.

Before the time of his correspondence with Comte, he had found himself obliged to give up the rigorous position of his father, set forth in the article on "Government". Macaulay's attack in the *Edinburgh Review* (1829) had convinced him that what he afterwards called the "geometrical method" of direct deduction from principles of human nature cannot give valid propositions applicable to the whole of a society. The purely experimental or "chemical" method (as he called it later) of Macaulay is, however, equally invalid. Specific experience is here too complicated to permit the application of the inductive methods. The method has to be some kind of scientific deduction. With abstract Political Economy he had no special difficulty. If men are assumed to be actuated only by one class of motives—in this case, those that refer to wealth—then the problem is sufficiently simplified to be treated in the manner of a deductive science like astronomy or physics. Having reached conclusions hypothetically valid, we can correct them by restoring the data provisionally set aside. When, however, all the phenomena of a society are to be taken into account at once, the *consensus* of its elements deprives us of the resource furnished by this kind of abstraction. For the problem of method thus left over, he found the solution, as has been said, in Comte. With some reserves intended to conciliate English prejudice regarding Comte's use of the term "theological", he also accepted his doctrine expressed in the "law of the three states". Further than this it cannot be said that he ever proceeded in Sociology as a science. The later developments of his own thought in its application to society were in Economics, in Politics considered as a practical art depending to some extent on philosophical principles, and in the theory of Ethics.

A project referred to in the correspondence with Comte, but not carried out, was a work on the science Mill called Ethology, or the formation of human character, regarded as derivative from Psychology, or the science of the elementary laws of mind. This, in Mill's view, would have been a step on the way to a scientific Sociology. The lines on which it was conceived were, however, "individualistic" in the sense in which Comte was now fully aware of his own advance on individualism. Mill came to perceive that his scheme was, at least for the present, impracticable, and turned instead to the subject of Political Economy, with the development of which, up to the point it had reached, he was perfectly familiar. Here again there was a divergence from Comte, who, though not condemning outright Mill's project of a treatise on economics, in reality thought the abstract science of the economists of very slight value. He had already expressed himself to this effect. The separate treatment of the phenomena of wealth, in his view, was the source of antithetic errors: industrial *laissez-faire* on the one side, and socialistic schemes for nationalising the instruments of production on the other. The only kind of social science that could henceforth give any true guidance was a science of social phenomena in their totality. Mill, however, seeing no clear light in this direction, and retaining his belief in economics within its own limits, now began his second great treatise, the *Principles of Political Economy*, which appeared in 1848. What gave the work its essential interest for him was the hope, by application of the new doctrines attained since Adam Smith by Ricardo and Malthus, to point the way to social reform. In particular, the doctrine of Malthus on population was applied by him to refute despairing views as to the future of the labouring classes. Population, it is true, by its unchecked increase tends to press on the means of subsistence, and thus to reduce the remuneration of the labourer to no more than will support life; but the standard of living can be raised, and the increase of population brought under control by prudence. All through, Mill showed himself anxious to mark the limitations of the economic view. If the laws of production of wealth are in the main fixed, the laws of its distribution differ according to the customs and the social order of different societies, and a better order may be thought out than that which exists. The present distribution is so unjust that even a scheme of communistic equality would be preferable; and, if communism can be reconciled with the free play of individuality, this may be the ideal order to be realised in the future. Mill, however, will not resign individual freedom. He puts forward no scheme of his own that can be called properly socialistic. In spite of the new influences under which he had come, his work could in fact be regarded as a text-book of the "classical" political economy, for which *laissez-faire* was the general rule admitting only of occasional exceptions.

Another point of difference between Mill and Comte related to the position and the mental qualities of women. On biological grounds, Comte argues that women are intellectually inferior to men. This Mill cannot admit. All actual differences are to be traced to circumstances, such as mode of education, opinion of society constantly impressed, and so forth. No legal or political difference ought to exist. This was afterwards the thesis maintained with passion in *The Subjection of Women* (1869). Mill came to think later that in the correspondence he had made too many concessions. The deep cleft, however, between his view and Comte's is manifest. The weakness of his position controversially is on the biological side. He will hardly admit at any time, whether in discussing sex or race, that any mental difference whatever can be traceable to the organism. His strength is in the feeling that justice between the sexes, as in every other relation, implies a certain equality as its condition. Economic dependence legally enforced, for example, is incompatible with this. In commenting on the deification of women in the *Positive Polity* as the "moral providence", he remarks that Comte concedes to them everything except justice. Comte's view about the importance of the relative superiorities on each side had to some extent changed, but his practical inference as regards social institutions remained the same.

In the sphere of politics, each point in turn could be treated as a case of antithesis between the two thinkers. Mill's *Representative Government* (1861), for instance, takes up the problem of developing precisely that political system which Comte regarded not only as transitional but as already superseded. For Comte, the way to the ideal order is henceforth through a series of dictatorships. Democracy as a permanent system is anarchical. Now Mill, while he was always a democrat, came to fear rather that the rule of the numerical majority would tend to suppress individual variation. Hence he shows himself eager to adopt any device that may be proposed for reducing this danger. Parliamentary institutions in general he accepts above all because of the educational value of voting and discussion for the individual citizen. A benevolent despotism, though not to be condemned in all times and places, since the historical relativity of institutions must be recognised, would not be the best form of government even if it were the most efficient. Whether the particular devices taken up by Mill are such as to promote the ends he had at heart is a disputed question; but events have not refuted either his own doctrine or that of the school from which he sprang, as far as their hopes lay in the development of a parliamentary as distinguished from a dictatorial system.

Mill's most famous contribution to the defence of individuality is of course the *Liberty* (1859). This is first of all a philosophical defence of freedom in the expression of opinion, especially when opposed to popular orthodoxy. Here at last Mill was able to plead with effect, as he had long desired, for intellectual liberty against the silencing, by social intolerance, of open disbelief in Christianity. In an often-quoted passage where the defects of Christian as contrasted with the best pagan ethics are insisted on, he gave an illustration of the freedom he claimed. The persuasiveness and eloquence of the writing helped to win the cause, in England, of free thought and speech. Although some who agree in Mill's general conclusion do not find the proof as stringent as might be desired, none deny the effectiveness of the plea at the time; and the *Liberty* has taken classical rank with Milton's argument for unlicensed printing. To a logical persecutor, doubtless, neither the *Liberty* nor the *Areopagitica* would carry conviction; but both came at a time when the public mind was slowly becoming more sensitive to the interests of truth and justice; and the literary rather than technically philosophical clothing of the arguments did not tell against them.

What has perhaps been most commented on in the *Liberty* is the contention for limitations on the control exercised by society over the actions of the individual. Not merely freedom of thought, but practical "experiments in living", ought, in Mill's view, to be encouraged as against the tendency, which he feared in modern civilisation and in political democracy, to an enforced uniformity. Here especially we see the thinker who had shown himself so sensitive in youth to the influences of the counter-revolution. Wordsworth and Coleridge, we must remember, were in reaction first against the European tyranny by which the Revolution was followed, and had cared much less about temporary anarchy. Again, through social interactions which it would take long to discuss, Mill's argument against pressing the coercion of public opinion too far has been taken up by later conservative thinkers. Hence this side of this thought, by enabling both parties to appeal to it, has indirectly helped to strengthen the authority of his name.

The principal statement of Mill's ethics is the *Utilitarianism*, which appeared first in *Fraser's Magazine* in 1861, and was separately published in 1863. While guarding himself against what he thinks the errors of Comte's teaching in so far as it overrides the claims of liberty and individuality, Mill here in effect adopts the Religion of Humanity. The supreme end of action is human happiness, under which is included (as also by Comte) the happiness of other sentient beings in relation with man. Of the properly philosophical positions connected with acceptance of this as the end, Mill attempts such proof as he thinks them capable of. There is an express argument against the "transcendentalist" view that justice is irreducible to utility (or conduciveness to happiness), and can only be derived from an immediate intuition of what is universally obligatory without reference to ends. The feeling for justice, like other moral sentiments, is found to have its origin in assignable circumstances of human history, and to acquire its peculiar character in the individual from the type of moral education that has been determined by those circumstances. In the case of the *Utilitarianism* as of the *Liberty*, those who are in general agreement with Mill's conclusions have not found his proofs in all respects satisfactory. What has been most frequently disputed from one side or the other is the modification attempted by him in Bentham's definition or description of happiness. For Bentham, happiness consists of pleasures quantitatively estimated, pains being deducted as negative. The net sum—the greatest possible happiness—is the end. Mill (after Plato in the *Republic*) proposes to distinguish pleasures as also qualitatively higher or lower. Yet happiness is still regarded by him as a sum. Thus, as opponents have pointed out, all the apparent simplicity of Benthamism is destroyed, while its principle is not expressly abandoned. Indeed, Mill incidentally accepts the most rigorous Benthamic view in the admission that the end is to maximise the sum without reference to its distribution. An adherent of utilitarianism like Professor Bain holds therefore that it would have been better tactics if Mill had declined to commit himself to any but the broadest statement of the utilitarian position, which is not specially Benthamic. The only difference of quality, relative to ethics, that Bain can admit, is the difference between egoistic and altruistic feelings. This too is a departure from rigorous Benthamism. An obvious objection to Mill's use of the principle of "inseparable association" to explain the origin of moral sentiments is that this seems to reduce them to illusions destructible by analysis. It is indeed paradoxical that Associationists, having shown how, for example, the love of money arises from association of means with the ends of action, till at last they come to be substituted for the ends themselves as the object of desire, should complacently argue that the regard for moral virtue is psychologically explicable in the same way. Mill is conscious of the difficulty, and in one place gives an answer by pointing out that love of virtue is so far natural to man as not to be dissolved by analysis when it has been acquired; but on the whole his hopes were so much in educability that he preferred to dwell on the power of teachers and legislators to produce by public or private education any type of character they choose. Since he wrote, ethical discussion has taken new forms through the entrance into the controversy of factors like "evolution" and the "social medium". Practically innate moral sentiments, according to the Spencerian theory of evolution, have their source in the experience of the race, though the experience of the individual cannot wholly account for them. Again, from the Positivist or the Hegelian point of view, if man is a social being before he is properly man, the attempt to derive the profoundest moral sentiments from an explicit mental process in the individual is an inversion of the true order. All this, however, belongs to the psychology of ethics rather than to ethics proper. The rational problem of ends and criteria remains. Of this the new factors furnish no ready-made solution; but only, like the Associationist psychology itself at an earlier stage, contribute materials for the ethical philosopher. It may be said of Mill that he was primarily a philosopher or logician rather than a psychologist, and in his time cleared the discussion of many irrelevancies.

THE ESSAYS ON RELIGION

The year 1873 saw the publication of Mill's *Autobiography*. In 1874 appeared the posthumous essays on "Nature", "The Utility of Religion", and "Theism". Of these the first two were composed during the period between 1850 and 1858, to which belongs also the composition of the *Liberty* and the *Utilitarianism*. The third was written much later, and had been very imperfectly revised. It was not the kind of work that had been expected either by Mill's friends or by his opponents; yet it is not really inconsistent with anything he had written elsewhere on religion.

While Mill is often classed as having the type of mind of the eighteenth century, the essay on Nature contains the strongest possible attack on a favourite abstraction of that period. Against every attempt to find moral guidance for man in nature unmodified by human agency, Mill proclaims war. Natural forces act in ways that would be regarded as involving the highest degree of criminality in human agents. When we turn to man himself, we find that what is best in him is artificial, being the comparatively late product of culture. "Nature's god" and the "noble savage" are sophistic fancies. The only morally admissible theory of Creation, in view of the facts both of nature and of human history, is that the Principle of Good is limited by extraneous conditions; that not otherwise than by struggle with the powers of evil, and by gradual growth, could the moral order of civilised human life be attained.

The next essay starts from the discussion in the work entitled *Analysis of the Influence of Natural Religion on the Temporal Happiness of Mankind*, by "Philip Beauchamp" (1822). This is now known to have been written by George Grote, with assistance from the fragmentary manuscripts of Bentham. Its conclusions are completely hostile to the utility of theism, and, by implication, of Christianity. Mill thinks that it presses many parts of the argument too hard; and his own view allows some value historically to the "supernatural sanction" as an aid to ethics. In the end, however, he points out the danger of associating sound moral precepts with doctrines intellectually unsustainable, and for himself explicitly accepts the Religion of Humanity, not as an imperfect substitute for the supernatural religions, but as equal to them in their best manifestations and superior to them in any of their others.

The essay on Theism develops the thought expressed incidentally in the first essay, that, notwithstanding the spectacle presented by nature, a moral theory of creation is admissible on the hypothesis that the Deity is limited in power. The limitation, Mill adds, may also be in knowledge, and even in benevolence. Yet, if there are any grounds for the belief in such a creative God, this kind of theism may aid and fortify the purely human religion which, with or without supernatural sanctions, he cannot doubt is destined to be the Religion of the Future.

The grounds that Mill finds for this hypothesis are essentially those that have always furnished a basis for the design-argument. The eye appears to have been made for seeing, and the ear for hearing. The Darwinian theory, he recognises, cannot be disregarded as one possible explanation of the apparent adaptations of organisms to their conditions; yet it does not seem to him to be more than plausible as a substitute for intelligent design. On the whole, a creative God working on matter is, he contends, still the theory for which, as a speculation, most can be said.

Matter is, of course, taken here in its common-sense meaning as something real and opposed to mind. Mill, however, could easily have adapted the argument to his own idealism. For the "permanent possibilities of sensation" into which matter is resolved by him metaphysically are not to be supposed correspondent to nothing at all. They may signify some non-rational conditions of the manifestation of intelligence. As to the nature of these conditions, Mill does not speculate. All that is necessary for him is that they should be limiting conditions. His creative Deity is clearly not the Absolute. He may be the most powerful being in the universe, but he is not to be identified with the reality of the whole. Mill, as was noted before, does not regard his own idealism as a possible foundation for ontology. The only definite use he makes of it is to show that it leaves room for a belief in the natural immortality of the individual soul. That it does not directly prove immortality he allows. At the same time he points out that mind, according to idealism, has a higher degree of reality than matter as phenomenally known. Thus it may, notwithstanding anything that is proved as to the impermanence of material combinations, survive the organism in association with which it has been temporarily manifested.

In theism, as distinguished from idealism, Mill finds very little to confirm the belief in immortality. The most that can be made out is that it permits the hope for a future state as a possibility. Generally his treatment here gives ground for the view that he would like to discover some residue of truth in the doctrines of "natural theology", though not for the inference that he felt any need of them himself. In pantheistic or evolutionary speculations it is clear that he felt no interest. Hence he remains in the end more in sympathy with the tenets common to Christian and non-Christian theists than Comte, the fictions of whose "subjective synthesis" have a decided affinity with the monistic ontology which he nevertheless completely repudiated. And Comte, with all his admiration for the Catholic type of life, makes no such concession to the claim that there is anything unique in Christian ethics as is made by Mill in the section of his last essay which he devotes to "Revelation".

To whichever side our sympathies may incline, both philosophers here give us less satisfaction than we have intellectually a right to expect, and point to something beyond themselves. Hypotheses or fictions may be permissible; but in philosophy we ought to have grounds for saying, as Plato did of his myths, that the meaning contained in them, though not any particular imagination we can clothe it with, is the truth of things. For a religion, Comte's dogmatic assertions, whether negative or positive, seem at any rate more satisfying than Mill's suspension of judgment. The Positivist "subjective immortality", or preservation in the memory of survivors, for example, is held out as a certainty. With Mill "objective immortality" is indeed a possibility, as it was not for Comte; but its realisation is quite uncertain. Yet it is here rather than in relation to personal theism that his philosophical principles gave him tenable grounds for an attitude not wholly suspensory.

ASPECTS OF LATER THOUGHT

The most genuinely philosophical advance made since Comte and Mill has consisted in a renewed effort to lay hold of the traditional speculative problems they had in different degrees set aside. While Mill was applying destructive dialectic to the conglomerate constructions of Hamilton and the attenuated Kantianism of Mansel, Herbert Spencer, with even less direct knowledge than Mill of German thought, was working out, from the very imperfect version of it before him, a metaphysical theory not wanting in universality. Taking the Absolute of Hamilton and Mansel seriously, and ignoring their Christian theism, he put forth as the prelude to a system of scientific philosophy the ontological doctrine that that which lies behind the phenomena accessible to science is a demonstrably positive but at the same time demonstrably unknowable real Being. The unknowable is the object of what is permanent in the religious sentiment, of which the essence is the consciousness of an insoluble mystery. This was as far as Spencer carried metaphysics; but later thinkers, not acquiescing in his resignation of further search into reality as distinguished from appearance, have tried again, with or without aid from newer scientific ideas, to grasp the whole. Some of these attempts could easily be brought into relation with the ideas of Comte and Mill last discussed. An atheological doctrine of personal immortality, for example, though it was not Mill's actual belief, had some affinity with his metaphysical conclusion regarding consciousness. And for a doctrine of pampsychism Comte's "fictions" might take the place of anticipatory Platonic myths.

To discuss this aspect of their thought is, however, to take both thinkers on their less characteristic side. The strength of both positively was in the ordering of scientific knowledge from general points of view, and its direction to rationalise the life of man. The difference that goes with this resemblance may perhaps best be put thus: that Comte was not more superior to Mill as a system-builder than Mill was to Comte as a critic, the word "critic" being taken in the widest sense. The observation of Professor Bain, though it may not have been made with Comte in view as the antithesis to Mill, seems here particularly apt. "A multitude of small impressions may have the accumulated effect of a mighty whole". Thus in a summary it is more difficult to do justice to Mill than to Comte. The essays, for example, collected in the four volumes of *Dissertations and Discussions*, which cannot well be brought into a short general view, would add more varied interest to the outline than Comte's subsidiary expositions of his system, such as the *Catéchisme Positiviste* or the *Appel aux Conservateurs*, to which reference has been similarly omitted.

But this is not all that there is to say. While Comte was essentially a systematiser, his system is at certain points demonstrably wrong, not merely from the imperfect knowledge of the time, but from the very nature of its exclusions. His doctrine is not in conception at the level of Platonism or Aristotelianism, failing as it does to give any adequate consideration to "dialectic" or "first philosophy". Doubtless it will be found to have less permanent aesthetic value. On the other hand, if we refuse to be compelled to take it or leave it as a whole, it remains profoundly suggestive both in relation to science and practice. The stimulative power that might seem to belong more naturally to the comparatively dispersive thinking of Mill, with his cultivated openness of mind, is now far more present in the rigorous dogmatism of the Positive Philosophy and Polity. Mill's miscellaneous work was for his own generation, and contributes little, directly or indirectly, to solve newer problems. To complete the antithesis, Mill, though he has left no system of philosophy, has done a single piece of work that marks a definitive step forward in human thought such as has not been taken by any of the great systematisers who appeared in his century. For Mill's Inductive Logic is unquestionably a "new organon", susceptible of common use by other minds. This cannot be said of Hegel's Logic. And Comte, to adopt the accurate distinction of his disciple Mr Frederic Harrison, has indeed "instituted", but he has not "constituted", Sociology. All that is definitive in his treatment is the discovery of the "historical method", which merely contributes one chapter to Mill's *Logic*.

That neither Mill nor Comte was affected by the evolutionary biology which had been rising into notice in Germany even before it received scientific proof from Darwin or speculative development from Spencer, does not seem important in relation to the special work of either. So far as the idea of organic development had a bearing on Comte's own work, he accepted it. "Social evolution" is a phrase that he constantly employs, perhaps before any one else. And the rational problems that Mill attacked in his theory of knowledge and in his ethics are not really solved by bringing in the experience of the race to supplement that of the individual. The full acceptance of biological evolution by Spencer before the appearance of the *Origin of Species*, and his cosmical extension of the idea, did not enable him to get rid of the individualism that Comte had left behind from the beginning. Thus his Sociology is in some respects belated as compared with Comte's. His "social organism" is thought of in biological terms, much like the "body politic" of Hobbes. For, of course, the term "individualism" is not used here in reference to a theory of government. The point is that Commonwealth, or the "social organism", whatever may be regarded as the ideal mode of its regulation, is conceived only as composite Man, and not also as in its social character a condition prior to the existence of its component units as human "individuals". Comte, we have seen, had fully attained this latter conception. Here at least no fault can be found with him from the evolutionary side. No doubt it was inevitable that evolution should at first seem to overshadow everything else; but we can now see that to social and political science the distinctively evolutionary thinkers contributed less than either Comte or Mill. It is not in relation to their distinctive work, but where that reaches its limit, that we shall find an advance due to evolutionary thought.

The real scientific advance made by Spencer on Comte is the result not of his evolutionism, but of his studies in subjective psychology, and his consequent recognition that this, and not biology, immediately precedes the science of society. Prior to sociology, it has been allowed, the individual cannot be properly known; but there is a preliminary science of the more elementary laws of mind, worked out subjectively, which does for the sociologist what Comte erroneously attributed to cerebral physiology. That in psychological introspection the observed and the observer are identical is no doubt a paradox from the point of view of the objective sciences; but introspection is not therefore illusory. Comte's own historical method is no less real because it cannot be applied in biology. The distinctiveness of his insight into the nature of history is undeniable; but he partially failed when he came to deal with the "pre-history" that is the more special province of

Spencer and the anthropologists. And his failure here was closely connected with his non-recognition of the introspective method. What he missed was precisely the "animism" which, according to Tylor and Spencer, was started by primitive man in order to explain the peculiarities of that subjective consciousness which psychologists regard as the material of a positive science. In Comte's view, as we have seen, all the theologies can be explained by derivation from a primitive theory that objects themselves are animated. The gods of polytheism being the result of generalisation from resemblances between objects of the same class, a god who, since he is common to all, can no longer be localised, comes to be thought of as separable from any object whatsoever. Now it cannot be absolutely denied that the notion of a separable deity might arise in this fashion. And, if it did, subsequent generalisation would no doubt suffice to explain monotheism also. A more natural explanation of the separability of the god seems, however, to be furnished by primitive animism. The notion of a separable soul is first evolved as an explanation of the phenomena of life and mind in man himself, and then (according to Tylor's form of the "ghost-theory") a similar soul is imaginatively projected into objects. The "ghost-soul" (according to both Tylor and Spencer) is at first conceived as a shadowy semblance of the bodily form, and is supposed to go away and return because this hypothesis seems required by the alternations of personal consciousness and unconsciousness, the imagery with which the separable entity is clothed being supplied by reflexions, shadows, and other accompaniments of the tangible person. Thus what is primitive is "animism", or the notion of a population of separable spirits. From these, the separable deities are derivative, directly or indirectly. "Fetishism", or the notion that there is a soul in certain objects, is secondary; and the idea of universally animated matter is a generalisation out of man's reach at the earliest stage. Now this "ghost-theory", since it has been founded on careful collation of evidence about the beliefs of savages at all stages, does not seem likely to be displaced as a whole. Had Comte's insight not been defective in pure psychology, it is probable that the hints of "metaphysical" precursors like Hobbes would have suggested it to him. As it is, no shade of a suggestion of it, so far as I recollect, occurs in any of his writings.

Yet it must be allowed that there is a tendency of late to regard the strictest interpretation of the "ghost-theory" as overstrained. The notion that the world of objects is itself animated, some modern theorists maintain, was directly suggested, apart from all ideas of ghosts, by the phenomena of moving things. To all things that are apparently active, life is directly ascribed by analogy with active persons. The case is, perhaps, one where combination of theories may be permissible. The ghost-theory undoubtedly, and perhaps even Comte's derivation of all later developments from fetishism, might with ingenuity be stretched to cover the facts; but we have no sound reason for attempting to work exclusively either with one or the other, if there is evidence, as there may be, of independent origins. The law called by Sir William Hamilton the "law of parsimony", as Mill pointed out, is not a law of nature, but only a methodological rule. We must not invent hypothetical causes where known causes suffice to explain the phenomena; and, if we have to recur to hypotheses, we must not multiply hypothetical causes without necessity; but, when we know of more than one, or of many experienced causal processes, we need not dismiss a portion of them for the mere sake of simplifying our explanations. The processes of nature are frequently complex.

This was fully recognised by Comte, who was himself strongly opposed to the chimerical unifications that are not content with carrying scientific explanation into everything, but aim at the reduction of all laws to one. The excess of system here can be redressed by his own principles. It is not the result of too great a striving after speculative unity, but of a too absorbing desire to unify human life. Neither in Comte nor in Mill do we meet with the barren formulae that seem to explain everything while actually explaining nothing.

Indeed, the demand for precision and applicability becomes on one side a defect, as limiting the speculative outlook. Both are too exclusively humanist. Here is the real failing in their philosophy that might have been corrected by application of evolutionary theories with their appeal to "cosmic emotion". In Mill, as in Comte, there is a theoretical opposition of man to the cosmos which seems to make of him a kind of miracle in nature. Evolution in its larger aspects restores a wholeness that both were sometimes too willing to renounce.

Selected Works

MAINLY BIOGRAPHICAL

Notice sur l'Œuvre et sur la Vie d'Auguste Comte. Par le Docteur Robinet. 2nd ed. 1864.

Auguste Comte et la Philosophie Positive. Par E. Littré. 2nd ed. 1864.

Lettres à M. Valat, 1870.

Testament d'Auguste Comte, 1884.

The Positive Philosophy of Auguste Comte. Freely translated and condensed by Harriet Martineau. With an Introduction by Frederic Harrison. 3 vols. 1896.

Correspondance de John Stuart Mill et d'Auguste Comte, avec une Introduction par L. Lévy-Bruhl, 1899.

J. S. Mill, *Autobiography*, 1873.

Correspondance inédite avec Gustave d'Eichthal, 1898.

John Stuart Mill. A Criticism: with Personal Recollections. By Alexander Bain, 1882.

Life of John Stuart Mill. By W. L. Courtney, 1889.

The English Utilitarians. By Sir Leslie Stephen (vol. iii: John Stuart Mill), 1900.

CHAPTER IV

SCHOPENHAUER

LIFE AND WRITINGS

ARTHUR SCHOPENHAUER may be distinctively described as the greatest philosophic *writer* of his century. So evident is this that he has sometimes been regarded as having more importance in literature than in philosophy; but this is an error. As a metaphysician he is second to no one since Kant. Others of his age have surpassed him in system and in comprehensiveness; but no one has had a firmer grasp of the essential and fundamental problems of philosophy. On the theory of knowledge, the nature of reality, and the meaning of the beautiful and the good, he has solutions to offer that are all results of a characteristic and original way of thinking.

In one respect, as critics have noted, his spirit is different from that of European philosophy in general. What preoccupies him in a special way is the question of evil in the world. Like the philosophies of the East, emerging as they do without break from religion, Schopenhauer's philosophy is in its outcome a doctrine of redemption from sin. The name of pessimism commonly applied to it is in some respects misleading, though it was his own term; but it is correct if understood as he explained it. As he was accustomed to insist, his final ethical doctrine coincides with that of all the religions that aim, for their adepts or their elect, at deliverance from "this evil world". But, as the "world-fleeing" religions have their mitigations and accommodations, so also has the philosophy of Schopenhauer. At various points indeed it seems as if a mere change of accent would turn it into optimism.

This preoccupation does not mean indifference to the theoretical problems of philosophy. No one has insisted more strongly that the end of philosophy is pure truth, and that only the few who care about pure truth have any concern with it. But for Schopenhauer the desire for speculative truth does not by itself suffice to explain the impulse of philosophical inquiries. On one side of his complex character, he had more resemblance to the men who turn from the world to religion, like St Augustine, than to the normal type of European thinker, represented pre-eminently by Aristotle. He was a temperamental pessimist, feeling from the first the trouble of existence; and here he finds the deepest motive for the desire to become clear about it. He saw in the world, what he felt in himself, a vain effort after ever new objects of desire which give no permanent satisfaction; and this view, becoming predominant, determined, not indeed all the ideas of his philosophy, but its general complexion as a "philosophy of redemption".

With his pessimism, personal misfortunes had nothing to do. He was, and always recognised that he was, among the most fortunately placed of mankind. He does not hesitate to speak sometimes of his own happiness in complete freedom from the need to apply himself to any compulsory occupation. This freedom, as he has put gratefully on record, he owed to his father, Heinrich Floris Schopenhauer, who was a rich merchant and banker of Danzig, where the philosopher was born on the 22nd of February, 1788. Both his parents were of Dutch ancestry. His mother, Johanna Schopenhauer, won celebrity as a novelist; and his sister, Adele, also displayed some literary talent. Generalising from his own case, Schopenhauer holds that men of intelligence derive their character from their father and their intellect from their mother. With his mother, however, he was not on sympathetic terms, as may be read in the biographies. His father intended him for a mercantile career, and with this view began to prepare him from the first to be a cosmopolitan man of the world. The name of Arthur was given to him because it is spelt alike in the leading European languages. He was taken early to France, where he resided from 1797 to 1799, learning French so well that on his return he had almost forgotten his German. Portions of the years 1803 to 1804 were spent in England, France, Switzerland, and Austria. In England he was three months at a Wimbledon boarding-school kept by a clergyman. This experience he found extremely irksome. He afterwards became highly proficient in English: was always pleased to be taken for an Englishman, and regarded both the English character and intelligence as on the whole the first in Europe; but all the more deplorable did he find the oppressive pietism which was the special form taken in the England of that period by the reaction against the French Revolution. He is never tired of denouncing that phase of "cold superstition", the dominance of which lasted during his lifetime; for the publication of Mill's *Liberty* and of Darwin's *Origin of Species*, which may be considered as marking the close of it, came only the year before his death.

The only real break in the conformity of Schopenhauer's circumstances to his future career came in 1805, when he was placed in a merchant's office at Hamburg, whither his father had migrated in disgust at the annexation of his native Danzig, then under a republican constitution of its own, by Prussia in 1793. Soon afterwards his father died; but out of loyalty he tried for some time longer to reconcile himself to commercial life. Finding this at length impossible, he gained permission from his mother, in 1807, to leave the office for the gymnasium. At this time he seems to have begun his classical studies, his education having hitherto been exclusively modern. They were carried on first at Gotha and then at Weimar. In 1809 he entered the university of Göttingen as a student of medicine. This, however, was with a view only to scientific studies, not to practice; and he transferred himself to the philosophical faculty in 1810. Generally he was little regardful of academical authority. His father's deliberately adopted plan of letting him mix early with the world had given him a certain independence of judgment. At Göttingen, however, he received an important influence from his teacher, G. E. Schulze (known by the revived scepticism of his *Aenesidemus*), who advised him to study Plato and Kant before Aristotle and Spinoza.

From 1811 to 1813 he was at Berlin, where he heard Fichte, but was not impressed. In 1813 the degree of Doctor of Philosophy was conferred on him at Jena for the dissertation *On the Fourfold Root of the Principle of Sufficient Reason* (*Ueber die vierfache Wurzel des Satzes vom zureichenden Grunde*, 2nd ed., 1847). This was the first result of his Kantian studies. In the same year he began to be acquainted with Goethe at Weimar, where his mother and sister had gone to reside in 1806. A consequence of this acquaintance was that he took up and further developed Goethe's theory of colours. His dissertation *Ueber das Sehen und die Farben* was published in 1816. A second edition did not appear till 1854; but in the meantime he had published a restatement of his doctrine in Latin, entitled *Theoria Colorum Physiologica* (1830). This, however, was an outlying part of his work. He had already been seized by the impulse to set forth the system of philosophy that took shape in him, as he says, by some formative process of which he could give no conscious account. His great work, *Die Welt als Wille und Vorstellung*, was ready for publication before the end of 1818, and was published with the date 1819. Thus he is one of the most precocious philosophers on record. For in that single volume, written before he was thirty, the outlines of his whole system are fixed. There is some development later, and there are endless new applications and essays towards confirmation from all sources. His mind never rested, and his literary power gained by exercise. Still, it has been said with truth, that there never was a greater illusion than when he thought that he seldom repeated himself. In reality he did little but repeat his fundamental positions with infinite variations in expression.

After completing his chief work, Schopenhauer wrote some verses in which he predicted that posterity would erect a monument to him. This prediction was fulfilled in 1895; but, for the time, the work which he never doubted would be his enduring title to fame seemed, like Hume's *Treatise*, to have fallen "deadborn from the press". This he attributed to the hostility of the academical philosophers; and, in his later works, attacks on the university professors form a characteristic feature. The official teachers of the Hegelian school, he declared, were bent only on obtaining positions for themselves by an appearance of supporting Christian dogma; and they resented openness on the part of any one else. Yet on one side he maintained that his own pessimism was more truly Christian than their optimism. The essential spirit of Christianity is that of Brahmanism and Buddhism, the great religions that sprang from India, the first home of our race. He is even inclined to see in it traces of Indian influence. What vitiates it in his eyes is the Jewish element, which finds its expression in the flat modern "Protestant-rationalistic optimism". As optimistic religions, he groups together Judaism, Islam, and Graeco-Roman Polytheism. His antipathy, however, extends only to the two former. He was himself in great part a child of Humanism and of the eighteenth century, rejoicing over the approaching downfall of all the faiths, and holding that a weak religion (entirely different from those he admires) is favourable to civilisation. Nothing can exceed his scorn for nearly everything that characterised the Middle Ages. With Catholicism as a political system he has no sympathy whatever; while on the religious side the Protestant are as sympathetic to him as the Catholic mystics. What is common to all priesthoods, he holds, is to exploit the metaphysical need of mankind (in which he also believes) for the sake of their own power. Clericalism, "Pfaffenthum", whether Catholic or Protestant, is the object of his unvarying hatred and contempt. If he had cared to appreciate Hegel, he would have found on this point much community of spirit; but of course there was a real antithesis between the two as philosophers. No "conspiracy" need be invoked to explain the failure of Schopenhauer to win early recognition. Belief in the State and in progress was quite alien to him; and Germany was then full of political hopes, which found nourishment in optimistic pantheism. What at length gave his philosophy vogue was the collapse of this enthusiasm on the failure of the revolutionary movement in 1848. Once known, it contained enough of permanent value to secure it from again passing out of sight with the next change of fashion.

The rest of Schopenhauer's life in its external relations may be briefly summed up. For a few years, it was diversified by travels in Italy and elsewhere, and by an unsuccessful attempt at academical teaching in Berlin. In 1831 he moved to Frankfort, where he finally settled in 1833. He lived unmarried there till his death on the 21st of September, 1860. The monument, already spoken of, was unveiled at Frankfort on the 6th of June, 1895.

The almost unbroken silence with which his great work was received, though it had a distempering effect on the man, did not discourage the thinker. The whole series of Schopenhauer's works, indeed, was completed before he attained anything that could be called fame. Constantly on the alert as he was to seize upon confirmations of his system, he published in 1836 his short work *On the Will in Nature*, pointing out verifications of his metaphysics by recent science. In 1839 his prize essay, *On the Freedom of the Human Will* (finished in 1837), was crowned by the Royal Scientific Society of Drontheim in Norway. This and another essay, *On the Basis of Morality*, *not* crowned by the Royal Danish Society of Copenhagen in 1840, he published in 1841, with the inclusive title, *Die beiden Grundprobleme der Ethik*. In 1844 appeared the second edition of his principal work, to which there was added, in the form of a second volume, a series of elucidations and extensions larger in bulk than the first. This new volume contains much of his best and most effective writing. His last work, *Parerga und Paralipomena*, which appeared in 1851 (2 vols.), is from the literary point of view the most brilliant. It was only from this time that he began to be well known among the general public; though the philosophic "apostolate" of Julius Frauenstädt, who afterwards edited his works, had begun in 1840. His activity was henceforth confined to modifying and extending his works for new editions; an employment in which he was always assiduous. In consequence of this, all of them, as they stand, contain references from one to another; but the development of his thinking, so far as there was such a process after 1818, can be easily traced without reference to the earlier editions. There is some growth; but, as has been said, it does not affect many of the chief points. A brief exposition of his philosophy can on the whole take it as something fixed. The heads under which it must fall are those assigned to the original four books of *Die Welt als Wille und Vorstellung*.

Although Schopenhauer discountenanced the attempt to connect a philosopher's biography with his work, something has to be said about his character, since this has been dwelt on to his disadvantage by opponents. There is abundant material for a personal estimate in the correspondence and reminiscences published after his death by his disciples Julius Frauenstädt and Wilhelm Gwinner. The apparent contradiction is at once obvious between the ascetic consummation of his ethics and his unascetic life, carefully occupied in its latter part with rules for the preservation of his naturally robust health. He was quite aware of this, but holds it absurd to require that a moralist should commend only the virtues which he possesses. It is as if the requirement were set up that a sculptor is to be himself a model of beauty. A saint need not be a philosopher, nor a philosopher a saint. The science of morals is as theoretical as any other branch of philosophy. Fundamentally, character is unmodifiable, though knowledge, it is allowed, may change the mode of action within the limits of the particular character. The passage to the state of asceticism cannot be effected by moral philosophy, but depends on a kind of "grace". After all, it might be replied, philosophers, whether they succeed or not, do usually make at least an attempt to live in accordance with the moral ideal they set up. The best apology in Schopenhauer's case is that the fault may have been as much in his ideal as in his failure to conform to it. The eloquent pages he has devoted to the subject of holiness only make manifest the inconsequence (which he admits) in the passage to it. For, as we shall see, this has nothing in common with the essentially rational asceticism of the schools of later antiquity; which was a rule of self-limitation in view of the philosophic life. He did in a way of his own practise something of this; and, on occasion, he sets forth the theory of it; but he quite clearly sees the difference. His own ideal, which he never attempted to practise, is that of the self-torturing ascetics of the Christian Middle Age. Within the range of properly human virtue, he can in many respects hold his own, not only as a philosopher but as a man. If his egoism and vanity are undeniable, he undoubtedly possessed the virtues of rectitude and compassion. What he would have especially laid stress on was the conscientious devotion to his work. With complete singleness of purpose he used for a disinterested end the leisure which he regarded as the most fortunate of endowments. As he said near the close of his life, his intellectual conscience was clear.

Of Schopenhauer's expositions of his pessimism it would be true to say, as Spinoza says of the Book of Job, that the matter, like the style, is not that of a man sitting among the ashes, but of one meditating in a library. This of course does not prove that they are not a genuine, if one-sided, rendering of human experience. All that can be said is that they did not turn him away from appreciation of the apparent goods of life. His own practical principle was furnished by what he regarded as a lower point of view; and this gives its direction to the semi-popular philosophy of the *Parerga*. From what he takes to be the higher point of view, the belief that happiness is attainable by man on earth is an illusion; but he holds that, by keeping steadily in view a kind of tempered happiness as the end, many mistakes may be avoided in the conduct of life, provided that each recognises at once the strength and weakness of his own character, and does not attempt things that, with the given limitations, are impossible. Of the highest truth, as he conceived it, he could therefore make no use. Only by means of a truth that he was bound to hold half-illusory could a working scheme be constructed for himself and others. This result may give us guidance in seeking to learn what we can from a thinker who is in reality no representative of a decadence, but is fundamentally sane and rational, even in spite of himself.

THEORY OF KNOWLEDGE

The title of Schopenhauer's chief work is rendered in the English translation, *The World as Will and Idea.* Here the term "idea" is used in the sense it had for Locke and Berkeley; namely, any object of mental activity. Thus it includes not merely imagery, but also perception. Since Hume distinguished "ideas" from "impressions", it has tended to be specialised in the former sense. The German word, *Vorstellung*, which it is used to render, conveys the generalised meaning of the Lockian "idea", now frequently expressed in English and French philosophical works by the more technical term "presentation" or "representation". By Schopenhauer himself the word "Idea" was used exclusively in the sense of the Platonic Idea, which, as we shall see, plays an important part in his philosophy. The distinction is preserved in the translation by the use of a capital when Idea has the latter meaning; but in a brief exposition it seems convenient to adopt a more technical rendering of *Vorstellung*; and, from its common employment in psychological text-books, I have selected "presentation" as the most suitable.

The first proposition of Schopenhauer's philosophical system is, "The world is my presentation". By this he means that it presents itself as appearance to the knowing subject. This appearance is in the forms of time, space, and causality. Under these forms every phenomenon necessarily appears, because they are *a priori* forms of the subject. The world as it presents itself consists entirely of phenomena, that is, appearances, related according to these forms. The most fundamental form of all is the relation between object and subject, which is implied in all of them. Without a subject there can be no presented object.

Schopenhauer is therefore an idealist in the sense in which we call Berkeley's theory of the external world idealism; though the expressions used are to some extent different. The difference proceeds from his following of Kant. His Kantianism consists in the recognition of *a priori* forms by which the subject constructs for itself an "objective" world of appearances. With Berkeley he agrees as against Kant in not admitting any residue whatever, in the object as such, that is not wholly appearance. But while he allows that Berkeley, as regards the general formulation of idealism, was more consistent than Kant, he finds him, in working out the principle, altogether inadequate. For the modern mind there is henceforth no way in philosophy except through Kant, from whom dates the revolution by which scholastic dualism was finally overthrown. Kant's systematic construction, however, he in effect reduces to very little. His is a much simplified "Apriorism". While accepting the "forms of sensible intuition", that is, time and space, just as Kant sets them forth, he clears away nearly all the superimposed mechanism. Kant's "Transcendental Aesthetic", he says, was a real discovery in metaphysics; but on the basis of this he for the most part only gave free play to his architectonic impulse. Of the twelve "categories of the understanding", which he professed to derive from the logical forms of judgment, all except causality are mere "blind windows". This alone, therefore, Schopenhauer adopts; placing it, however, not at a higher level but side by side with time and space, Kant's forms of intuition. These three forms, according to Schopenhauer, make up the understanding of men and animals. "All intuition is intellectual". It is not first mere appearance related in space and time, and waiting for understanding to organise it; but, in animals as in man, it is put in order at once under the three forms that suffice to explain the knowledge all have of the phenomenal world.

To Reason as distinguished from Understanding, Schopenhauer assigns no such exalted function as was attributed to it in portions of his system by Kant, and still more by some of his successors. The name of "reason", he maintains, ought on etymological grounds to be restricted to the faculty of abstract concepts. This, and not understanding, is what distinguishes man from animals. It discovers and invents nothing, but it puts in a generalised and available form what the understanding has discovered in intuition.

For the historical estimation of Schopenhauer, it is necessary to place him in relation to Kant, as he himself always insisted. Much also in his chief work is made clearer by knowledge of his dissertation *On the Fourfold Root of the Principle of Sufficient Reason*, to which he is constantly referring. Later, his manner of exposition became more independent; so that he can be read by the general reader with profit simply by himself, and without reference to antecedents. Still, it will always be advisable for an expositor to follow his directions, at least to the extent of giving some short account of the dissertation. This I proceed to give approximately in the place to which he has assigned it in his system.

The name of the principle (*principium rationis sufficientis*) he took over from Leibniz and his successor Wolff, but gave it a new amplitude. With him, it stands as an inclusive term for four modes of connexion by which the thoroughgoing relativity of phenomena to one another is constituted for our intelligence. The general statement adopted is, "Nothing is without a reason why it should be rather than not be". Its four forms are the principles of becoming (*fiendi*), of knowing (*cognoscendi*), of being (*essendi*), and of acting (*agendi*). (1) Under the first head come "causes". These are divided into "cause proper", for inorganic things; "stimulus", for the vegetative life both of plants and animals; and "motive", for animals and men. The law of causation is applicable only to changes; not to the forces of nature, to matter, or to the world as a whole, which are perdurable. Cause precedes effect in time. Not one thing, but one state of a thing, is the cause of another. From the law of causation there results an infinite series *a parte ante* as well as *a parte post.* (2) The principle of sufficient reason of knowing is applicable to concepts, which are all derived from intuition, that is, from percepts. The laws of logic, which come under this head, can yield nothing original, but can only render explicit what was in the understanding. (3) Under the third head come arithmetical and geometrical relations. These are peculiar relations of presentations, distinct from all others, and only intelligible in virtue of a pure *a priori* intuition. For geometry this is space; for arithmetic time, in which counting goes on. Scientifically, arithmetic is fundamental. (4) As the third form of causality was enumerated "motive" for the will; but in that classification it was viewed from without, as belonging to the world of objects. Through the direct knowledge we have of our own will, we know also from within this determination by the presentation we call a motive. Hence emerges the fourth form of the principle of sufficient reason. This at a later stage makes possible the transition from physics to metaphysics.

All these forms alike are forms of necessary determination. Necessity has no clear and true sense but certainty of the consequence when the ground is posited. All necessity therefore is conditional. In accordance with the four expressions of the principle of sufficient reason, it takes the fourfold shape of physical, logical, mathematical, and moral necessity.

The sharp distinction between logical and mathematical truth, with the assignment of the former to conceptual and of the latter to intuitive relations, comes to Schopenhauer directly from Kant. So also does his view that the necessary form of causation is sequence; though here his points of contact with English thinkers, earlier and later, are very marked. Only in his statement of the "law of motivation" as "causality seen from within" does he hint at his own distinctive metaphysical doctrine. Meanwhile, it is evident that he is to be numbered with the group of modern thinkers who have arrived in one way or another at a complete scientific phenomenism. Expositors have noted that in his earlier statements of this he tends to lay more stress on the character of the visible and tangible world as mere appearance. The impermanence, the relativity, of all that exists in time and space, leads him to describe it, in a favourite term borrowed from Indian philosophy, as Maya, or illusion. Later, he dwells more on the relative reality of things as they appear. His position, however, does not essentially alter, but only finds varying expression as he turns more to the scientific or to the metaphysical side. From Hume's view on causation he differs not by opposing its pure phenomenism, but only by recognising, as Kant does, an *a priori* element in the form of its law. German critics have seen in his own formulation an anticipation of Mill, and this is certainly striking as regards the general conception of the causal order, although there is no anticipation of Mill's inductive logic. On the same side there is a close agreement with Malebranche and the Occasionalists, pointed out by Schopenhauer himself. The causal explanations of science, he is at one with them in insisting, give no ultimate account of anything. All its causes are no more than "occasional causes"—merely instances, as Mill expressed it afterwards, of "invariable and unconditional sequence". From Mill of course he differs in holding its form to be necessary and *a priori*, not ultimately derived from a summation of experiences; and, with the Occasionalists, he goes on to metaphysics in its sense of ontology, as Mill never did. The difference here is that he does not clothe his metaphysics in a theological dress.

In the later development of his thought, Schopenhauer dealt more expressly with the question, how this kind of phenomenism is reconcilable with a scientific cosmogony. On one side the proposition, "No object without subject", makes materialism for ever impossible; for the materialist tries to explain from relations among presentations what is the condition of all presentation. On the other side, we are all compelled to agree with the materialists that knowledge of the object comes late in a long series of material events. Inorganic things existed in time before life; vegetative life before animal life; and only with animal life does knowledge emerge. Reasoned knowledge of the whole series comes only at the end of it in the human mind. This apparent contradiction he solves by leaving a place for metaphysics. Our representation of the world as it existed before the appearance of life was indeed non-existent at the time to which we assign it; but the real being of the world had a manifestation not imaginable by us. For this, we substitute a picture of a world such as we should have been aware of had our "subject", with its *a priori* forms of time, space, and causality, been then present. What the reality is, is the problem of the thing-in-itself (to use the Kantian term). This problem remains over; but we know that the metaphysical reality cannot be matter; for matter, with all its qualities, is phenomenal. It exists only "for understanding, through understanding, in understanding". These discriminations made, Schopenhauer offers us a scientific cosmogony beginning with the nebular hypothesis and ending with an outline of organic evolution. This last differs from the Darwinian theory in supposing a production of species by definite steps instead of by accumulation of small individual variations. At a certain time, a form that has all the characters of a new species appears among the progeny of an existing species. Man is the last and highest form to be evolved. From Schopenhauer's metaphysics, as we shall see, it follows that no higher form of life will ever appear.

A word may be said here on a materialistic-sounding phrase which is very prominent in Schopenhauer's later expositions, and has been remarked on as paradoxical for an idealist. The world as presentation, he often says, is "in the brain". This, it must be allowed, is not fully defensible from his own point of view, except with the aid of a later distinction. The brain as we know it is of course only a part of the phenomenon of the subject—a grouping of possible perceptions. How then, since it is itself only appearance, can it be the bearer of the whole universe as appearance? The answer is that Schopenhauer meant in reality "the being of the brain", and not the brain as phenomenon. He had a growing sense of the importance of physiology for the investigation of mind; and his predilection led him to adopt a not quite satisfactory shorthand expression for the correspondence we know scientifically to exist between our mental processes and changes capable of objective investigation in the matter of the brain.

In science his distinctive bent was to the borderland between psychology and physiology. Hence came the attraction exercised on him by Goethe's theory of colours. To his own theory, though, unlike his philosophical system, it has always failed to gain the attention he predicted for it, the merit must be allowed of treating the problem as essentially one of psycho-physics. What he does is to attempt to ascertain the conditions in the sensibility of the retina that account for our actual colour-sensations. This problem was untouched by the Newtonian theory; but Schopenhauer followed Goethe in the error of trying to overthrow this on its own ground. He had no aptitude for the special inquiries of mathematics and physics, though he had gained a clear insight into their general nature as sciences. On the psycho-physical side there is to-day no fully authorised theory. The problem indeed has become ever more complex. Schopenhauer's attempt, by combination of sensibilities to "light" and "darkness", to explain the phenomena of complementary colours, deserves at least a record in the long series of essays of which the best known are the "Young-Helmholtz theory" and that of Hering. It marks an indubitable advance on Goethe in the clear distinction drawn between the mixture, in the ordinary sense, that can only result in dilution to different shades of grey, and the kinds of mixture from which, in their view, true colours arise.

A characteristic position in Schopenhauer's theory of knowledge, and one that is constantly finding new expression in his writings, is the distinction between abstract and intuitive knowledge already touched on. Intuitive knowledge of the kind that is common to men and animals, as we have seen, makes up, in his terminology, the "understanding"; while "reason" is the distinctively human faculty of concepts. When he depreciates this, as he often does, in comparison with "intuition", it must be remembered that he does not limit this term to perception of particulars, but ascribes to what he calls the "Platonic Idea" a certain kind of union between reason and "phantasy", which gives it an intuitive character of its own. Thus intuition can stand, though not in every case for what is higher, yet always for that which is wider and greater and more immediate. Whatever may be done with reflective reason and its abstractions, every effectual process of thought must end, alike for knowledge and art and virtue, in some intuitive presentation. The importance of reason for practice is due to its generality. Its function is subordinate. It does not furnish the ground of virtuous action any more than aesthetic precepts can enable any one to produce a work of art; but it can help to preserve constancy to certain maxims, as also in art a reasoned plan is necessary because the inspiration of genius is not every moment at command. Virtue and artistic genius alike, however, depend ultimately on intuition: and so also does every true discovery in science. The nature of pedantry is to try to be guided everywhere by concepts, and to trust nothing to perception in the particular case. Philosophy also Schopenhauer regards as depending ultimately on a certain intuitive view; but he allows that it has to translate this into abstractions. Its problem is to express the *what* of the world in abstract form: science dealing only with the *why* of phenomena related within the world. This character of philosophy as a system of abstract concepts deprives it of the immediate attractiveness of art; so that, as he says in one place, it is more fortunate to be a poet than a philosopher.

METAPHYSICS OF THE WILL

We have seen that scientific explanation does not go beyond presentations ordered in space and time. This is just as true of the sciences of causation—the "aetiological" sciences—as it is of mathematical science. All that we learn from Mechanics, Physics, Chemistry and Physiology, is "how, in accordance with an infallible rule, one determinate state of matter necessarily follows another: how a determinate change necessarily conditions and brings on another determinate change". This knowledge does not satisfy us. We wish to learn the significance of phenomena; but we find that from outside, while we view them as presentations, their inner meaning is for ever inaccessible.

The starting-point for the metaphysical knowledge we seek is given us in our own body. The animal body is "the immediate object of the subject": in it as presentation the "effects" of "causes" in the order of presentations external to it are first recognised. Now in virtue of his body the investigator is not pure knowing subject standing apart from that which he knows. In the case of the particular system of presentations constituting his organism, he knows what these presentations signify, and that is his *will* in a certain modification. The subject appears as individual through its identity with the body, and this body is given to it in two different ways: on one side as object among objects, and subjected to their laws; on the other side as the will immediately known to each. The act of will and the movement of the body are not two different states related as cause and effect; for the relation of cause and effect belongs only to the object, the phenomenon, the presentation. They are one and the same act given in different manners: the will, immediately to the subject; the movement, in sensible intuition for understanding. The action of the body is the objectified act of will. Called at first the immediate object of presentation, the body may now, from the other side, be called "the objectivity of the will".

Thus, as was said, the "law of motivation" discloses the inner nature of causality. In causality in general we know only relations of phenomena; but in the case of our own body we know something else that those relations express; namely, the act of will determined by motives. Now there are in the world as presentation other systems like that which we call our body. Unless all these are to be supposed mere phantoms without inner reality, we must infer by analogy, in correspondence with like phenomena, other individual wills similar to that which we know in ourselves. This inference from analogy, universally admitted in the case of human and animal bodies, must be extended to the whole corporeal world. The failure to take this step is where the purely intellectual forms of idealism have come short. Kant's "thing-in-itself", which is not subject to the forms by which presentations become experience, but which experience and its forms indicate as the reality, has been wrongly condemned by his successors as alien to idealism. It is true that Kant did in some respects fail to maintain the idealistic position with the clearness of Berkeley; but his shortcoming was not in affirming a thing-in-itself beyond phenomena. Here, in Schopenhauer's view, is the metaphysical problem that he left a place for but did not solve. The word of the riddle has now been pronounced. Beyond presentation, that is, in itself and according to its innermost essence, the world is that which we find in ourselves immediately as will. By this it is not meant that a falling stone, for example, acts from a motive; knowledge and the consequent action from motives belongs only to the determinate form that the will has in animals and men; but the reality in the stone also is the same in essence as that to which we apply the name of will in ourselves. He who possesses this key to the knowledge of nature's innermost being will interpret the forces of vegetation, of crystallisation, of magnetism, of chemical affinity, even of weight itself, as different only in phenomenal manifestation but in essence the same; namely, that which is better known to each than all else, and where it emerges most clearly is called will. Only the Will is thing-in-itself. It is wholly different from presentation, and is that of which presentation is the phenomenon, the visibility, the objectivity. Differences affect only the degree of the appearing, not the essence of that which appears.

While the reality everywhere present is not will as specifically known in man, the mode of indicating its essence by reference to this, Schopenhauer contends, is a gain in insight. The thing-in-itself ought to receive its name from that among all its manifestations which is the clearest, the most perfect, the most immediately illumined by knowledge; and this is man's will. When we say that every force in nature is to be thought of as Will, we are subsuming an unknown under a known. For the conception of Force is abstracted from the realm of cause and effect, and indicates the limit of scientific explanation. Having arrived at the forces of nature on the one side and the forms of the subject on the other, science can go no further. The conception of Will can make known that which was so far concealed, because it proceeds from the most intimate consciousness that each has of himself, where the knower and the known coincide.

By this consciousness, in which subject and object are not yet set apart, we reach something universal. In itself the Will is not individualised, but exists whole and undivided in every single thing in nature, as the Subject of contemplation exists whole and undivided in each cognitive being. It is entirely free from all forms of the phenomenon. What makes plurality possible is subjection to the forms of time and space, by which only the phenomenon is affected. Time and space may therefore be called, in scholastic terminology, the "principle of individuation". While each of its phenomena is subject to the law of sufficient reason, which is the law of appearance in these forms, there is for the Will as thing-in-itself no rational ground: it is "grundlos". It is free from all plurality, although its phenomena in space and time are innumerable. It is one, not with the unity of an object or of a concept, but as that which lies outside of space and time, beyond the *principium individuationis*, that is, the possibility of plurality. The individual, the person, is not will as thing-in-itself, but phenomenon of the will, and as such determined. The will is "free" because there is nothing beyond itself to determine it. Further, it is in itself mere activity, without end, a blind striving. Knowledge appears only as the accompaniment of its ascending stages.

Here we have arrived at the thought which, in its various expressions, constitutes Schopenhauer's metaphysics. That this cannot be scientifically deduced he admits; but he regards it as furnishing such explanation as is possible of science itself. For science there is in everything an inexplicable element to which it runs back, and which is real, not merely phenomenal. From this reality we are most remote in pure mathematics and in the pure *a priori* science of nature as it was formulated by Kant. These owe their transparent clearness precisely to their absence of real content, or to the slightness of this. The attempt to reduce organic life to chemistry, this again to mechanism, and at last everything to arithmetic, could it succeed, would leave mere form behind, from which all the content of phenomena would have vanished. And the form would in the end be form of the subject. But the enterprise is vain. "For in everything in nature there is something of which no ground can ever be given, of which no explanation is possible, no cause further is to be sought." What for man is his inexplicable character, presupposed in every explanation of his deeds from motives, that for every inorganic body is its inexplicable quality, the manner of its acting.

The basis of this too is will, and "groundless", inexplicable will; but evidently the conception here is not identical with that of the Will that is one and all. How do we pass from the universal to that which has a particular character or quality? For of the Will as thing-in-itself we are told that there is not a greater portion in a man and a less in a stone. The relation of part and whole belongs exclusively to space. The more and less touches only the phenomenon, that is, the visibility, the objectivation. A higher degree of this is in the plant than in the stone, in the animal than in the plant, and so forth; but the Will that is the essence of all is untouched by degree, as it is beyond plurality, space and time, and the relation of cause and effect.

The answer to the question here raised is given in Schopenhauer's interpretation of the Platonic Ideas. These he regards as stages of objectivation of the Will. They are, as Plato called them, eternal forms related to particular things as models. The lowest stage of objectivation of the Will is represented by the forces of inorganic nature. Some of these, such as weight and impenetrability, appear in all matter. Some are divided among its different kinds, as rigidity, fluidity, elasticity, electricity, magnetism, chemical properties. They are not subject to the relation of cause and effect, but are presupposed by it. A force is neither cause of an effect nor effect of a cause. Philosophically, it is immediate objectivity of the will; in aetiology, *qualitas occulta*. At the lowest stages of objectivation, there is no individuality. This does not appear in inorganic things, nor even in merely organic or vegetative life, but only as we ascend the scale of animals. Even in the higher animals the specific enormously preponderates over the individual character. Only in man is the Idea objectified in the individual character as such. "The character of each individual man, so far as it is thoroughly individual and not entirely comprehended in that of the species, may be regarded as a particular Idea, corresponding to a peculiar act of objectivation of the Will."

Schopenhauer warns us against substituting this philosophical explanation for scientific aetiology. The chain of causes and effects, he points out, is not broken by the differences of the original, irreducible forces. The aetiology and the philosophy of nature go side by side, regarding the same object from different points of view. Yet he also gives us in relation to his philosophy much that is not unsuggestive scientifically. His doctrine is not properly evolutionary, since the Ideas are eternal; but he has guarded incidentally against our supposing that all the natural kinds that manifest the Ideas phenomenally must be always represented in every world. For our particular world, comprising the sun and planets of the solar system, he sets forth in the *Parerga* an account of the process by which it develops from the nebula to man. This was referred to in the preceding section. In his fundamental work he describes a struggle, present through the whole of nature, in which the phenomenal manifestations of the higher Ideas conquer and subjugate those of the lower, though they leave them still existent and ever striving to get loose. Here has been seen an adumbration of natural selection: he himself admits the difficulty he has in making it clear. We must remember that it is pre-Darwinian.

Knowledge or intelligence he seeks to explain as an aid to the individual organism in its struggle to subsist and to propagate its kind. It first appears in animal life. It is represented by the brain or a large ganglion, as every endeavour of the

Will in its self-objectivation is represented by some organ; that is, displays itself for presentation as such and such an appearance. Superinduced along with this contrivance for aid in the struggle, the world as presentation, with all its forms, subject and object, time, space, plurality and causality, is all at once there. "Hitherto only will, it is now at the same time presentation, object of the knowing subject." Then in man, as a higher power beyond merely intuitive intelligence, appears reason as the power of abstract conception. For the most part, rational as well as intuitive knowledge, evolved originally as a mere means to higher objectivation of the Will, remains wholly in its service. How, in exceptional cases, intellect emancipates itself, will be discussed under the heads of Aesthetics and Ethics.

That this view implies a teleology Schopenhauer expressly recognises. Indeed he is a very decided teleologist on lines of his own, and, in physiology, takes sides strongly with "vitalism" as against pure mechanicism. True, the Will is "endless" blind striving, and is essentially divided against itself. Everywhere in nature there is strife, and this takes the most horrible forms. Yet somehow there is in each individual manifestation of will a principle by which first the organism with its vital processes, and then the portion of it called the brain, in which is represented the intellect with its *a priori* forms, are evolved as aids in the strife. And, adapting all the manifestations to one another, there is a teleology of the universe. The whole world, with all its phenomena, is the objectivity of the one and indivisible Will; the Idea which is related to all other Ideas as the harmony to the single voices. The unity of the Will shows itself in the unison of all its phenomena as related to one another. Man, its clearest and completest objectivation, is the summit of a pyramid, and could not exist without this. Inorganic and organic nature, then, were adapted to the future appearance of man, as man is adapted to the development that preceded him. But in thinking the reality, time is to be abstracted from. The earlier, we are obliged to say, is fitted to the later, as the later is fitted to the earlier; but the relation of means to end, under which we cannot help figuring the adaptation, is only appearance for our manner of knowledge. And the harmony described does not get rid of the conflict inherent in all will.

In this account of Schopenhauer's metaphysical doctrine, I have tried to make the exposition as smooth as possible; but at two points the discontinuity can scarcely be concealed. First, the relation of the universal Will to the individual will is not made clear; and, secondly, the emergence of the world of presentation, with the knowledge in which it culminated, is left unintelligible because the will is conceived as mere blind striving without an aim. As regards the first point, disciples and expositors have been able to show that, by means of distinctions in his later writings, apparent contradictions are to some extent cleared away; and, moreover, that he came to recognise more reality in the individual will. On the second point, I think it will be necessary to admit that his system as such breaks down. But both points must be considered in their connexion.

One of the most noteworthy features of Schopenhauer's philosophy is, as he himself thought, the acceptance from first to last of Kant's distinction between the "empirical" and the "intelligible" character of the individual. Every act of will of every human being follows with necessity as phenomenon from its phenomenal causes; so that all the events of each person's life are determined in accordance with scientific law. Nevertheless, the character empirically manifested in the phenomenal world, while it is completely necessitated, is the expression of something that is free from necessitation. This "intelligible character" is out of time, and, itself undetermined, manifests itself through that which develops in time as a chain of necessary causes and effects. That this doctrine had been taken up, without any ambiguity as regards the determinism, by Schelling as well as by himself, he expressly acknowledges; and he finds it, as he also finds modern idealism, anticipated in various passages by the Neo-Platonists. His adaptation of it to his doctrine of the Ideas is distinctly Neo-Platonic in so far as he recognises "Ideas of individuals"; but of course to make Will the essence belongs to his own system. "The intelligible character", he says, "coincides with the Idea, or, yet more precisely, with the original act of will that manifests itself in it: in so far, not only is the empirical character, of each man, but also of each animal species, nay, of each plant species, and even of each original force of inorganic nature, to be regarded as phenomenon of an intelligible character, that is, of an indivisible act of will out of time." This is what he called the "*aseitas*" of the will; borrowing a scholastic term to indicate its derivation (if we may speak of it as derived) from itself (*a se*), and not from a supposed creative act. Only if we adopt this view are we entitled to regard actions as worthy of moral approval or disapproval. They are such not because they are not necessitated, but because they necessarily show forth the nature of an essence the freedom of which consists in being what it is. Yet he could not but find a difficulty in reconciling this with his position that the one universal Will is identical in all things, and in each is "individuated" only by space and time. For the Ideas, like the thing-in-itself, are eternal, that is, outside of time as well as space; and all the things now enumerated, forces of nature, plant and animal species, and individual characters of men, are declared to be in themselves Ideas.

He in part meets this difficulty by the subtlety that time and space do not, strictly speaking, determine individuality, but arise along with it. The diremption of individualities becomes explicit in those forms. Yet he must have perceived that this is not a complete answer, and various modifications can be seen going on. His first view clearly was that the individual is wholly impermanent, and at death simply disappears; nothing is left but the one Will and the universal Subject of contemplation identical in all. Metempsychosis is the best mythological rendering of what happens, but it is no more. Later, he puts forward the not very clearly defined theory of a "palingenesia" by which a particular will, but not the intellect that formerly accompanied it, may reappear in the phenomenal world. And the hospitality he showed to stories of magic, clairvoyance, and ghost-seeing, is scarcely compatible with the view that the individual will is no more than a phenomenal differentiation of the universal Will. A speculation (not put forward as anything more) on the appearance of a special providence in the destiny of the individual, points, as Professor Volkelt has noted, to the idea of a guidance, not from without, but by a kind of good daemon or genius that is the ultimate reality of the person. On all this we must not lay too much stress; but there is certainly one passage that can only be described as a definite concession that the individual is real in a sense not at first allowed. Individuality, it is said in so many words (*Parerga*, ii. §117), does not rest only on the "principle of individuation" (time and space), and is therefore not through and through phenomenon, but is rooted in the thing-in-itself. "How deep its roots go belongs to the questions which I do not undertake to answer."[1]

This tends to modify considerably, but does not overthrow, Schopenhauer's original system. In very general terms, he is in the number of the "pantheistic" thinkers; and it is remarkable, on examination, how these, in Europe at least, have nearly always recognised in the end some permanent reality in the individual. This is contrary to first impressions: but the great names may be cited of Plotinus, John Scotus Erigena, Giordano Bruno, Spinoza (in Part v of the *Ethics*), and finally of Schopenhauer's special aversion, Hegel, who has been supposed most unfavourable of all to any recognition of individuality as real. It is more true, Hegel maintains, that the individuality determines its world than that it is determined by it; and there is no explanation why the determination should be such and such except that the individuality was already what it is.[2] And, if Schopenhauer's more imaginative speculations seek countenance from the side of empiricism, there is nothing in them quite so audacious as a speculation of

[1] *Werke*, ed. Frauenstädt, vi. 243.

[2] *Phänomenologie des Geistes*, Jubiläumsausgabe, ed. G. Lasson, pp. 201–203.

J. S. Mill on disembodied mind, thrown out during the time when he was writing his *Logic*.[1]

The association with pantheism Schopenhauer accepts in principle, though the name is not congenial to him. In his system the Will is one and all, like the "Deus" of Spinoza. The difference is that, instead of ascribing perfection to the universe that is its manifestation, he regards the production of a world as a lapse from which redemption is to be sought. His doctrine has been rightly described, in common with the predominant philosophical doctrines of his period, as a resultant of the deepened subjective analysis brought by Kant into modern philosophy on the one side, and of the return to Spinoza in the quest for unity of principle on the other. Why, then, it may be asked, are Fichte, Schelling, and Hegel the constant objects of his attack? The true explanation is not the merely external one, that they were his successful rivals for public favour, but is to be found in a real antithesis of thought. Within the limits of the idealism they all hold in common, Schopenhauer is at the opposite pole. In spite of his attempt to incorporate the Platonic Ideas, and in spite of his following of Kant, whose "intelligible world" was in essence Platonic or Neo-Platonic, he could find no place in his system for a rational order at the summit. Now this order was precisely what Fichte and Hegel aimed at demonstrating. If Schopenhauer is less unsympathetic in his references to Schelling, that is because Schelling's world-soul appeared to him to prefigure his own attempt to discover in nature the manifestation of a blindly striving will or feeling rather than reason. Suspicious as he shows himself of possible plagiarisms by others, the charge cannot be retorted against himself. The supreme principle of Fichte, it has been pointed out, has an actively volitional character and was formulated before

[1] Letter to Robert Barclay Fox, May 10, 1842. Printed in Appendix to *Letters and Journals of Caroline Fox*, 3rd ed., ii. 331–333. "To suppose that the eye is *necessary* to sight", says Mill, "seems to me the notion of one immersed in matter. What we call our bodily sensations are all in the mind, and would not necessarily or probably cease, because the body perishes."

Schopenhauer's: but then it is essentially rational. For Hegel, what is supreme is the world-reason. Hence they are at one with Plato in holding that in some sense "mind is king". For Schopenhauer, on the contrary, mind, or pure intellect, is an emancipated slave. Having reached its highest point, and seen through the work of the will, it does not turn back and organise it, but abolishes it as far as its insight extends.

Yet to say merely this is to give a wrong impression of Schopenhauer. Starting though he does with blind will, and ending with the flight of the ascetic from the suffering inherent in the world that is the manifestation of such a will, he nevertheless, in the intermediate stages, makes the world a cosmos and not a chaos. And the Platonists on their side have to admit that "the world of all of us" does not present itself on the surface as a manifestation of pure reason, and that it is a serious task to "rationalise" it. Where he completely fails is where the Platonic systems also fail, though from the opposite starting-point. His attempt to derive presentation, intellect, knowledge, from blind striving, is undoubtedly a failure. But so also is the attempt of the Platonising thinkers to deduce a world of mixture from a principle of pure reason without aid from anything else empirically assumed. Not that in either case there is failure to give explanations in detail; but in both cases much is taken from experience without reduction to the principles of the system. What we may say by way of comparison is this: that if Schopenhauer had in so many words recognised an immanent Reason as well as Will in the reality of the universe, he would have formally renounced his pessimism; while it cannot be said that on the other side a more explicit empiricism in the account of the self-manifestation of Reason would necessarily destroy the optimism.

AESTHETICS

A portion of Schopenhauer's system by which its pessimism is considerably mitigated is his theory of the Beautiful and of Fine Art. The characteristic of aesthetic contemplation is, he finds, that intellect throws off the yoke and subsists purely for itself as clear mirror of the world, free from all subjection to practical purposes of the will. In this state of freedom, temporary painlessness is attained.

The theory starts from his adaptation of the Platonic Ideas. Regarded purely as an aesthetic theory, it departs from Plato, as he notes; for, with the later Platonists, who took up the defence of poetic myths and of the imitative arts as against their master, he holds that Art penetrates to the general Idea through the particular, and hence that the work of art is no mere "copy of a copy". The difference of the Idea from the Concept is that it is not merely abstract and general, but combines with generality the characters of an intuition.

The Ideas, as we have seen, constitute the determinate stages of objectivation of the Will. The innumerable individuals of which the Ideas are the patterns are subject to the law of sufficient reason. They appear, that is to say, under the forms of time, space, and causality. The Idea is beyond these forms, and therefore is clear of plurality and change. Since the law of sufficient reason is the common form under which stands all the subject's knowledge so far as the subject knows as individual, the Ideas lie outside the sphere of knowledge of the individual as such. If, therefore, the Ideas are to be the object of knowledge, this can only be by annulling individuality in the knowing subject.

As thing-in-itself, the Will is exempt even from the first of the forms of knowledge, the form of being "object for a subject". The Platonic Idea, on the other hand, is necessarily an object, something known, a presentation. It has laid aside, or rather has not taken on, the subordinate forms; but it has retained the first and most general form. It is the immediate and most adequate possible objectivity of the Will; whereas particular things are an objectivation troubled by the forms of which the law of sufficient reason is the common expression.

When intellect breaks loose from the service of the will, for which it was originally destined in the teleology of nature, then the subject ceases to be merely individual and becomes pure will-less subject of knowledge. In this state the beholder no longer tracks out relations in accordance with the principle of sufficient reason—which is the mode of scientific as well as of common knowledge—but rests in fixed contemplation of the given object apart from its connexion with anything else. The contemplator thus "lost" in the object, it is not the single thing as such that is known, but the Idea, the eternal form, the immediate objectivity of the Will at this stage. The correlate of this object—the pure Subject exempt from the principle of sufficient reason—is eternal, like the Idea.

The objectivation of the Will appears faintly in inorganic things—clouds, water, crystals—more fully in the plant, yet more fully in the animal, most completely in man. Only the essential in these stages of objectivation constitutes the Idea. Its development into manifold phenomena under the forms of the principle of sufficient reason, is unessential, lies merely in the mode of knowledge for the individual, and has reality only for this. It is not otherwise with the unfolding of that Idea which is the completest objectivation of the Will. To the Idea of Man, the occurrences of human history are as unessential as the shapes they assume to the clouds, as the figures of its whirlpools and foam-drift to the stream, as its frost-flowers to the ice. The same underlying passions and dispositions everlastingly recur in the same modes. It is idle to suppose that anything is gained. But also nothing is lost: so the Earth-spirit might reply to one who complained of high endeavours frustrated, faculties wasted, promises of world-enlightenment brought to nought; for there is infinite time to dispose of, and all possibilities are for ever renewed.

The kind of knowledge for which the Ideas are the object of contemplation finds its expression in Art, the work of genius. Art repeats in its various media the Ideas grasped by pure contemplation. Its only end is the communication of these. While Science, following the stream of events according to their determinate relations, never reaches an ultimate end, Art is always at the end. "It stops the wheel of time; relations vanish for it: only the essence, the Idea, is its object." The characteristic of genius is a predominant capacity for thus contemplating things independently of the principle of sufficient reason. Since this requires a forgetting of one's own person and the relations between it and things, the attitude of genius is simply the completest "objectivity". The "subjectivity" opposed to this, in Schopenhauer's phraseology, is preoccupation with the interests of one's own will. It is, he says, as if there fell to the share of genius a measure of intelligence far beyond the needs of the individual will: and this makes possible the setting aside of individual interests, the stripping off of the particular personality, so that the subject becomes "pure knowing subject", "clear world-eye", in a manner sufficiently sustained for that which has been grasped to be repeated in the work of art. A necessary element in genius is therefore Imagination. For without imagination to represent, in a shape not merely abstract, things that have not come within personal experience, genius would remain limited to immediate intuition, and could not make its vision apprehensible by others. Nor without imagination could the particular things that express the Idea be cleared of the imperfections by which their limited expression of it falls short of what nature was aiming at in their production. "Inspiration" is ascribed to genius because its characteristic attitude is intermittent. The man of genius cannot always remain on a height, but has to fall back to the level of the common man, who can scarcely at all regard things except as they affect his interests —have a relation to his will, direct or indirect.

This is the statement in its first outline of a theory that became one of Schopenhauer's most fruitful topics. Many are the pages he has devoted to the contrast between the man of genius and "the wholesale ware of nature, which she turns out daily by thousands". The genius is for him primarily the artist. Scientific genius as a distinctive thing he does not fully recognise; and he regards men of action, and especially statesmen, rather as men of highly competent ability endowed with an exceptionally good physical constitution than as men of genius in the proper sense. Philosophers like himself, who, as he frankly says, appear about once in a hundred years, he classes in the end with the artists; though this was left somewhat indeterminate in his first exposition. The weakness of the man of genius in dealing with the ordinary circumstances of life he allows, and even insists on. Genius, grasping the Idea in its perfection, fails to understand individuals. A poet may know man profoundly, and men very ill. He admits the proximity of genius to madness on one side, and explains it in this way. What marks the stage of actual madness, as distinguished from illusion or hallucination, is complete disruption of the memory of past life, of the history of the personality as something continuous; so that the particular thing is viewed by itself, out of relation. This gives a kind of resemblance to the attitude of genius, for which present intuition excludes from view the relations of things to each other. Or, as we may perhaps sum up his thought in its most general form, "alienation" or dissolution of personality has the resemblance often noted between extremes to the impersonality, or, as he calls it, "objectivity", that is super-personal.

In spite of his contempt for the crowd, he has to admit, of course, that the capacity of genius to recognise the Ideas of things and to become momentarily impersonal must in some measure belong to all men; otherwise, they could not even enjoy a work of art when produced. Genius has the advantage only in the much higher degree and the greater prolongation of the insight. Since, then, the actual achievement of the artist is to make us look into the world through his eyes, the feelings for the beautiful and the sublime may be treated irrespectively of the question whether they are aroused by nature and human life directly or by means of art.

Aesthetic pleasure in contemplation of the beautiful proceeds partly from recognition of the individual object not as one particular thing but as Platonic Idea, that is, as the enduring form of this whole kind of things; partly from the consciousness the knower has of himself not as individual, but as pure, will-less Subject of Knowledge. All volition springs out of need, therefore out of want, therefore out of suffering. No attained object of will can give permanent satisfaction. Thus, there can be no durable happiness or rest for us as long as we are subjects of will. "The Subject of Will lies continually on the turning wheel of Ixion, draws ever in the sieve of the Danaides, is the eternally thirsting Tantalus. But in the moment of pure objective contemplation, free from all interest of the particular subjectivity, we enter a painless state: the wheel of Ixion stands still." The Flemish painters produce this aesthetic effect by the sense of disinterested contemplation conveyed in their treatment of insignificant objects. There are certain natural scenes that have power in themselves, apart from artistic treatment, to put us in this state; but the slightest obtrusion of individual interest destroys the magic. Past and distant objects, through their apparent detachment, have the same power. The essential thing aesthetically, whether we contemplate the present or the past, the near or the distant, is that only the world of presentation remains; the world as will has vanished.

The difference between the feelings of the Beautiful and of the Sublime is this. In the feeling of the beautiful, pure intelligence gains the victory without a struggle, leaving in consciousness only the pure subject of knowledge, so that no reminiscence of the will remains. In the feeling of the sublime, on the other hand, the state of pure intelligence has to be won by a conscious breaking loose from relations in the object that suggest something threatening to the will; though there must not be actual danger; for in that case the individual will itself would come into play, and aesthetic detachment would cease. Elevation above the sense of terror has not only to be consciously won but consciously maintained, and involves a continuous reminiscence, not indeed of any individual will, but of the will of man in general, so far as it is expressed through its objectivity, the human body, confronted by forces hostile to it. Pre-eminently this feeling arises from contrast between the immensities of space and time and the apparent insignificance of man. It means in the last resort that the beholder is upheld by the consciousness that as pure subject of knowledge (not as individual subject) he himself bears within him all the worlds and all the ages, and is eternal as the forces that vainly seem to threaten him with annihilation.

On the objective side, and apart from the subjective distinction just set forth, the sublime and the beautiful are not essentially different. In both cases alike, the object of aesthetic contemplation is not the single thing, but the Idea that is striving towards manifestation in it. Whatever is viewed aesthetically is viewed out of relation to time and space: "along with the law of sufficient reason the single thing and the knowing individual are taken away, and nothing remains over but the Idea and the pure Subject of Knowledge, which together make up the adequate objectivity of the Will at this stage". There is thus a sense in which everything is beautiful; since the Will appears in everything at some stage of objectivity, and this means that it is the expression of some Idea. But one thing can be more beautiful than another by facilitating aesthetic contemplation. This facilitation proceeds either from the greater clearness and perfection with which the particular thing shows forth the Idea of its kind, or from the higher stage of objectivation to which that Idea corresponds. Man being the highest stage of objectivation of the Will, the revelation of his essence is the highest aim of art. In aesthetic contemplation of inorganic nature and vegetative life, whether in the reality or through the medium of art, and in appreciation of architecture, the subjective aspect, that is to say, the enjoyment of pure will-less knowledge, is predominant; the Ideas themselves being here lower stages of objectivity. On the other hand, when animals and men are the object of aesthetic contemplation or representation, the enjoyment consists more in the objective apprehension of those Ideas in which the essence of the Will is most clearly and fully manifested.

Of all Schopenhauer's work, its aesthetic part has met with the most general appreciation. Here especially he abounds in observations drawn directly, in his own phrase, from intuition. To make a selection of these, however, is not appropriate to a brief sketch like the present. I pass on, therefore, to those portions of his theory of Art by which he makes the transition, in terms of his system, to Morality.

From Architecture onward the arts are obliged to represent the Will as divided. Here, at the first stage, its division subsists only in a conflict of inorganic forces which have to be brought to equilibrium. The conflict between weight and rigidity is in truth the only aesthetic material of architecture as a fine art. When we come to animal and lastly to human life, which, in the Plastic Arts and in Poetry, as form, individualised expression, and action, is the highest object of aesthetic representation, the vehemence of divided will is fully revealed; and here too is revealed the essential identity of every will with our own. In the words of the Indian wisdom, "Tat twam asi"; "that thou art". Under the head of Ethics it will be shown expressly that by this insight, when it reacts on the will, the will can deny itself. For the temporary release from its striving, given in aesthetic contemplation, is then substituted permanent release. To this "resignation", the innermost essence of all virtue and holiness, and the final redemption from the world, Art itself, at its highest stages, points the way.

The summits of pictorial and poetic art Schopenhauer finds in the great Italian painters so far as they represent the ethical spirit of Christianity, and in the tragic poets, ancient and modern. It is true that the poverty of their sacred history or mythology puts the Christian artists at a disadvantage; but events are merely the accidents of their art. Not in these, as related according to the law of sufficient reason, is the essence, but in the spirit we divine through the forms portrayed. In their representation of men full of that spirit, and especially in the eyes, we see mirrored the knowledge that has seized the whole essence of the world and of life, and that has reacted on the will, not so as to give it motives, but as a "quietive"; whence proceeds complete resignation, and with it the annulling of the will and of the whole essence of this world. Of tragedy, the subject-matter is the conflict of the will with itself at its highest stage of objectivity. Here also the end is the resignation brought on by complete knowledge of the essence of the world. The hero, on whom at last this knowledge has acted as a quietive, gives up, not merely life, but the whole will to live. "The true meaning of tragedy is the deeper insight, that what the hero expiates is not his particular sins, but original sin, that is, the guilt of existence itself." To illustrate this position Schopenhauer is fond of quoting a passage from Calderon which declares that the greatest sin of man is to have been born.

It seems strange that, after deriding as he does the popular notion of "poetic justice", so detached a thinker should imagine an at least equally one-sided view to receive its final confirmation from the Spanish dramatist's poetic phrasing of a Christian dogma. The great tragic poets, for Schopenhauer also, are Aeschylus, Sophocles and Shakespeare. Now it is safe to say that by none of these was any such general doctrine held either in conceptual or in intuitive form. The whole effect of any kind of art, of course he would admit, cannot be packed into a formula; but if we seek one as an aid to understanding, some adaptation of his own theory of the sublime would probably serve much better as applied to tragedy than his direct theory of the drama. In the case of pictorial art, all that is proved by what he says about the representation of ascetic saintliness, is that this, like many other things, can be so brought within the scope of art as to make us momentarily identify ourselves with its Idea in the impersonal manner he has himself described. His purely aesthetic theory is quite adequate to the case, without any assumption that this is the representation of what is best. Art, pictorial or poetic, can no more prove pessimism than optimism. We pick out expressions of one or the other for quotation according to our moods or subjective preferences; but, if we have the feeling for art itself, our sense of actual aesthetic value ought to be independent of these.

Schopenhauer's aesthetic theory, however, does not end here. There follows the part of it by which he has had an influence on artists themselves. For him, a position separate from all the other arts is held by music. While the rest objectify the Will mediately, that is to say, by means of the Ideas, Music is as immediate an objectivation of the whole Will as the world itself, or as the Ideas, of which the pluralised phenomenon constitutes the sum of particular things. The other arts speak of the shadow, music of the substance. There is indeed a parallelism, an analogy, between Music and the Ideas; yet Music never expresses the phenomenon in which these are manifested, but only the inner essence behind the appearance, the Will itself. In a sense it renders not feeling in its particularity, but feeling *in abstracto*; joy, sorrow, not a joy, a sorrow. The phenomenal world and music are to be regarded as two different expressions of the same thing. The world might be called embodied Music as well as embodied Will. "Melodies are to a certain extent like general concepts, an abstract of reality." A complete explanation of music, that is, a detailed repetition of it in concepts, were this possible, would be a complete explanation of the world (since both express the same thing) and therefore a true and final philosophy. As music only reaches its perfection in the full harmony, "so the one Will out of time finds its perfect objectivation only in complete union of all the stages which in innumerable degrees of heightened distinctness reveal its essence". But here, too, Schopenhauer adds, the Will is felt, and can be proved, to be a divided will; and the deliverance wrought by this supreme art, as by all the others, is only temporary.

ETHICS

Permanent redemption from the suffering of the world is to be found only in the holiness of the ascetic; but to this there are many stages, constituting the generally accepted human virtues. Of these Schopenhauer has a rational account to give in terms of his philosophy; and if the last stage does not seem to follow by logical sequence from the others, this is only what is to be expected; for it is reached, in his view, by a sort of miracle. To the highest kind of intuitive knowledge, from which the ascetic denial of the will proceeds, artistic contemplation ought to prepare the way; and so also, on his principles, ought the practice of justice and goodness. Yet he is obliged to admit that few thus reach the goal. Of those that do reach it, the most arrive through personal suffering, which may be deserved. A true miracle is often worked in the repentant criminal, by which final deliverance is achieved. Though the "intelligible character" is unalterable, and the empirical character can only be the unfolding of this, as every great dramatist intuitively recognises, yet the "convertites", like Duke Frederick in *As You Like It*, are not to be regarded as hypocrites. The "second voyage" to the harbour, that of the disappointed egoist, on condition of this miracle, brings the passenger to it as surely as the first, that of the true saints, which is only for the few. And in these equally a miraculous conversion of the will has to be finally worked.

At the entrance to his distinctive theory of ethics, Schopenhauer places a restatement of his metaphysics as the possible basis of a mode of contemplating life which, he admits, has some community with an optimistic pantheism. The Will, through the presentation and the accompanying intelligence developed in its service, becomes conscious that that which it wills is precisely the world, life as it is. To call it "the will to live" is therefore a pleonasm. "Will" and "will to live" are equivalent. For this will, life is everlastingly a certainty. "Neither the will, the thing-in-itself in all phenomena, nor the subject of knowledge, the spectator of all phenomena, is ever touched by birth and death." It is true that the individual appears and disappears; but individuality is illusory. Past and future exist only in conceptual thought. "The form of life is a present without end, howsoever the individuals, phenomena of the Idea, come into existence and vanish in time, like fugitive dreams." Only as phenomenon is each man different from the other things of the world: as thing-in-itself he is the Will, which appears in all, and death takes away the illusion that divides his consciousness from the rest. "Death is a sleep in which the individuality is forgotten: everything else wakes again, or rather has remained awake." It is, in the expression adopted by Schopenhauer later, an awakening from the dream of life: though this bears with it somewhat different implications; and, as has been said, his theory of individuality became modified.

With the doctrine of the eternal life of the Will are connected Schopenhauer's theories, developed later, of the immortality of the species and of individualised sexual love. The latter is by itself a remarkable achievement, and constitutes the one distinctly new development brought to completion in his later years; for the modifications in his theory of individuality are only tentative. His theory of love has a determinate conclusion, of great value for science, and not really compatible, it seems to me, with his pessimism. In its relation to ethics, on which he insisted, it is rightly placed in the position it occupies, between the generalised statement of his metaphysics just now set forth on the one side, and his theory of human virtue on the other.

The teleology that manifests itself in individualised love is, in his view, not related in reality to the interests of the individual life, but to those of the species. That this is immortal follows from the eternity of the Idea it unfolds.[1] The end sought is aimed at unconsciously by the person. Fundamentally, for Schopenhauer, teleology must of course be unconscious, since the will is blind, and will, not intelligence, is primordial. Its typical case is the instinct of animals; but the "instinctive" character belongs also to the accomplishment of the highest aims, as in art and virtue. What characterises individualised love internally is the aim, attributed to "nature" or "the species", at a certain typical beauty or perfection of the offspring. The lover is therefore deluded in thinking that he is seeking his own happiness. What looks through the eyes of lovers is the genius of the race, meditating on the composition of the next generation. It may, in the complexity of circum-

[1] The disappearance of species in time raises difficulties in more than one way for his philosophy; but he formally escapes refutation by the suggestion, already noted, that the Idea need not always be manifested phenomenally in the same world. This, however, he did not work out.

stances, be thwarted. When it reaches its end, often personal happiness is sacrificed. Marriages dictated by interest tend to be happier than love-matches. Yet, though the sacrifice of the individual to the race is involuntary in these, egoism is after all overcome; hence they are quite rightly the object of a certain admiration and sympathy, while the prudential ones are looked upon with a tinge of contempt. For here too that element appears which alone gives nobility to the life either of intellect or of art or of moral virtue, namely, the rising above a subjective interest of the individual will.

No doubt there are touches of pessimism in this statement; but the general theory does not seem reconcilable finally with pessimism as Schopenhauer understands it. For it is a definitely stated position of his that nature keeps up the process of the world by yielding just enough to prevent discontinuance of the striving for an illusory end. Yet he admits here in the result something beyond bare continuance of life; for this is already secured without the particular modification of feeling described. What the feeling is brought in to secure is a better realisation of the type in actual individuals; and such realisation is certainly more than bare subsistence with the least possible expenditure of nature's resources.

As the immediate preliminary to his ethics proper, Schopenhauer restates his doctrine on the intelligible and the empirical character in man, and lays down a generalised psychological position regarding the suffering inherent in life. Everything as phenomenon, we have seen already, is determined because it is subject to the law of sufficient reason. On the other hand, everything as thing-in-itself is free; for "freedom" means only non-subjection to that law. The intelligible character of each man is an indivisible, unalterable act of will out of time; the developed and explicit phenomenon of this in time and space is the empirical character. Man is his own work, not in the light of knowledge, but before all knowledge; this is secondary and an instrument. Ultimately, freedom is a mystery, and takes us beyond even will as the name for the thing-in-itself. In reality, that which is "will to live" need not have been such (though we cannot see how this is so), but has become such from itself and from nothing else. This is its "*aseitas*". Hence it is in its power to deny itself as will to live. When it does this, the redemption (like the fall) comes from itself. This denial does not mean annihilation, except relatively to all that we know under the forms of our understanding. For the will, though the nearest we can get to the thing-in-itself, is in truth a partially phenomenalised expression of this. As the will to live expresses itself phenomenally, so also does the denial of the will to live, when this, by special "grace", is achieved. Only in man does the freedom thus attained find phenomenal expression. That man can attain to it proves that in him the will has reached its highest possible stage of objectivation; for, after it has turned back and denied itself, there is evidently nothing more that we can call existence, that is to say, phenomenal existence, beyond. What there is beyond in the truth of being is something that the mystics know—or rather, possess, for it is beyond knowledge—but cannot communicate.

The psychological reason that can be assigned for the ascetic flight from the world is that all pleasure, happiness, satisfaction, is merely negative. The will is a striving that has no ultimate aim. It is sustained only by hindrances. Hindrance means suffering; and every satisfaction attained is only temporary, a mere liberation from need, want, pain, which is positive. Suffering increases with the degree of consciousness. The life of civilised man is an alternation between pain and *ennui*, which can itself become as intolerable a suffering as anything. The problem of moral philosophy, then, is ultimately how redemption from such a world is to be attained, but only so far as this is a matter of conceptual knowledge. For philosophy, being from beginning to end theoretical, cannot work the practical miracle by which the will denies itself.

The intuitive, as distinguished from merely conceptual, knowledge by which the return is made, consists essentially in a clear insight into the identity of the suffering will in all things and the necessity of its suffering as long as it is will to live.

This, then, is the true foundation of morality. The universe as metaphysical thing-in-itself, as noumenon, has an ethical meaning. All its stages of objectivation, though in the process what seems to be aimed at is preservation of the will as manifested, have in truth for their ultimate aim its redemption by suppression of the phenomenal world in which it manifests itself.

Affirmation of the will is affirmation of the body, which is the objectivity of the will. The sexual impulse, since it affirms life beyond the death of the individual, is the strongest of self-affirmations. In it is found the meaning of the mythical representation that has taken shape in the theological dogma of original sin. For by this affirmation going beyond the individual body, suffering and death, as the necessary accompaniment of the phenomenon of life, are reaffirmed, and the possibility of redemption this time declared fruitless. But through the whole process there runs eternal justice. The justification of suffering is that the will affirms itself; and the self-affirmation is justified by payment of the penalty.

Before the final redemption—which is not for the world but for the individual—there are many stages of ethical progress. These consist in the gradual overcoming of egoism by sympathy. And here Schopenhauer proceeds to set forth a practical scheme for the social life of man, differing from ordinary utilitarianism only by reducing all sympathy to pity, in accordance with his view that there can be no such thing as positive happiness.

He begins with a theory of justice, legal and moral, very much on the lines of Hobbes, except that he regards it as up to a certain point *a priori*. Here he is consistent throughout. As in his philosophical account of mathematics and physics, so also in his aesthetics and ethics, he retained, side by side with a strong empirical tendency, belief in certain irreducible *a priori* forms without which our knowledge cannot be constituted. The pure ethical theory of justice, he says, bears to the political theory the relation of pure to applied mathematics. Injustice he holds to be the positive conception. It means the breaking into the sphere of another person's will to live. The self-affirmation of the will that appears in one individual body is extended to denial of the will that appears in other bodies. Justice consists in non-encroachment. There is a "natural right", or "moral right", of resistance to injustice by infliction of what, apart from the attempted encroachment, would be wrong. Either force or deception may be used; as either may be the instrument of injustice. The purely ethical doctrine of justice applies only to action; since only the not doing of injustice depends on us. With the State and its laws, the relation is reversed. The object of these is to prevent the suffering of injustice. The State is not directed against egoism, but has sprung out of a rationalised collective egoism. It has for its purpose only to avoid the inconvenient consequences of individual aggressions on others. Outside of the State, there is a right of self-defence against injustice, but no right of punishment. The punishment threatened by the State is essentially a motive against committing wrong, intended to supply the place of ethical motives for those who are insufficiently accessible to them. Actual infliction of it is the carrying out of the threat when it has failed, so that in general the expectation of the penalty may be certain. Revenge, which has a view to the past, cannot be justified ethically: punishment is directed only to the future. There is no right in any one to set himself up as a moral judge and inflict pain; but man has a right to do what is needful for social security. The criminal's acts are of course necessitated; but he cannot justly complain of being punished for them, since it is ultimately from himself, from what he is, that they sprang.

With the doctrine of "eternal justice", touched on above, we pass into a different region of thought. What is responsible for the guilt in the world is the Will by which everything exists, and the suffering everlastingly falls where the guilt is. Take the case of apparently unpunished injustice (from the human point of view) expressing itself in the extreme form of deliberate cruelty. Through this also, eternal justice, from which there is no escape, is fulfilled. "The torturer and the tortured are one. The former errs in thinking he has no share in the torture; the latter in thinking he has no share in the guilt." For all the pain of the world is the expiation of the sin involved in the self-affirmation of will, and the Will as thing-in-itself is one and the same in all.

If this could satisfy any one, there would be no need to go further. The whole being as it ought to be, why try to rectify details that are absolutely indifferent? But of course the implication is that individuality is simply illusory; and this, as has been said, was a position that Schopenhauer neither could nor did consistently maintain. Indeed, immediately after setting forth this theory of "eternal justice", he goes on to a relative justification of those acts of disinterested vengeance by which a person knowingly sacrifices his own life for the sake of retribution on some extraordinary criminal. This, he says, is a form of punishment, not mere revenge, although it involves an error concerning the nature of eternal justice. Suicide involves a similar error, in so far as it supposes that the real being of the individual can be assailed through its phenomenal manifestation. It is not a denial of the will to live, but a strong affirmation of it, only not in the given circumstances: different circumstances are desired with such intensity that the present cannot be borne. Therefore the individual manifestation of the will is not suppressed. Yet, one might reply, if individuality is an illusion attached to the appearance in time and space of a particular organism, it would seem that, with the disappearance of this, all that distinguishes the individual must disappear also.

Schopenhauer had no will thus to escape from life; nor did he afterwards devote himself to expounding further his theory of eternal justice. What he wrote later, either positively or as mere speculation, implies both greater reality in the individual and more of cosmic equity to correspond. His next step, even at his first stage, is to continue the exposition of a practicable ethics for human life. His procedure consists in adding beneficence to justice, with the proviso already mentioned, which is required by his psychology, that all beneficence can consist only in the relief of pain. For Schopenhauer, as for Comte, what is to be overcome is "egoism", an excessive degree of which is the mark of the character we call "bad". The "good" is what Comte and Spencer call the "altruistic" character. This difference between characters Schopenhauer goes on to explain in terms of his metaphysics. The egoist is so deluded by the principle of individuation that he supposes an absolute cleft between his own person and all others. The remorse of conscience from which he suffers proceeds in part from an obscure perception that the principle of individuation is illusory. Genuine virtue springs out of the intuitive (not merely abstract) knowledge that recognises in another individuality the same essence as in one's own. The characteristic of the good man is that he makes less difference than is customary between himself and others. Justice is an intermediate stage between the encroaching egoism of the bad and positive goodness. In the renunciation of rights of property, and provision for all personal needs without aid from others, practised by some religious and philosophical ascetics, it is passing over into something more. There is, however, a certain misunderstanding involved in so interpreting strict justice; for there are many ways in which the rich and powerful can be positively beneficent. At the other extreme, when they simply live on their inherited wealth, without doing anything in return, their mode of life is morally, though not legally, unjust. Rights of property Schopenhauer derived from labour spent on the things appropriated. The injustice, in many ways, of the present social order he quite recognises. If he has no sympathy with revolutions, it is because he has no belief in the realisation of an ideal state. This follows from his view of history. Human life, it is his conviction, never has been and never will be different as a whole. Redemption from evil can be attained only by the individual. All that the State can do is to provide certain very general conditions of security under which there will be no hindrance to those who desire to live in accordance with a moral ideal.

Yet there are qualifications to make. Many passages in

Schopenhauer's writings prove his firm belief in the future triumph of reason over superstition. It is to the honour of humanity, he says, that so detestable a form of evil as organised religious persecution has appeared only in one section of history. And, in his own personal case, he has the most complete confidence that the truths he has put forth cannot fail sometime to gain a hearing. In all cases, error is only temporary, and truth will prevail. His language on this subject, and indeed often on others, is indistinguishable from that of an optimist.

In the last resort, his pessimism entrenches itself behind the psychological proposition that every satisfaction is negative, being only the removal of a pain. If this is unsustainable, there is nothing finally in his Metaphysics of Will to necessitate the pessimistic conclusion drawn. The mode of deduction by which he proceeds is to argue first to the position already noticed: that all that love of others on which morality is based is fundamentally pity. True benevolence can only be the desire to relieve others' pain, springing from the identification of this with our own. For that reason, moral virtue must finally pass over into asceticism—the denial of the will to live. In others, if we are able to see through the principle of individuation, we recognise the same essence as in ourselves, and we perceive that as long as this wills it must necessarily suffer. The end then is to destroy the will to live. This is to be done by *askesis*, self-mortification. The first step is complete chastity. If, says Schopenhauer, the highest phenomenon of will, that is, man, were to disappear through a general refusal to affirm life beyond the individual body, man's weaker reflexion in the animal world would disappear also, and the consciousness of the whole would cease. Knowledge being taken away, the rest would vanish into nothingness, since there is "no object without subject". That this will come to pass, however, he certainly did not believe. He has no cosmogony, like that of Hartmann, ending in a general redemption of the universe by such a collective act. Nor did he hold, like his later successor Mainländer, that through the conflict and gradual extinction of individualities, "this great world shall so wear out to nought". The world for him is without beginning and without end. But the exceptional individual can redeem himself. What he does when he has reached the height of holiness is by voluntary poverty and all other privations, inflicted for their own sake, to break and kill the will, which he recognises as the source of his own and of the world's suffering existence. In his case not merely the phenomenon ends at death, as with others, but the being is taken away. To be a "world-overcomer" in this sense (as opposed to a "world-conqueror") is the essence of sanctity when cleared of all the superstitious dogmas by which the saints try to explain their mode of life to themselves.

The absolutely pure expression of this truth is to be found only in philosophy; but of the religions Buddhism comes nearest to expressing it without admixture. For the Buddhist saint asks aid from no god. True Christianity, however—the Christianity of the New Testament and of the Christian mystics—agrees both with Buddhism and with Brahmanism in ultimate aim. What spoils it for Schopenhauer is the Judaic element. This, on one side, infects it with the optimism of the Biblical story of creation, in which God "saw everything that he had made, and, behold, it was very good". On the other side, it contaminates the myth of original sin, which bears in itself a profound philosophical truth, by this same doctrine of a creative God; from which follows all the injustice and irrationality necessarily involved in the Augustinian theology, and not to be expelled except with its theism. Nevertheless, the story of the Fall of Man, of which that theology, in its fundamentally true part, is a reasoned expression, is the one thing, Schopenhauer avows, that reconciles him to the Old Testament. The truth that it clothes he finds also among the Greeks; Empedocles, after the Orphics and Pythagoreans, having taught that the soul had been doomed to wander because of some antenatal sin. And the mysticism that accompanies all these more or less pure expressions of one metaphysical truth he finds represented by the Sufis even in optimistic Islam; so that he can claim for his philosophy a world-wide consent.

Religion, if we take this to include mysticism, at once rises above philosophy and falls below it. As "metaphysics of the people", it is a mythological expression of philosophical truth: as mysticism, it is a kind of "epi-philosophy". Beyond pure philosophy Schopenhauer does not profess to go; but he accepts what the mystics say as the description of a positive experience which becomes accessible when supreme insight is attained intuitively. For the philosopher as such, insight into that which is beyond the forms of our knowledge and even beyond the will itself, remains only conceptual; though it is within the province of philosophy to mark out the place for this. The "something else" that is left when the will has been denied, is indicated by the "ecstasy", "illumination", "union with God", spoken of by the mystics. Paradoxically, some of the mystics themselves even have identified it with "nothing"; but the result of the denial of the will to live is to be called nothing only in relation to the world as we know it. "On the other hand, to those in whom the will has turned back and denied itself, this so very real world of ours with all its suns and milky ways is—nothing."

In this terminus of his philosophy, Schopenhauer recognised his kinship with Indian thought, of which he was a lifelong student. To call his doctrine a kind of Buddhism is, however, in some ways a misapprehension. Undoubtedly he accepts as his ideal the ethical attitude that he finds to be common to Buddhism and the Christianity of the New Testament; but metaphysical differences mark him off from both. We have seen that he rejects the extra-mundane God of Semitic derivation, adopted by historical Christianity. Indeed he is one of the most pronounced anti-Jehovists of all literature. But equally his belief in a positive metaphysical doctrine marks him off from Buddhism, according to the account given of it by its most recent students, who regard it either as ultimately nihilistic or as having no metaphysics at all, but only a psychology and ethics. Nor can he be precisely identified with the Vedantists of orthodox Hinduism. Their ultimate reality, if we are to find an analogue for it in European metaphysics, seems to resemble the hypostasised *ego* of Fichte, or the Kantian "transcendental unity of apperception", much more than it resembles Schopenhauer's blindly striving will as thing-in-itself. Even in practical ethics, he does not follow the Indian systems at all closely. Philosophical doctrines of justice are of course purely European; and Schopenhauer himself points out the sources of his own theory. In his extension of ethics to animals, on which he lays much stress, he cites the teachings of Eastern non-Semitic religions as superior to the rest; but he does not follow the Indians, nor even the Pythagoreans, so far as to make abstinence from flesh part of the ideal. He condemns vivisection on the ground that animals have rights: certain ways of treating them are unjust, not simply uncompassionate. The discussion here again is of course wholly within European thought. Thus, in trying to determine his significance for modern philosophy, we may consider his system in its immediate environment, leaving it to more special students to determine how far it received a peculiar colouring from the Oriental philosophies, of which, in his time, the more exact knowledge was just beginning to penetrate to the West.

HISTORICAL SIGNIFICANCE

Schopenhauer is not one of the philosophers who have founded a school, though he has had many disciples and enthusiastic admirers. The pessimism that was for a time a watchword with certain literary groups has passed as a mode, and his true significance must be sought elsewhere. Of the thinkers who have followed him in his pessimism, two indeed stand out as the architects of distinct systems, Eduard von Hartmann and Philipp Mainländer (both already incidentally referred to); but while they are to be classed unquestionably as philosophers, their systems contain an element that their master would have regarded as mythological. Schopenhauer declared as clearly as any of the Greeks that the phenomenal world is without beginning and without end. Kant's positing of an "antinomy" on this point he regarded as wholly without rational justification. What Kant calls the "antithesis", namely, the infinite series, can be logically proved for phenomena. The "thesis", which asserts a beginning in time, is defended by mere fallacies. Now Hartmann and Mainländer both hold, though in different fashions, that there is a world-process from a beginning to an end, namely, the extinction of consciousness. This is the redemption of the world. Their affinity, therefore, seems to be with the Christian Gnostics rather than with the pure philosophers of the Greek tradition, continued in modern times by Bruno, Spinoza, and Schopenhauer.

Whatever may be thought of the pessimism by which Schopenhauer's mood is distinguished from that of his precursors, few will fail to recognise that special doctrines of his system contain at least a large portion of truth. His theories of Art, of Genius, and of Love are enough to found an enduring reputation for any thinker, even if there were nothing else of value in his writings. But there is much else, both in systematic construction and in the illumination of detail. I have been inclined to put forward first of all the translation into idealistic terms of the universal sentiency held by the Ionian thinkers to be inherent in the primordial elements of nature. While they viewed the world as an objective thing having psychological qualities, Schopenhauer, after the long intermediate process of thought, could treat it as phenomenal object with a psychological or subjective essence. For both doctrines alike, however, mind or soul is immanent. Still, it must be allowed that a difference remains by which Schopenhauer was even more remote than they were from the later Greek idealism. As they were not materialists, so they did not exclude reason from the psychical properties of their substances. Schopenhauer, while he rejected the materialism of their ancient and modern successors alike, took the step of formally derationalising the elements of mind. This, no doubt, is unsustainable ultimately, if reason is ever to emerge from them.

Yet the one-sidedness of the position has had a peculiar value in combating an equally one-sided rationalistic idealism. This is recognised by clear-sighted opponents. And Schopenhauer's calling the non-rational or anti-rational element in the world "will" helps to make plainer the real problem of evil. There is truth in the Hegelian paradox that "pessimism is an excellent basis for optimism". An optimist like Plotinus saw that, even if good comes of evil, the case of the optimist must fail unless evil can be shown to be a necessary constituent of the world. The Platonic and Neo-Platonic "matter", a principle of diremption or individuation, like time and space for Schopenhauer, was an attempt to solve this problem; but something more positive seemed to be needed as the source of the stronger manifestations of evil. To the strength of these Plato drew attention in a passage (*Republic*, x, 610[1]) where it is acknowledged that injustice confers a character of vitality and sleeplessness upon its possessor. In the notion of a blind and vehement striving, Schopenhauer supplies something adequate; only, to maintain a rational optimism, it must be regarded as a necessary element in a mixture, not as the spring of the whole.

Much might be said on the teleology by which he tries to educe intelligence from the primordial strife. Against his view, that it is evolved as a mere instrument for preserving races in a struggle, another may be set that is ready to hand in a dialogue of Plutarch.[2] The struggle among animals, it is there incidentally argued, has for its end to sharpen their intelligence. Both these theories are on the surface compatible with evolution. If, leaving aside the problem of mechanism, we try to verify them by the test of results, the latter undoubtedly seems the more plausible. For if the struggle was a means to the improvement of intelligence, nature has succeeded more and more; whereas, if her intention was to preserve races, she has continually failed. This argument is at

[1] Cited in one of the introductory essays to Jowett and Campbell's edition, vol. ii.

[2] *De Sollertia Animalium*, 27.

any rate perfectly valid against Schopenhauer himself; for he holds in common with the optimistic teleologists that "nature does nothing in vain".

I will conclude with a few detached criticisms on the ethical doctrine which he regarded as the culmination of his system. The antithesis, it may first be noted, between the temporary release from the vehemence of the will that is gained through art, and the permanent release through asceticism, is not consistently maintained. Schopenhauer admits that the knowledge which for the ascetic is the "quietive" of the will has to be won anew in a perpetual conflict. "No one can have enduring rest on earth." Again, revision of his doctrine concerning the reality of the individual would, I think, necessitate revision also of the position that not only asceticism but "all true and pure love, nay, even freely rendered justice, proceeds from seeing through the *principium individuationis*". If the individual is in some sense ultimately real, then love must be to a certain extent literally altruism. We are brought down to the elementary fact, in terms of the metaphysics of ethics, that the object of love is a real being that is itself and not ourselves, though having some resemblance to us and united in a larger whole. An objection not merely verbal might indeed be taken to Schopenhauer's metaphysics of ethics strictly on his own ground. If it is purely and simply the essence of ourselves that we recognise in everything, does not this reduce all love finally to a well-understood egoism? The genuine fact of sympathy seems to escape his mode of formulation. And, in the end, we shall perhaps not find the ascetic to be the supreme ethical type. Of the self-tormenting kind of asceticism, it is not enough to say with Schopenhauer that, since it is a world-wide phenomenon of human nature, it calls for some account from philosophy. The account may be sufficiently rendered by historical psychology; the result being to class it as an aberration born of the illusions incident to a certain type of mind at a certain stage. Indeed, that seems to be the conclusion of the Buddhists, who claim to have transcended it by finding it superfluous for the end it aims at. Let us then take, as our example of the completed type, not the monks of the Thebaid, but the mild ascetics of the Buddhist communities. Does not this type, even in its most attractive form, represent a "second best"? Is not the final judgment that of Plato, that to save oneself is something, but that there is no full achievement unless for the life of the State also the ideal has been brought nearer realisation? When there is nothing in the world but irredeemable tyranny or anarchy, flight from it may be the greatest success possible as far as the individual life is concerned; but this is not the normal condition of humanity. Finally, may not some actual achievement, either practical or, like that of Schopenhauer, speculative, even if accompanied by real imperfections of character, possess a higher human value than the sanctity that rests always in itself?

Selected Works

ENGLISH TRANSLATIONS

The World as Will and Idea. Translated by R. B. Haldane and J. Kemp. 3 vols. 1883–1886.

Two Essays: I. On the Fourfold Root of the Principle of Sufficient Reason. II. On the Will in Nature. Bohn's Philosophical Library, 1889.

Religion: A Dialogue, and other Essays. Selected and translated by T. Bailey Saunders. 3rd ed. 1891. [A series of other volumes of selections excellently translated by Mr Saunders has followed.]

Selected Essays of Arthur Schopenhauer. With a Biographical Introduction and Sketch of his Philosophy. By E. Belfort Bax. 1891.

The Basis of Morality. Translated with Introduction and Notes by A. B. Bullock. 1903.

BIOGRAPHICAL AND EXPOSITORY

Arthur Schopenhauer: His Life and Philosophy. By Helen Zimmern. 1876.

Life of Arthur Schopenhauer. By Professor W. Wallace. 1890.

La Philosophie de Schopenhauer. Par Th. Ribot. 1874. [Probably still the best general introduction to Schopenhauer's philosophy.]

Arthur Schopenhauer. Seine Persönlichkeit, seine Lehre, sein Glaube. Von Johannes Volkelt. 3rd ed. 1907.

Schopenhauer-Lexikon. Von Julius Frauenstädt. 2 vols. 1871.

The best critical edition of Schopenhauer's complete works is that of Ed. Grisebach, who did much better what had been commenced by Frauenstädt.

CHAPTER V

VICO'S NEW SCIENCE OF HUMANITY[1]

I

To write for posterity has been a not infrequent ambition. Giambattista Vico combined with this, in perfect seriousness, the intention long afterwards humorously expressed by Charles Lamb, to write for antiquity.[2] In natural accordance with these aims, constantly held before himself, his name has remained at once great and isolated. He has been thought to belong in spirit to Greek or Roman antiquity, or to the sixteenth or seventeenth century, rather than to the early eighteenth in which he wrote; and there is no doubt that he prefigured some characteristic ideas of the nineteenth. This is part of the interest of his work; but it is not the whole. He did, as he himself conceived, found an actually new science, not anticipated by any ancient or modern thinker; and, if he was a remarkable anticipator of later ideas, his system comprises also generalised views more adequately thought out by himself than by any of his successors, and reasoned positions corrective of some illusions of the age that was to follow his own.

In order to show this, I propose to give an account of the *Scienza Nuova* founded on a study of the recent elaborate edition by Dr Fausto Nicolini.[3] The separate treatment of Vico's great work is both desirable and possible: desirable be-

[1] This phrase, though not in the title of his great work, is used once or twice by Vico himself.

[2] "La prima pratica è stata:—come riceverebbono queste cose ch'io medito un Platone, un Varrone, un Quinto Muzio Scevola?—La seconda pratica è stata quella:—come riceverà queste cose ch'io scrivo la posterità?" (*Scienza Nuova*, "Idea dell' opera", ed. Nicolini, p. 51).

[3] Giambattista Vico, *La Scienza Nuova* giusta l' edizione del 1744, con le varianti dell' edizione del 1730 e di due redazioni intermedie inedite, e corredata di Note storiche. A cura di Fausto Nicolini. 3 vols. Bari: Laterza, 1911, 1913, 1916. Pp. lxxix, 1273 (paging continuous).

cause he himself more than once expressed indifference to the survival of any of his other works; and possible because, whatever the defects of his exposition, as unsparingly animadverted on by Italian as by foreign critics, he has in reality brought his "New Science" into a form in which it stands by itself, perfectly clear of every metaphysical doctrine, including even his own occasionally very interesting suggestions.

These may be found adequately set forth in the two standard monographs on his life and thought, by Flint[1] and by Croce.[2] The most remarkable of them are: (1) an anticipation of Kant's doctrine that we *make* mathematical truth—in Vico's phrase, *verum* is *factum*; (2) a similar but not identical position as regards the science of man. In mathematical truth, according to Vico, there is an element of arbitrariness, since we choose certain abstractions, rather than others, from which to set out. In the science of man, we know from within the subject-matter with which we deal; whence our constructions have a concrete fulness not attainable in mathematical science.[3] His method he calls the combination of philosophy with philology; that is, of meditation on ideas with study of the facts of history and pre-history as known from literary records and other monuments, or inferred from the deeper implications of these discovered by comparison of languages, myths and fragments of tradition. Such comparison brings us to the underlying unity (not without difference) of human

[1] R. Flint, *Vico* (Blackwood's Philosophical Classics), 1884; translated into Italian, 1888.

[2] B. Croce, *La Filosofia di Giambattista Vico*, 1911, 2nd ed. 1922. The English translation (1913) has an additional appendix in the form of a lecture on "The Sources of Vico's Theory of Knowledge", not included in the second Italian edition.

For Croce's tribute to Flint's work, see p. 327 (2nd ed.). Flint, not being so far removed in time, found it possible to say a word in praise of Michelet, whose translations (or paraphrases) offend the Italian critics by a style so completely alien to the original. He still remembered that the French historian did more than any one else to carry Vico's fame through France to all Europe in the early nineteenth century. Weber's German translation (1822), which Nicolini praises, was found so unreadable in its literalness that, as he is obliged to admit, the Germans themselves preferred to read Vico in Michelet's French.

[3] *Scienza Nuova*, i. 187–188.

nature. Man himself makes history, and therefore he can think it and know it.

To go further into Vico's own metaphysical system, which in his minor writings he develops from a theory of knowledge into an ontology, is unnecessary except for very special students. And a rapid indication of the character of his actual method for the science of man will suffice. All students of his work have noticed that he was as much attracted by Bacon as he was repelled by Descartes; and incidentally he claims to have carried over the Baconian method from the things of external nature to the things of human civility.[1] He was, in fact, so far as he was methodical, an inductive, not a deductive, thinker; but, unlike Bacon as well as Descartes, he had no hope of formulating a procedure which, simply in virtue of its methodical character, would infallibly yield true results. He was quite conscious that what he had himself achieved was done by the reading of facts in the light of a kind of scientific intuition, not by the application of any formulated rules. This means that he was not in effect wrong in seeking inspiration from Bacon, who preached method but whose own mind was, like Vico's, intuitive and inexact. The affinity comes out in Vico's excursions into the aphoristic mode of statement, as also in many phrases indicating close familiarity with Bacon's thought.

His peculiar scientific intuition was in the first place arrived at by the study of Roman law, the growth of which he came to see as what we should now call an "evolution". That is to say, he saw it as a social product, and explained it by changes in the social factors from age to age. There were not in the beginning codes wrought out by great legislators. The notion of the Twelve Tables, for example, as a definitive document ascribable to particular persons, was a "poetic" fiction of later times. The laws of the Twelve Tables belong in their origin to different ages. They came into being by a slow growth in response to the varying needs of a society that was constantly undergoing modifications. And the same

[1] i. 126–127.

formula did not mean the same thing for successive ages: not only laws but the interpretations of laws became modified. Words changed their meanings: "king", "people", and "liberty" meant one thing at the beginning and another thing at the end of a long political development. So it was in relation to everything. Early societies see the whole social world, external nature and the order of the universe in a way different from the way in which they present themselves to later societies. These differences are not arbitrary. All the phenomena can be reduced to a certain uniformity because they are correlated and change in such a manner that given one set of factors, or one set of antecedents, the other factors, or the consequents, will be the same in the same circumstances. And so we rise to the most general position. "This civil world", says Vico,[1] "was certainly made by men; whence there can be found, because there ought to be found, its principles within the modifications of our own human mind."

His science of man is thus a subjective science as distinguished from the objective sciences of inorganic or even of organic nature. Its facts, that is to say, retain in them, as essential parts, thoughts, desires and feelings. It is also fundamentally a science of human nature conceived as social. This sociality is never simply that of an animal species. Man, when he has once emerged (by whatever process) from the merely animal life, constructs for himself a world of imaginations and memories which, at first fluctuating and predominantly fictitious, pass at length into definable ways of thinking and acting and determinate historical traditions. These become capable of investigation through the continuity of the tradition in each society, preserved especially in its literature and laws. Vico's aim is to bring out the consensus at each social phase, and to establish a definite sequence of transitions from one phase to another. The stages of development, it must be added in order to distinguish his general view clearly from that of his successors, are not those of Humanity as a whole, but of the separate peoples which, becoming by degrees civil

[1] i. 172–173.

communities in the form of cities and nations, manifest in their changes the qualities of a common human nature. This common human nature is indeed modifiable both by innate differences of peoples and by external circumstances; but it has certain "eternal properties" which make it the object of a science. For where there is uniformity science is possible.

Of all this, from beginning to end of the *Scienza Nuova*, Vico has a firm grasp. Where he fails in comparison with his successors is not in insight; for if in positive ideas they are superior to him in some respects, they have also lost from view some things that he saw clearly. His misfortune was to be unable to put his remarkable conceptions into an order that should give the sense of movement from point to point. All the aspects of his thought are always more or less mingled. Now Comte, and even Hegel, resolute reading though they require, always give the impression that there is an end at which we shall arrive, if we follow them step by step. As they had besides a world to appeal to that was better prepared for them, we cannot be surprised that Vico has scarcely come into view in the history of thought except as partially their anticipator.

It is not, however, too late to seek for him an independent standing. The recent movement of philosophical thought in Italy, largely Hegelian in inspiration, may almost be said to have rediscovered him. His fame, for a time extending little beyond Naples and then mainly Italian, is now European. The greatness of his name therefore gives an opening for a new attempt to set forth intelligibly his far-reaching ideas. In my exposition I shall roughly follow the order of his work, omitting in each section, where it is possible, statements that properly have their place elsewhere. Some repetition will on this plan be unavoidable; but as there is really in the *Scienza Nuova* an implicit logic, I thought the proposed method more hopeful than an endeavour to compress the philosopher's ideas into a framework not his own.

GENERAL VIEW

With his successors of the nineteenth century, Vico shares the idea of an "immanent teleology" of the human race. While he is himself a theist, his conception of the divine providence manifested in history differs from that which Comte formulates as the "human providence" only in so far as the immanent end is for Comte progress, for Vico conservation. For both alike, all goes on with uniformity according to laws of cause and effect within the world; but their more specific idea of cause within humanity is direction of its course by something equivalent to a general mind that makes use of the purposes of individuals for ends above those that they consciously aim at. Essentially this is Hegel's view also.

Within certain limits, Vico recognises progress in the past; but he does not look forward to any future stage beyond that which has been reached already by the most civilised nations; and he does not recognise any total movement of humanity. Contact between nations as a factor in their movement is admitted occasionally; but the predominant view is that their "common nature" expresses itself in similar movements uninfluenced by the others. This view, in the circumstances of the time, gave Vico a scientific advantage over most of his contemporaries; for he was able in virtue of it to reject totally that doctrine of "the learned" which explained "the religions of the Gentiles" as corruptions of Hebrew religion. As it is only the Gentiles with whom Vico proposes to deal, he is thus able to treat all the origins with which he is concerned as completely non-supernatural; the Hebrews being usually left out as an exception because their religion only was revealed. If he ever touches on their history, it is to find (perhaps inadvertently) resemblances to the "poetic" history of the Gentiles.[1] When he comes to Christianity, he strongly insists

[1] One opinion he expresses is that if there were derivation on either side, it would be more probable that the Hebrews borrowed the names of the letters from the Greeks than that the Greeks borrowed them from the Hebrews: he thinks, however, that the Phoenician origin of all the "vulgar letters" is established. See i. 288–290.

on the element it contains of Platonic and Aristotelian philosophy. Of this, which in its generalised form he regards as the ultimately true philosophy, he seeks the origin exclusively in Greek thought; not at all, as some of his learned contemporaries still did, in borrowings from the Jews. In this attitude there was no subterfuge or conscious evasion. Vico was the most open and candid of men and he desired to be a good Christian and Catholic; but, as his biographers have observed, it was not in his power really to care for anything in Catholicism or Christianity except the philosophy incorporated in its historic system. From popular superstition, as Croce puts it, he averted his eyes as if from the faults of a beloved person; and his own philosophy, while the "liberals" have been sympathetic, has always aroused distrust in "less liberal but more coherent Catholics".[1]

There is no doubt, however, about the importance assigned to religion in Vico's story of the beginnings of human civilisation. Taking up a saying which he somewhat transforms in a manner not infrequent with him in quotations, he declares that, as against the opinion of Polybius, that if there had been philosophers there would have been no need of religions,[2] the true view is that without religions philosophers could not have existed; for philosophers can exist only in a political state, and every political state was founded on a religion.

Religions, according to Vico, arise spontaneously from the first imaginations of dawning humanity about the universe. The state of mind which he conceives to be that of primitive men is very much the same as Comte's "fetishism". This

[1] See Croce, *op. cit.* pp. 325–326. Flint also finds that in one way "his spirit was far more Greek and Roman than Christian" (*Vico*, p. 48), and describes him as a theological but not a theocratic thinker.

[2] Vico often returns to the point. What Polybius says amounts really to this: that if it were possible to bring together a political community consisting of philosophers (in the sense of sages) perhaps there would be no need of religion, but that, human nature being what it is, the statesmen of Rome have done well to maintain its practices and beliefs for the sake of the multitude. *ἐμοί γε μὴν δοκοῦσι τοῦ πλήθους χάριν τοῦτο πεποιηκέναι. εἰ μὲν γὰρ ἦν σοφῶν ἀνδρῶν πολίτευμα συναγαγεῖν, ἴσως οὐδὲν ἦν ἀναγκαῖος ὁ τοιοῦτος τρόπος* (vi. 56).

"childhood of the human race" is revived in the imaginations of the poets. "The most sublime labour of poetry is to give to insensate things sense and passion; and it is proper to children to take things without sense in their hands and to talk to them in play as if they were living persons."[1] This poetic or mythological side of early religion, however, is not the only side that he sees. He draws no idyllic picture of a Golden Age in religion or in anything else. He has already the sensitiveness to the darker side of religion that has come to the most modern anthropologists through seeing as its centre not myth but cult. With the nineteenth century in general, he completely rejects the notion that imposture was the source of religions. False religions, he says, did not spring from the imposture of others, but from the credulity of the men themselves who imagined them. It was thus with the sanguinary religions and their principles of sacrifice, which, among the fierce and cruel men of early times, began with human victims. He has no objection to the saying of Petronius, which he often quotes, that fear first made gods in the world. Yet he never quotes without protest the words of Lucretius about the evil to which religion persuaded mankind. It was really the frightful religions (*le spaventose religioni*), the religions, in various forms, of Jupiter the god of the thunderbolt, that first drove the human race, by the shock of terror, to take the path to civilisation. Thus the "semi-bestial giants", the ancestors, in the post-diluvial age,[2] of the pagan nations, were startled out of a state of promiscuous vagabondage into fixed marriages; whence came, by degrees, settled communities with recognition of private property. Common to all nations of men, from the time when they became men, are religious and matrimonial and funeral ceremonies. The religious practices on which Vico specially fixes his attention are those of augury, of taking the auspices. The gods, it was thought by the first founders of families and of a settled order, intended to say

[1] i. 133.

[2] Vico's deluge is ostensibly that of the Book of Genesis, but it might equally well be that of Plato or the Stoics. Where he differs is in giving his primitive race more of fierce savagery.

something to them; and augury was the formulation of what was supposed to be revealed. This was the beginning of a human life regulated by law.

There was a certain nobility in these giants on the way to humanity, whose grandiose imaginations founded the Gentile religions. They had a poetry born of ignorance and wonder. It was "divine" from its subject-matter; for what they wondered at they called "gods". We can get some insight into their minds from the things told about the aborigines of America, from what is recorded of the ancient Germans by Tacitus, and from what we observe in children. They at once feigned and believed, with a marvellous sublimity that sprang from their robust ignorance, things profoundly disturbing to them, which were brought forth by imaginations immersed in the corporeal. Thus they were poets in the Greek sense of creators. With this creative faculty went the desire for uniformity, expressing itself, however, not in abstractions, but in a kind of fabulous unities.[1] The more robust giants on the mountains, when it lightened and thundered, looked up to the sky; and, interpreting the effect by their own violent passions, they feigned the heaven to be an animated body, and called it "Jove". Curiosity, the daughter of ignorance and the mother of science, led them to attribute other feelings of theirs to things; as when they supposed in the loadstone an occult sympathy with iron; and so the whole of nature became for them a vast animated body which feels affections. This notion of a sympathetic nature as an immeasurable woman we can barely understand and cannot imagine; even the popular mind being now too much withdrawn from sense by the abstractions of which languages are full, and too subtilised by the art of writing and as it were spiritualised by the use of counting.

While the imaginations of the first men were vast, they were also limited. For the primitive theological poets, Jupiter was no higher than the mountain-tops. It was from thence that he was supposed to give the signs interpreted by the art of divination as his commands. Men called him the Saviour because he did not destroy them with his thunderbolts.

[1] i. 214.

The proper material of early poetry as of all poetry is the "credible impossible". It is impossible that bodies should be minds; but to early men, not yet capable of abstraction from sensible things, it was credible that the thundering heaven should be a god with mind and will. Man, in the age of metaphysical phantasy which came before reasoned metaphysic, made in his own image all things in nature through not understanding.[1] This activity of mind is more creative than that which comes later, when man by understanding explains his own mind and comprehends things.

All early stories were held to be true. Tropes, and in particular metaphors, supposed to be ingenious inventions of authors, were necessary modes of expression for the first poetic nations. No facile abstractions being ready, a vehement effort was necessary to utter what was meant. Poetic diction arose precisely through poverty of language and need of explanation.[2] It resulted from a kind of strength in weakness.

In the early religions there was something that may be called a philosophy; but this philosophy existed as poetic thought, not as recondite wisdom formulated in abstract terms, which the men of the first ages did not possess even when they were founders and legislators.[3]

The insight into the minds of early men thus summed up caused Vico flatly to reject the view universal among the learned of his time, and only with difficulty expelled by discoveries made long after, that a deep philosophy lay hidden beneath the Egyptian hieroglyphics. The opinion, he says, must be wholly uprooted that "hieroglyphics were invented by philosophers to conceal therein the mysteries of deep abstruse wisdom".[4] Hieroglyphic writing, in which pictorial

[1] i. 251–252. [2] ii. 305.

[3] See i. 191, where Vico incidentally contrasts "la sapienza volgare di tutti i legislatori e la sapienza riposta degli più riputati filosofi". In principle, Vico holds, the legislators and the Platonic philosophers agree in the belief in a divine providence and in the immortality of the soul; but the legislators drew on the primary and "poetic" wisdom, while the procedure of the philosophers was secondary and reflective, not creative. Belief in immortality was much older than Plato, who did not first diffuse it among the peoples, but took it over from them. [4] i. 278.

representations are used, is characteristic of the early age of man, and could contain nothing but the "poetic wisdom" of religious myth and the "vulgar wisdom", or common sense put in order, of practical legislators.

The reputation of the theological poets for wisdom has come largely from the philosophers, who found it convenient to take up expressions from them in setting forth their own meditated doctrines, which they were thus able to support by the authority of traditional religion. What the poets had felt touching common wisdom, that the philosophers understood in the way of recondite wisdom; so that the poets may be called the sense, and the philosophers the intellect, of the human race. The beginning is always from sense.

As we shall see in more detail later, Vico, in dismissing the notion that early thought was philosophical in the proper meaning of the term, does not in the least intend to depreciate it. On the contrary, what he is apt to depreciate is too much method and system, which he finds repressive of genius. And it is in a classification of the ages furnished by what he knew of the Egyptian annals drawn from Manetho that he finds a basis for his own "eternal ideal history". To this we must now pass on.

Egyptian history was divided by the annalists into the ages of gods, heroes and men. Taking over this division, Vico proceeds to divide the history of every people, so far as it is determined from within, into the "divine", the "heroic", and the "human" ages. These, unless extraneous causes intervene, follow one another of necessity in this order; though for different peoples the corresponding ages are not necessarily simultaneous. The Greeks, for example, made the transitions in advance of the Romans. The first age, the "age of the gods", he sometimes calls "theocracy"; but, in dealing with it in detail, he is much more preoccupied with cult and myth than with mode of government, which begins to interest him distinctively only in the second or "heroic" age. In fact, he has no conception of the difference between government through a priestly caste, as in the East, and the mere permeation of life by religious sanctions wielded by heads of households and by civil magistrates, as among the Greeks and Romans. For him, so far as religion is concerned, the second age continues the first, except that he tacitly supposes the creativeness of phantasy to have sunk, and the rising social interest to be in political government. Vico's "heroic age" is essentially military aristocracy, in which those rule who are held to be more allied in race to the gods. From this political form, a government by men of forceful action, the transition is to democracy, or recognition of equal legal rights on the ground of a common humanity; but democracy is only the first form of the "human age". Generalising from the case of Rome, Vico conceives the democratic republic as culminating in a monarchy. By the imperial monarchy the law of equal justice was continually extended; and this kind of monarchy he finds to have been restored, after the collapse of the Empire and the long reign of the "returned barbarism" in Europe, by the "enlightened despotisms" (as they have since been called) of the Continent in his own time. The culminating monarchy of this type is to be completely distinguished from the early "heroic" monarchies, in which the king was simply the chief of a "severely aristocratic republic". A remains of that order he finds, among contemporary nations, in England and in Poland, which he classes together because of their surviving element of political aristocracy. Examples of modern democracies are the "free cities" included in the federal systems of Holland, Switzerland, and Germany.[1]

The ages of gods, heroes and men have different characteristic modes of figured expression. The language of the first is hieroglyphic or sacred or divine; of the second, symbolic or by signs or heroic emblems (*e.g.*, on shields); of the third, epistolary, to communicate at a distance the ordinary needs of life. On spoken language, Vico adopts the view of those ancient thinkers who held that in the first languages there must have been some resemblance between word or sign and thing signified. From this, he observes, it does not follow

[1] iii. 1028–1029.

that there must have been one universal language; for, while the utilities and necessities of human life are the same everywhere, the different peoples have differences, as well as communities, of nature which express themselves in languages as in customs. Conventional language, in which the sign has become simply a sign, belongs to the third period. Hieroglyphic signs, in which external things are figured, in whatever people they appear, come first, and belong to the stage of poetic or mythologic thought. For Homer, in the heroic age, the "language of the gods" means a language more ancient than his own. Vico allows that in all this there is something of abstraction. In concrete reality, one kind of age and one mode of language does not wholly displace another. The germs of all coexist from the beginning; for those who fabricated the gods and believed their own nature to have in it a mixture of the divine were, after all, men.

In Vico's theory of political changes, the Romans, as all who have dealt with his work are careful to impress on their readers, were his model. Yet, though he early gave up the direct study of Greek, he knew well the difference between Roman and Greek civilisation, which he always treats as more refined and more humane; and he has subtle remarks on the different modes of development within the general likeness presupposed by his doctrine. The Greeks, he says, through their more rapid passage to a refined civilisation, retained, side by side with this, the myths, divine and heroic, of their time of barbarism, while the slower-moving Romans forgot theirs. The French, among modern nations, he finds to be most like the Greeks. Thus, in the transition from the returned barbarism that followed the break-up of the Roman Empire, poems of Homeric kind could be written among them while the subtlest scholasticism was going on. In the simultaneity, in the twelfth century, of poetic literature drawn directly from mythical and legendary sources with the pursuit of philosophy in the school of Paris, they restored the Atticism of the Greeks.[1]

[1] i. 124 (and elsewhere).

POETIC CHARACTERS

Such continuance of an older age in a newer supplies Vico with some of the hints for his profoundly original theory of "poetic characters". He was not, of course, the first to maintain that some personages supposed to have been historical were really mythical. Aristotle, as quoted by Cicero, denied that Orpheus was historical; and Vico knew this denial. No one, however, before him had done anything to generalise the notion of such a quasi-historical but really "poetical" or mythical character; and even those who in the nineteenth and twentieth centuries have adopted similar views in particular cases have perhaps never generalised their explanation as Vico did. For Vico thinks of his explanation not as applicable to any age whatever without definition of its place in the series of times, but distinctively to ages or nations on the borders of civilisation and barbarism, in which vivid fancy is still socially creative. By "poetic characters" he means personages who, with or without the nucleus of some "particular man in nature", were imagined in the late, rather than the early, myth-making age as representatives of legislative or political systems or as symbolising phases of culture. Of these are the Hermes Trismegistus of the Egyptians, the Orpheus and Daedalus of the Greeks, the Zoroaster of the Persians, all of whom became for the learned of after-times, as he puts it, particular men replete with deepest abstruse wisdom. Being the effective discoverer of this as a generalised mode of explanation, Vico naturally applies it too widely. Compared with what has been made out since his time, his knowledge of the relevant facts was slight; and, even if he had always borne it in mind, he could have made little use then of the precaution dictated by logical method, that each case must be submitted to a separate empirical investigation. Figures that seemed to him much alike turn out, when closely examined, to have quite different degrees of historical reality. Pythagoras, for example, might in Vico's age seem classifiable with Orpheus as simply the ideal representative of a movement. Yet for us, though no authentic record is preserved of anything written or spoken by him, he has become increasingly a tangible historical figure; while Orpheus remains wholly mythical. Again, Solon is a known personage in Athenian history and the author of verses which remain, while Lycurgus as actual legislator of Sparta is at least very doubtful. In qualification, however, of this criticism, it must be said that Vico is rarely dogmatic in denying every trace of "historicity"; though he is quite peremptory in setting against the prejudices of "the learned" the complete predominance, in the most typical cases, of the imaginary over the historical features. And in detail he often (with or without precursors) exactly hits the mark. Special scholars agree that the Zoroastrian oracles, the *Poemander* of Hermes Trismegistus, the Orphic verses, and the *Golden Verses* ascribed to Pythagoras, are all compositions of which the ascription was false. In the Greek writings ascribed to Zoroaster, Vico, like Porphyry, finds a doctrine that was new vended as old. The Zoroastrian oracles, in common with the Orphic verses, he says, savour too much of Platonic and Pythagorean philosophy.[1] The name itself of Zoroaster he takes to be a generalised name for founders of peoples in the East, as Hercules was a name for their leaders in the West.[2] The earliest form of Zoroaster, he concludes, was the Bactrian; as the earliest form of Orpheus was the Thracian. The later Orpheus, who brings the wild beasts of Greece to humanity, is "a vast den of a thousand monsters".[3] Discussing what is related of the life of Pythagoras, he makes it the occasion of an argument against the supposed extensive travels of the Greek sages and the carrying over of detailed traditions from one people to another; and especially against the asserted derivation of the fables of other nations from corruption of the sacred stories of the Hebrews. He admits likeness, however, and the impetus of his own thought occasionally carries him on to comparisons which, if sustained, would have removed the boundary that he had set for himself and brought him, on

[1] ii. 684. [2] i. 72.
[3] i. 85: "un vasto covile di mille mostri".

another line, into more dangerous collision with consecrated positions.

His celebrated "discovery of the true Homer" is set forth at a later stage of his work, after he has dealt more circumstantially with the characteristics of poetic thought. To that stage we must leave the question in what sense Vico held that the "prince and father of all poets" was himself a "poetic character" and how far his theory or that of his successors is tenable.

II

PRIMEVAL OR POETIC THOUGHT

The first nations, says Vico, thought in poetic characters, spoke in fables, and wrote in hieroglyphics;[1] taking external things or acts for signs. Poetic or mythological thought, thus described in general terms, he proceeds to treat under the successive heads of poetic metaphysics, logic, morals, economics, politics, physics, cosmography, astronomy, chronology, and geography.

The metaphysic of the earliest ages, though altogether poetic or mythological, yet had a generalising thought beneath it. All the "Gentile nations" observed the heaven under the "aspect of Jove", whom they regarded as legislating by counsels and commands given in the auspices. For the belief of the Romans, Ennius is quoted: "Aspice hoc sublime candens quem omnes invocant Iovem". Chaldeans, Persians, Egyptians, Greeks, ancient Germans, all in the same way looked up to the sky and called it God. And in modern European languages God is often spoken of by the name of Heaven.

While the early ideas differed totally from the later metaphysical idea of the ubiquity of God, there was in them a kind of universality, though not yet detachable from sense and from particulars. In all things the discovery of unity and universality proceeds by genius,[2] whether that of peoples at their formative stage or of the discoverers who arise in creative

[1] i. 269.
[2] ii. 347: "il ritruovare è propietà dell' ingegno".

periods. It comes before judgment or criticism; and this, when it assumes too much the ratiocinative form, represses originality. There was too much of it, Vico thought, in Cartesianism. What is needed is a kind of *autopsia.*[1] Each thing must be taken in as a whole and seen in one glance. Vico thinks of the Baconian inductive logic, and of English experimental science, as going back to this kind of direct perceptive vision for the ground of its conclusions. Taking especially the case of law, his own fundamental study, he finds that the early rulers and legislators dealt only with individual cases, on which they gave their decisions in imperative form. Yet, by means of the particulars, the "intelligible universals" were understood; and so the impersonality of law came by degrees to be recognised: *legibus, non exemplis, est iudicandum.*[2]

Metaphysic, with logic, we see, is treated simply as the object of an evolutionary theory tracing the origin and growth of general ideas from their beginnings in perception. "Poetic morality", that is, morality immersed in myth, is dealt with in its turn from the same point of view. Religious fear, according to Vico, first made morals as well as gods. Morality did not arise among perfectly isolated individual egoists. We have to suppose human beings with a sense of shame. This was set in motion by some shock that was attributed to a deity. When the men of the early ages, emerging from promiscuous vagabondage, were impelled to take to themselves each a single mate, the human mind came to know itself in the god whose commands seemed to come from without. Piety in matrimony is the school where the first rudiments of all great virtues are learned.[3] The actual virtues of early times, however, were "virtues through sensation, a mixture of religion and savage cruelty".[4] Those times were neither the Golden Age of the later "effeminate poets" nor of the philosophers; neither an age in which all did as they pleased, nor in which they read in the breast of Jove the eternal laws of the just; but an age of which we may form a notion from the race of

[1] ii. 353. [2] ii. 362. [3] ii. 379.

[4] ii. 389: "virtù per sensi, mescolate di religione ed immanità".

Cyclopes as described in the *Odyssey* (ix. 112–115) or from the Scythians of Herodotus. The innocence of the Golden Age, Vico repeats from beginning to end,[1] is a vain opinion. The first men to emerge from the early promiscuity were as yet cityless (τοῖσιν δ' οὔτ' ἀγοραὶ βουληφόροι οὔτε θέμιστες). Monogamic patriarchs (who had carried off their wives by violence), living each apart from the others in caves on the mountain-tops, ruled their own families with a stern despotism sanctioned by the religion of fear that had been started in their minds by the thunderbolts of the sky-god. Their letting one another alone was in appearance justice, but in fact savagery. They were temperate, brave, industrious, and magnanimous; but, in place of the innocence imagined by the learned as characterising the early ages, there was a "fanaticism of superstition".[2] Beginning with the child-sacrifices of the Phoenicians, Vico observes that the Greeks, with their sacrifice of Iphigenia, agreed in the "impiously pious" custom. Moloch-worship did not spread, as some have tried to show, from the Phoenicians to the rest of the world. There were similar sacrifices in early Latium and among the ancient Germans, impenetrable then to foreign nations; and they have been found among the recently discovered natives of America. He notices in particular the sacrifices of their sons by kings to appease the celestial anger; and finds in the power of a Roman father to put to death his new-born child another example of the "cyclopian" model. But finally, citing the question of Plutarch, whether it is a less evil to worship the gods so impiously or not to believe in them at all, he answers it differently; not, however, on any religious ground, but purely on the social ground that only from such terrors could civilisation arise; so profoundly impressed is he with the conviction that strong fear of an imaginary divinity was necessary to hold the first men in some order. So much, he says in conclusion, for "divine morals"; heroic morals will be the subject of discourse later; that is, when it is shown how the aristocratic republics, which

[1] Cf. iii. 1009–1010.
[2] ii. 395.

were the first cities, arose through the association of the patriarchs in communities for self-defence.

This development is sketched out in the sections on "poetic economics"; by which we are to understand the government of families and the beginnings of larger communities in the myth-making age, which continues from the "divine" into the "heroic" period. Vico sets before us men thinking about and attending to material utilities, but unable to detach the thought of them from their imaginative beliefs about themselves and the world.

The first patriarchal "kings" were not monarchs in the later sense. The kind of regal power they had over their own families, ill-understood, gave origin to the mistaken notion that the first form of civil government was monarchy; and the monarchies established in civil communities have erroneously been explained as the result of force or fraud. This was not the case with the earliest of them; and if afterwards some were thus acquired, they could not be preserved by the same methods, but in the long run only by justice and clemency.

Kings in the "heroic" sense were those among the heads of families who took the lead in founding the communities that first departed from the "cyclopian" life. All the patriarchal rulers (as in Homer the heroes) were called "kings" as being in some sense descended from gods. The early founders of cities did not lie when they called themselves sons of earth (*i.e.*, of the soil of their country) but spoke with a noble simplicity what they believed. Livy, in treating such an assertion as a deliberate fiction of Romulus and his companions, "makes that become in their mouths an impudent lie which in the founders of the first peoples had been a heroic truth".[1] The historian himself wrote in good faith, merely following his sources, *viz.*, writers who had constructed for themselves a plausible account, according to the modes of thought of their own age, of what characters like Orpheus and Amphion and Romulus might be supposed to have said and done. These, however, were not "particular men in nature", but "poetic

[1] ii. 424–425.

characters", representing the heroic kings as a class.[1] To Romulus, the imaginary founder of Rome, were attached the qualities belonging to many founders of the first cities of Latium. These founders, in offering an asylum to refugees, did not act by "counsel", that is, with a definite plan in view of the future that actually resulted (as Livy or his sources made out), but by an impulse of nature subservient to the providence that rules in history.

The refugees to whom an asylum was offered by the founders of civic communities were the weaker among the vagabonds left outside the first monogamic families. Fleeing from the violent in the "great forest of the earth", they were received as "clients" in the early aristocratic republics, which consisted of patriarchs united by the necessity of self-defence against those same "violenti robusti". The status of the clients at that time was not practically different from slavery; but no more was the status of the sons, who were equally subject to the rigorous discipline of the *patres*. An accession to the ranks of the subject-class came later from the wars of the cities, when the prisoners were made slaves by the conquerors.

For the first nobility of the nations, constituted as has been seen, wealth sprang from agriculture. "Gold", in the early heroic stories, as of the golden fleece and the golden apples, refers to the fruits of the earth, and especially to corn. Virgil's "golden bough" (*aureus ramus*) mythically signifies "poetic gold", the grain that was harvested. Connected with this gold of the Golden Age were the worships of Saturn[2] and of Cybele or Berecyntia, identified with "the goddess Vesta, armed with fierce religion", on whose altars human victims (*Saturni hostiae*) were sacrificed. To early societies, perennial springs were one fundamental need; and so Actaeon is to be interpreted as the sacrificial victim of "the fearful religion of

[1] At ii. 429 the editor notes that Vico, forgetting as he does sometimes the separate place of the Hebrews in his formal scheme, puts the genealogies of the patriarchs in *Genesis* side by side with those of the Greek heroes.

[2] ii. 451: "detto *a satis*, da' seminati".

water-springs".[1] Such were "the most strong bridles of frightful religions" under which early societies grew up. Religion is appealed to when help from nature fails.[2] The first divisions of land could be established among fierce barbarians, where there was no public force, only by the sanctions of a religion of fear; not by deliberate convention in accordance with justice and observed with good faith. Contracts by mere consent were impossible in the early heroic ages, because the men of that time, being occupied with the necessary things of life, and being, as it were, all body, had the rudeness which is born of ignorance and is therefore distrustful.

Religion, with its terrors, has to be taken as the starting-point of the new science of man because it sets going the movement away from mere nature.[3] Both ethically and aesthetically, according to Vico, movement away from nature is a precondition of the higher feelings. Beyond the "heroism of nature", which exists in primitive societies, is the "heroism of virtue", expressed in the Roman "parcere subiectis et debellare superbos". Nature herself as beautiful is not appreciated by early man. Venus is, to begin with, "a character of civil beauty". After civil comes natural beauty, which presupposes mental comprehension for its perception; peasants or clownish men having little or no discernment of beautiful form. Lastly comes the beauty of virtue, understood only by philosophers.[4]

This, of course, belongs to the third or "human" age, at which we have not yet arrived in the regular course, and does not spring without intermediary from the "fearful religions" of primeval times and the "terrible paternal dominions" that were their pendant. In a long section on "poetic politics" Vico traces part of the process, going now into more detail about the early history of Rome. This furnishes him with the

[1] ii. 416: "la spaventosa religione de' fonti". [2] ii. 474.

[3] It is not *nature*, Vico says incidentally against an argument of Socrates (Xen. *Mem.* iv. 4, 22–23), that forbids incestuous relations, but *human nature*. The ultimate reason against them is not that worse offspring is to be expected, but that they are unfitted to ordered human life in society. [4] ii. 479–480.

model of the first polity that arose out of the archaic domestic governments. The Rome of the kings, as we have seen, is in his sense fundamentally an aristocracy. Having rejected the reconstructions (as he finds them to be) set out by Livy and Dionysius of Halicarnassus, he proceeds himself to reconstruct (as has been generally acknowledged) in the spirit of Niebuhr and later modern students. In flatly denying that the early history of Rome could be accurately known by writers under the late Republic or in the age of Augustus, he argues from a comparison with the history of Greece. How can we suppose, he asks, that the Romans, a rough and barbarous people, had by divine privilege an exact knowledge of their own antiquities which the acute and humane Greeks had not? Founding his own opinion on a declaration of Thucydides, together with an incidental concession of Livy, he holds that relatively accurate history began among the Greeks with the Peloponnesian War, and among the Romans with the Second Punic War.[1] From thence to the origins is a long way back, as he perfectly sees; and the Romans are in date further away from archaic society than the historic Greeks. Nevertheless he finds them as a people better adapted for an investigation of the political beginnings, not indeed by greater accuracy of records, but because, as known historically, they are more "heroic" in his sense, that is, nearer to militant barbarism. This refers to the nature of their language and manners, not to preservation of myths; which, as we have seen, he finds to have been better preserved among the Greeks. The Etruscans too, he says, were in advance of the Romans in civilisation, their monarchy being of the later "civic" type—that is, nearing the terminal stage of absolutism—as contrasted with the "heroic monarchy" of early Rome. It was through the belated "heroic" character of the Romans that they were able to conquer peoples who were passing on to the refinement of later societies.

The *patria potestas*, or power of life and death and despotic right over all acquisitions of sons and slaves, was not, however, an archaism peculiar to Rome, but was common to all

[1] ii. 597–598.

the early aristocratic republics, including those that existed among the Gauls and Germans. The first king in the distinctive sense, not at Rome but further back in the ages, Vico takes to have been a leader of the optimates in repressing a revolt of the "clients", who found themselves less humanely treated as time went on; but the king as yet remained simply a chief of the aristocracy, and not their master. The first *patria* was a combination of the interests of the *patres* or nobles, who were then the only "citizens".[1] Their order was the only "people", the *plebs* being at first the miscellaneous multitude of those outside the order. In the definitely formed aristocracies of optimates, these submit their individual sovereign powers to the order formed by them collectively, so that each may retain as much as possible of what has been acquired by virtue (as understood in those ages). By "liberty" is to be understood, as at Sparta, the liberty of the optimates, defended there by the ephors, who were its official custodians. Athens, too, Vico finds to have been at first an aristocratic republic.[2]

Here comes in one of those "civic" interpretations of myths which Vico tends more and more to substitute for the naturalistic ones with which he began. If, he says, Minerva attempts a conspiracy against Jupiter, that is in the manner of the republic of optimates, whose chief is not to be allowed to make himself an absolute monarch. To the period of the city figured in this poetic form belongs the praise of tyrannicide. Under a definitive monarchy of the later type established by Augustus at Rome, those who would formerly have been called tyrannicides would have had to be called rebels.[3]

The origin of Rome was comparatively late; and there the revolts of the subject-class came later than the heroic monarchy, which by the expulsion of the Tarquins had been displaced to make way for a State aristocratic in form as well as in substance. The excluded class called the *plebs* was able gradually, by means of concessions wrung from the *patres*, especially in the series of agrarian laws, to change the meaning of the word "people" and to bring the republic to a "popular"

[1] ii. 500–501. [2] ii. 512–513. [3] ii. 518.

form in our sense. The original armed "Roman people", the people of Mars, consisted only of nobles; the plebeians, as elsewhere, having no share in the government. It was an anachronism of later times to take *populus* in the sense of the whole multitude.[1] The *plebs*, Vico says, had an "instinct of revolution". The two classes of nobles and plebeians, he puts it in one place,[2] have two eternal contrary properties, the plebeians to wish ever to be changing States, and the nobles to preserve them as they are. That from the conflicts of classes a "universal civic good" should have come forth without the conscious design of men, he finds to be explicable only from some more general direction than can be given by human will; that is, by the wills of individuals aiming at their private good. For men are at first particular in their interests and understand only the particular. The nobles, caring at first only for the interest of their families, constitute a public order to protect these, and this becomes the earliest commonwealth or common good. The plebeians, claiming to possess equal capacity for virtue, bring in the idea of impartial justice and of equity, which rules in the next order of the State. Movements, however, pass into their opposites. Felicity was the result of the plebeian struggle for liberty, dissolution the result of the later struggle for power;[3] but then the civil monarchy arrives to control the anarchy of factions, carrying forward, under the dominance of a single person, the idea of equal legal rights for all.

That such an abstract outline as this should be presented under the head of "poetic politics" would seem rather surprising if we did not remember that Vico, in speaking of poetry, usually refers not to its properly aesthetic aspect, but to its substance as composed of mythological imagery. It is largely from the fables put into form by the poets that he tries to retrace the course of early history or pre-history. Two more illustrations may be added to that of Minerva cited above. Antaeus subdued by Hercules represents, according to Vico, the subject-class in revolt, brought by Hercules as

[1] ii. 593–594. [2] ii. 537. [3] ii. 589–590, n. 5.

the representative of the "heroes" under the dominion of the republic of optimates.[1] Again, treating combats about song in the myths as meaning "heroic combats about the auspices", he makes Marsyas stand for the plebeians striving for a share and defeated by Apollo as god of the science of divination, which was the appanage of the nobles. The punishment inflicted marks the ferocity of penalties in the heroic age.[2]

Whatever may be thought of these interpretations in detail, there can be no doubt about the keenness of Vico's insight into the nature of the problem. In steering clear of the prejudices of scholars in his time, he avoids falling into the opposite error of treating the heroic age simply as "a past that was never present". Thus he smiles at the diligence of the writers of Attic antiquities, who have found out the exact year and month and day on which Theseus returned to Athens after triumphing over the Minotaur,[3] but finds nevertheless in the "poetic character" of Theseus a reminiscence of the building of a fleet by the Athenians to hold in check the Cretan pirates, figured by the "ugly monster". By this method of conjectural search, many secrets of the past are now being unveiled.

What is wanting in Vico's story of the development from the "divine" to the "human" age is a more exact appreciation of the mode in which the power of religion came to be limited. We have seen how the auspices figure in his story; and he has caught more than a glimpse of the view so strongly insisted on by modern anthropologists, that the first kingdoms were everywhere kingships of priests.[4] "In the beginning, wisdom, priesthood and kingship were one and the same." The primeval wisdom being the "science of divination", it seemed fitting that those who were interpreters and ministers of the gods should possess the kingdom over men.[5] And so, Vico

[1] ii. 546–547. [2] ii. 582–583.

[3] ii. 570. With this may be compared the passing sarcasm (iii. 938) on the notion that among the Romans the form of giving up a besieged town was appointed by a particular king, Tarquinius Priscus. [4] ii. 528.

[5] ii. 404, n. 1. Here, as occasionally elsewhere, I have made use of pointed expressions quoted by the editor from Vico's preparatory writings. In the last sentence, the Baconian influence on the language is very distinctly perceptible.

reasons, the patricians supported their own political power by the claim to an exclusive right in the auspices. In particular, they denied to the plebeians the right of *conubium*; which, in his view, was not the right of intermarriage between patricians and plebeians, but the right of the plebeians to have solemn marriages among themselves like those of the patricians, as distinguished from mere "natural" marriages.[1] The actual claim, he holds, was to citizenship. Not till their marriages were regularly solemnised could the property of plebeians be willed or inherited.[2] With the communication of solemn marriage and citizenship to those who at first had no part in the city, the heroic age of the nations ends and the historical age begins.[3]

It must be left to special students of Roman history, when they have determined the point, to tell us who and what the plebeians precisely were. Vico always thinks of them as oppressed masses struggling for civil equality; and his theory about the *conubium* is constantly repeated. Now there may be in this an element of "eternal ideal history" separable from disputed facts, the "city of the rich" and the "city of the poor", as Plato said, having existed side by side everywhere; but it must be remarked by way of qualification that the religious conservatism of the Roman nobility was as far as possible from being zeal for religion. Vico is wrong, for example, in treating the wars among the ancient cities, because archaistic religious forms were used in proclaiming them, as similar to the "religious wars" of the "returned barbarism", and therefore peculiarly atrocious. Secular motives were consciously uppermost, especially in the case of the Roman Republic, and the hardness was normal at the time. Sporadic cases indeed are recorded of atrocious superstition, but they died down. Now in the "divine" or religious age that Vico has so brilliantly reconstructed, savage rites

[1] Cf. iii. 871.

[2] The direction in which human desires go, says Vico, is (1) riches, (2) honours (that is, offices of state), (3) nobility; not the reverse, as the ordinary view of Roman history supposes.

[3] ii. 592, n. 1.

were not merely sporadic but were a custom. This seems to establish a more important division in ideal history between the divine and the heroic ages, when these are contrasted, than between the aristocratic and the democratic republic. Indeed, Vico says in one place[1] that the "heroic" were the first "human" governments; a position not in the least inconsistent with his own general doctrine. His phraseology, quoted above, could easily be applied to the case. All the governments of the ancient cities, it might be said, from the heroic period through the aristocracies and on to the democracies, not by "counsel" but by an impulse of nature, acted as if they had a definite plan to prevent the priesthoods and specialised religion from controlling civic life. And even on the political side there was a certain continuity between the early and the later meaning of "people" and "liberty". What came about by degrees was an extension in the application of the terms; and for a time the democracies became more fiercely "tyrant-hating" than the aristocracies. On the other hand, the democracies were more suspicious of freethought; but it was when a master arrived that the aid of the "frightful" religions began to seem again indispensable. Tarquinius Superbus, according to an anecdote in Macrobius, reintroduced a rite of child-sacrifice in obedience to an oracle; and, after the expulsion of the Tarquins, Junius Brutus, the founder of the aristocratic republic, got rid of it by an ingenious interpretation. The approximately contemporary sons of Pisistratus at Athens, in the opinion of Ed. Meyer,[2] were sincerely devoted to revelations connected with the darker chthonian religions superficially displaced by the Olympian religion of the Achaean aristocracy. And, to come to quite solid historical ground, we know that Augustus, after establishing the new monarchy, systematically promoted religious reaction, and that his stringent marriage laws caused a reign of terror. Cato, on the other hand, whom Vico treats as a living anachronism come down from the aristocratic republic, thus drawing from his editor the ambiguous compliment that he anticipates

[1] ii. 561. [2] *Geschichte des Alterthums.*

Mommsen,[1] is represented by Lucan as refusing to consult a famous oracle in Africa, on the ground that the moral law within is the only oracle needed; a philosophical religion which Vico himself shares with the "human" age.

In the next section, on "poetic physics", Vico gives us some examples of his highly-developed "civic" interpretation of myths. The myths of early man are here referred largely to the utilities of human life that were the beginnings of civilisation. Some, however, are treated as merely indicating a simplicity like that of children. Dismissing curtly the philosophic fancy that Proteus in the *Odyssey* means "first matter", he explains that as children, when they look into a mirror, try to grasp the image, so primitive men, when they saw all that they did imaged in the water, thought there was a man there who changed himself into various forms.[2] He becomes more definitely civic when he says that Pan and the satyrs, who do not inhabit the cities but the woods, represented the semi-bestial vagabonds left outside the first ordered communities and still wandering through the great forest of the earth. Apollo, by contrast, meant civil light, by which civil beauty is discerned. Venus was civil beauty itself, afterwards taken by the physical philosophers for the beauty of nature. The "four civil elements" of the world, represented by Jupiter, Diana, Vulcan, and Cybele or Berecyntia, afterwards taken for the natural elements,[3] were at first those of the divine ceremonies: auspices; water of perennial springs; fire with which the woods are cleared; the cultivated earth with its grain. "But the greatest and most important part of physics is the contemplation of the nature of man."[4] Of this too the theological poets furnished a kind of rude analysis, adding to the names of the bodily organs such expressions as *anima*, *animus*, and *mens animi*. Always in the order of nature discovery comes first, judgment after. Therefore it was fitting to the childhood of the world to make the first discoveries in the

[1] ii. 608.
[2] ii. 620–621.
[3] Here we may see an allusion to the mythological names given to the elements by Empedocles.
[4] ii. 626.

science of man. Exercising themselves, to begin with, on the first operation of the human mind, the poet-theologians made memory, about which phantasy or imagination is entirely occupied, "the mother of the Muses", that is, of the arts of humanity, all of which arose before the coming of philosophers. The passions they associated with the humours, and thence with the blood; and so it is easily explained why they should assign thought to the heart; for the men of the heroic age did not think about the things that it was possible to do except when shaken by passions.[1]

By means especially of Latin etymology, Vico arrives at the conclusion that the primitive psychologists recognised an active element in "sensing". This he shows by the uses of verbs such as *cernere, tangere, olfacere, sapere*. The senses, he says, *make* the qualities which are called sensible. This truth, established by the natural philosophers, confirms the observations of those who first reflected on the operations of their own minds.[2]

On "poetic cosmography", Vico begins with the general remark that the heaven, imagined by the theological poets as no higher than the tops of the mountains, was thought to be upheld by them as by columns. The underworld was similarly imagined as not far out of reach. Its deities were at first those of the perennial springs; the cult of which, he has told us before, had its share in the human victims of early religion. In her aspect as goddess of the underworld, the triform Diana was identical with Proserpine. The poets began by giving the name of "hell" to the sepulchre; an expression met with also in the Hebrew Scriptures.[3] Afterwards hell became the furrow that received the grain; into which Ceres, who is the same as Proserpine (the seed-corn), was carried off by Pluto. Pluto, the god of the underworld, was called Dis, the god of riches, because the cultivated fields yield the true riches of peoples. The "golden bough", by which Aeneas descends, points to the golden grain, in the early days of agriculture the type of all that is precious. Developing further

[1] ii. 635. [2] ii. 640. [3] ii. 649.

this idea which has already emerged, Vico ascribes to the pious hero[1] the sacrifice of his companion Misenus as a means to the "descent into hell" attributed to all early founders of peoples. Though this is altogether a misunderstanding of what Virgil relates,[2] Vico may have had in his mind some reminiscence of the sacrifice of prisoners of war attributed to Aeneas as part of the funeral ceremonies at the tomb of Pallas. Here we may find one premonitory symptom,[3] in the poet of the new monarchy, of its affinity with that which Vico calls the "divine", as distinguished from the human age, though Virgil, for the rest, was a true poet of humanity.

Touching on "poetic astronomy", Vico admits, by way of exception from his general view, an advance due to contact between peoples. The old cosmic system had lasted down to the time of Homer; but the observations of the Chaldeans (made for the sake of divination) gave the Greeks truer notions of the height of the stars.

An interesting remark on "poetic chronology" is that times for our knowledge empty of facts must have been full of them. Thus the age of the gods, in which we have found, so to speak, all the rudiments of human civilisation, passes with the learned Varro for the "obscure time".[4] Returning to the distinction of times in Egyptian chronology, Vico recapitulates his "uniform rules of the course of nations"; identifying the age of the gods with the "obscure time", of the heroes with the "fabulous time", and of men with the "historical time". In conjunction with these, he recapitulates his political stages of theocracy, aristocracy, democracy, and definitive monarchy;

[1] ii. 653: "con sanguinosa religione pio".

[2] Cf. ii. 466, n. 2. Vico's imagination, his editor observes, "farebbe del pio eroe virgiliano il più scellerato ipocrita di questo mondo".

[3] An earlier symptom has been put on record by Dio Cassius: see an article by W. Warde Fowler in the *Classical Review*, May, 1916, on "An Unnoticed Trait in the Character of Julius Caesar", *viz.*, his interest in *caerimonia*. In 46 B.C., the historian relates, Caesar punished two mutinous soldiers "in a sort of priestly fashion": "the fact is that they were sacrificed (ἐτύθησαν) in the Campus Martius in the presence of the pontifices and the Flamen Martialis, and their heads were afterwards fixed up on the Regia".

[4] ii. 670.

noting, however, that the Phoenicians, being a maritime nation, had an exceptional course of development as contrasted with the monarchies of the East, and fixed themselves in popular government.

The section on "poetic geography" has special interest in relation to Vico's celebrated Homeric theory, which comes next after it. Both here and in the Homeric theory proper, he has not only anticipations of truths now admitted, but also of later theses that have not found general acceptance. The Greeks, he says, like other nations, carried over to distant countries, when they came to know them, names at first applied to cities, mountains, rivers, and so forth, within their native land; and this transference has distorted the meaning of their early records. Of the actual countries called by the historic Greeks Egypt and Phoenicia, Homer can have known nothing. These were in the Homeric time names of districts in Greece itself, and were only later given to countries with relative situations in the great world resembling those of the Greek "Egypt" and "Phoenicia" in the little world of Greece. This has an obvious analogy with the theory of some Biblical critics, in particular of Cheyne, that the Hebrew names for Egypt and Babylon were at first names of small countries in North Arabia, and were thence transferred to the great empires. Amid such conjectures and connected with one of them, there occurs an example of extraordinary perspicacity. According to Vico's theory of the Aeneas legend, the Aeneas of Italy was, to begin with, the hero of a Greek city founded in very early times on the borders of Latium, and afterwards destroyed by the Romans when its population had been annexed. When the Greeks much later spread abroad the fame of the siege of Troy, the Romans identified the local Aeneas with the Trojan hero, making him remotely their founder. But how could this be, since the Aeneas of Latium is supposed to have been a Greek? Vico replies that it is simply a common error of the learned to hold that the Trojans were not Greeks, and that "Phrygian", their supposed language, was a language different from Greek. Homer has given them no occasion to fall into this error; for he calls the Greeks of Europe "Achaeans", not as a synonym for Greeks in general, but as one group within the Greek people, in distinction from their kindred of Asia Minor. Thus the philosopher, by resolutely using his own eyes (without much knowledge of Greek) in reading Homer's story, anticipated that which, in the early twentieth century, has become the common view of scholars.

THE HOMERIC THEORY

On Vico's "Discovery of the True Homer", I am glad to find myself in agreement with Flint, with Croce, and with Vico's most recent editor, Nicolini. The views of all are to the same effect: that the kind of criticism known as "Wolfian" was completely anticipated by Vico, on whom his successors have made no essential advance; and that the importance of his theory consisted not in the denial of a personal Homer, but in the recovery of the modes of thought and feeling of the age reflected in the Homeric poems; in fact, of the age of Greece which was for Vico "poetic" in his own sense, that is, mythological in thought, primitive in manners, and ignorant of the "recondite wisdom" of the philosophers.[1] He demonstrated, too, that the poems not only belong to an age in which the ideas of historic Greece are inapplicable, but that there is in them a stratification of manners; some of the customs implied belonging to a deeper barbarism and some to dawning civilisation. Hence he concluded that the *Iliad* and the *Odyssey* were finally put into form near the end of the heroic age; their material having grown or been prepared all through it. Their metre, their use of simile, the stories they relate—which were not in basis pure fiction, but history passing into legend—had all emerged before they took the shape in which the later Greeks knew them. Thus the poems seem to Vico to be more a social product than the work of a single poet. The "true Homer" is in a sense the Greek people. Yet Vico, though he

[1] Cf. ii. 599–600. Poets living in or near the heroic age could not have given their personages "justice reasoned with maxims of Socratic morals".

sometimes comes near it, does not finally deny that there was also a Homer who was a "particular man in nature", not simply "un poeta d'idea", the ideal or imaginary founder of Greek poetry. That the name of Homer meant only the early men in Greece who sang their stories, he says,[1] must be "half-affirmed". The truth, in his opinion (of which he is sometimes only half-conscious), is more complex.

The explanation of this ambiguity lies partly in the fact that Vico had an imperfect sense for Homer's art, as some in Vico's own age had an imperfect sense for Dante's or Shakespeare's.[2] Homer was for him, in a phrase already quoted, the prince and father of all poets; but poetry here is to be taken in his own sense as referring to the matter of the fables, to the mythological language, to a certain sublimity of imagery that belongs at first to whole peoples and is their natural language because they want abstract vocables. Such is his sense of the greatness of this that he thinks it can never be equalled by later poets, and can only be approached by those who have again lived, like the final singer or singers of the Greek heroic age, on the verge of barbarous times. In this manner he explains the greatness of Dante, whom he calls "the Tuscan Homer". Dante, he quite recognises, was learned in the most recondite science of the scholastics; but he regards Dante's scholastic subtlety as extraneous to his genius. That he could take his place among the sublime poets is to be explained by partial contact with a more primitive age, that of the "returned barbarism", which was passing in his time but was still not far off. His relative primitiveness is indicated by his introduction of real persons and real facts into his story. For what was either history or supposed to be such was the material of all the first poets. Poets were everywhere the first historians; and they composed their verses because it was desired that the memory should be preserved of things that

[1] iii. 767.

[2] Mr A. W. Benn, in a review of Signor Croce's monograph in *Mind*, July, 1911 (N.S. xx. 441–442), showed, though in too depreciatory a way, that Vico did not wholly escape the limitations of taste that have come to be thought characteristic of the eighteenth century.

had really happened. Even Boiardo and Ariosto, coming in times when the world at large was illuminated by philosophies, as it was not in the time of the mediaeval schools, still took the subjects of their poems from stories told in early romances as real. Similarly, in the historic age of antiquity, the subjects of tragedy were personages of old poetic story who were held to have actually existed. Satire spoke evil of persons not only real but known. The Old Comedy introduced illustrious living persons into its fables. Not until the arrival of the New Comedy, born in times of the most subtle reflection, are characters simply fictitious, and invented all of a piece, put on the stage. It is only then that the dramatic poets begin to deal with private life. Loss of the public character is marked by disappearance of the chorus; for the chorus was itself a kind of "public".[1] In the development of Italian literature, the type of the New Comedy did not return till the beginning of the marvellously learned sixteenth century.

Here Vico's historical insight and the limitations of his aesthetic view come out together. His predilection for the art of the New Comedy as the outcome of a cultivated and, in his own sense, "human" (or humane) age, and for its wise maxims summing up the results of ethical reflection, causes him almost to deny self-conscious art to the "great and sublime poets" whose superior genius he nevertheless so much admires. Qualities like theirs, he says, can never be conferred by reflection or study. Their language retains a grandeur that cannot be given by the later poetical and critical arts, which impress a coldness and repress the power of invention. Yet, in spite of his view that relative barbarism is the very foundation of sublimity, he observes with what seems a touch of blame that to give delight by representations of barbarous manners like those of the *Iliad* is not the work of a philosophic poet, and that to collect for entertainment the fairy-tales of the *Odyssey* is incompatible with the grave thought of a philosopher. This of course only shows his preoccupation with content rather than form. The question that he always leaves

[1] iii. 779–780.

undiscussed is, whether the degree of self-conscious art, the degree of organic unity, in the *Iliad* and the *Odyssey* is or is not compatible with any hypothesis but that of personal authorship by an individual great poet. For my own part, I am content with Signor Croce's conclusion, that, as a rational hypothesis, the view that both the *Iliad* and the *Odyssey* owed their form, not to growth or compilation, but to the organising genius of a supreme poetic artist, still holds its own as against rival hypotheses.[1]

This, however, does not affect any serious estimate of the importance of Vico's Homeric theory. What he initiated was the scientific study of "sources"; of the accumulation of history transformed into legend; of the continuous tradition by which a literary language is formed; and in particular of the stratified record of manners and beliefs belonging originally to different ages. How little such stratification, which to many seems to tell most against unity of final authorship, is really inconsistent with it, may be seen by comparing the case of *Hamlet*. We know now that Shakespeare had sources, that he worked not only on a traditional story but with the aid of an older play, and we find a stratification of manners perhaps as deep as that which we find in Homer. Vico, if he had known Shakespeare, would have found the exclamation of the Prince of Denmark that he should, ere this, have "fatted all the region kites with this slave's offal", to belong not to the manners of a court where the maxims of Polonius are in place, but to those of the "returned barbarism" of Europe six centuries earlier. Exactly similar to this in the *Iliad* and *Odyssey* are the passages about leaving the dead to be devoured by dogs and carrion birds, and about the use of poisoned arrows. The mention of the savage customs has come down to the final poet with the tradition of what Vico calls the "first barbarism"; just as the passage in *Hamlet* is a reminiscence of the Denmark of the Vikings. Neither in the case of the ancient nor of the modern poet is it part of the superstructure; and in neither case, it seems to me, does such a relic of an older world

[1] *La Filosofia di Giambattista Vico*, cap. xvi.

disprove unity of final authorship. All that it proves is that the final poets were not the first inventors or singers of their fables, but had precursors of whose work they made use.

In the content of the heroic epics Vico finds simply a confirmation of the view he takes of heroic ages in general. The character of Homer's heroes he describes as violent, mobile, irrational, and fantastical.[1] To seek recondite wisdom in the representation of their passions and actions is idle. The real nature of the early poetry gives no support to the praises of Homer by rhetoricians as the founder of Greek civilisation. The less worthy things in him, however, do not make him any the less the father and prince of all the sublime poets.[2] This he was by the nature of his age. The heroic language was a mode of discourse by similes, images, comparisons, born of poverty in genera and species; consequently, by necessity of nature, born common to whole peoples. Summing up in accordance with this judgment, Vico concludes that not Homer as a man, but the "poetic thought" before philosophy, ordered Grecian polity and civility. There were poets before the date assigned to Homer; but Homer, as "poetic character", that is, as imaginary representative of all the early poets, has been acknowledged as head by all succeeding ages. The philosophers did not find their own doctrines in the *Iliad* and *Odyssey*, but put them there; yet it was "poetic wisdom", with its fables, that gave occasion to the philosophers to meditate their loftiest truths. For us, the *Iliad* and *Odyssey* are two great treasuries of customs in the most ancient times of Greece.

III

THE SEQUENCE OF THE AGES

After the long characterisation of the primeval age or ages, followed by the episodical Homeric theory, Vico enters upon a more detailed comparison between the three periods of "the course that the nations take, proceeding in all their so various and so diverse customs with constant uniformity upon the

[1] iii. 730. [2] iii. 754.

division of the three ages which the Egyptians said had passed before in their world, of *gods, heroes* and *men*".[1] These ages have three kinds of natures (imaginary natures of the world and of man); three kinds of customs; three kinds of natural rights or laws recognised by the men of the three ages; three kinds of civil States or commonwealths; three kinds of languages and of characters; three kinds of jurisprudence assisted by three kinds of authority and by as many kinds of reasons in as many of judgments, which judgments belong to three directions of human life[2] in the different ages.

The first "nature", to put Vico's thought in later language, was that of fetishists or animists on the way to create the gods of polytheism; who, with him as with Comte, are powers conceived to preside over species of things as distinguished from individual objects.[3] In his own language, nature was then made divine in substance by the poet-theologians who were the most ancient sages of all the Gentile nations. But nature for them, he adds, was all fierce and cruel. Because of their error of phantasy, they horribly feared the gods whom they themselves had feigned; and this is the condition of the prosperity of religions, that those who preside over them should themselves inwardly revere them. Similarly in the case of the heroic nature: the heroic race believed in its own natural nobility as being of divine origin; and so the heroes could regard themselves as the natural chiefs of mankind. The nature distinctive of the third age is human nature known as the common nature of man; intelligent and thence modest, benign, and reasonable; recognising for laws, conscience, reason, duty.

[1] iii. 785–786.

[2] This seems the nearest approach to an equivalent for "sètte di tempi"; which, the editor tells us (iii. 857, n. 1), is not quite correct Italian, since the phrase does not admit of a plural. What is meant is that the characteristic modes of feeling and acting in each age are as if derived from the doctrinal rule of a philosophical or religious sect concerning what is right or wrong, good or evil.

An expression similar in sound and sense, though of different origin etymologically, is cited in Murray's *New English Dictionary* from Samuel Daniel (1603): "the Set of the Time".

[3] Cf. i. 247–248.

This, however, Vico explains elsewhere, has its type debased by the multiplication of conflicting private interests, which were kept subordinate to an idea of the common good in the harder and sterner time when the nobles believed in themselves as a class and held together.[1]

The three corresponding kinds of customs are (1) tinged with religion and piety, (2) choleric and punctilious, (3) an affair of civil duty.

The rights or laws are congruous. On divine right follows the heroic, or the right of force, kept within bounds by religion where there are no human laws, or none that avail to curb it. It was in the order of providence that the first peoples, by nature fierce, should be brought by their religion, when they were as yet incapable of reason, to acquiesce in the rule of force, seeing in the determinations of fortune something divine. Only in the third stage comes recognition of human right dictated by explicit human reason.

Of the corresponding governments, the first or divine, says Vico, were called by the Greeks theocratic.[2] They are illustrated by the rule of the oracles. The second were heroic, or aristocratic, or "governments of optimates", such as in Greece those of the Spartans and Cretans. "The third are human governments, in which, by equality of the intelligent nature, which is the proper nature of man, all are accounted equal under the laws, since all are born free in their cities." These last comprise the "free popular cities" and those monarchies of which all the subjects are equal by law.

Of languages the first was a divine mental language by silent religious acts or divine ceremonies: which language

[1] Incidentally it may be observed that Vico conceives the successive ages of men as first considering the nature of the cosmos and then their own; but also as from the beginning interpreting the cosmos by what they feel in themselves.

[2] iii. 793. This is an error for once not noted by the editor, who usually points out Vico's inexactitudes. The name *θεοκρατία* was an invention of Josephus, as Vico knew (see ii. 561); but the Greeks had no use for it. It remained for the moderns, after new experience, to extend it from the polity of the Jews to priestly governments in general, including the "classic middle age" of the twelfth and thirteenth centuries.

belongs to religions by the eternal property that it concerns them more to be reverenced than to be reasoned.[1] The second was by heroic emblems, such as are still seen in military discipline. The third is by articulate speech. Everywhere hieroglyphics are the first form of writing; imaginative or poetic universals having everywhere preceded genera constituted by abstraction. The human mind, which delights in uniformity, when it could not achieve this by logical abstraction did it by a kind of fantastic portraiture. Imaginative genera passed into intelligible genera, whence afterwards the philosophers took their start. At the final stage of the art of writing were formed the "vulgar characters" that went in company with the "vulgar languages". These characters were not invented by particular persons, such as Cadmus; and monarchs cannot change them, as was seen in the case of the Emperor Claudius. On the contrary, the power of monarchs, in putting forth general laws for all classes, depends on the recognised usages of a common language.[2] This implies that, in the order of civil nature, the free popular republics, with their habits of discussion, preceded the monarchies.

From what Vico says it follows, though he does not lay stress on the paradox, that "recondite wisdom" arrives at expression in the "vulgar languages", while only "vulgar wisdom" is to be found beneath the hieroglyphic and emblematic languages. As we shall see shortly, he definitely traces the abstruse metaphysics of the later Greek schools to the dialectic that was fostered by the institutions of the Athenian democracy.

In jurisprudence the successive stages are: (1) strictness in performing ceremonies related to the "science of divination"; (2) caution in giving answers and punctilio in the use of verbal formulae; (3) regard to the truth of fact and to what is required by a benignant consideration for equality.

[1] iii. 796.

[2] Later (iii. 1158) Vico has the remark that peoples do not form themselves on the manners of princes, but princes on the manners of peoples.

The three kinds of authority are: (1) the divine, for which no reason is asked; (2) the heroic, consisting in the obligation to observe certain solemn legal formulae; (3) the human, resting on the trust placed in persons of special knowledge. This last is the "authority of counsel".[1]

In the true religion, indeed, says Vico in going on to distinguish expressly the three kinds of "reasons", divine reason and authority are identical; but this does not apply to the religion of the Gentiles, who, by the permission of Providence, received the authority of the auspices as a useful error when they could not yet understand reason. What Vico formally accepts as the true revealed religion is nowhere brought in by him from outside as a factor in the development of those Gentile nations with which alone he deals. In his own "eternal ideal history", its philosophical element arrives as the due culmination of an immanent process. This element he traces as the result of inward development in the thought of the Greeks and Romans passing from error to truth; and declares it to have been rightly received by the Christian Church from the schools that followed Plato and Aristotle; but of any beneficent influence from any peculiar dogma of the religion which he treats as alone revealed, he has nothing to say.

To the second or heroic period he assigns distinctively the "reason of State". The Roman Senate, he says, was a pre-eminent example of wisdom in this kind in the periods both of aristocratic and of popular liberty to the time of the Gracchi. Continuity was given through the deference still paid to the Senate in the time of popular liberty; though there was some change in the motives for seeking the public good. In the aristocratic period devotion to the commonwealth was more concentrated because then the *patria* consisted only of the *patres*, each of whom had a direct feeling of his own share in the good of the whole. In the "human" as distinguished from the "heroic" times, the idea of equal justice having permeated the general thought, there was so

[1] iii. 811: "di credito o di riputazione in sapienza, e perciò autorità di consiglio".

far an advance to a superior because wider outlook; but there was a diminution of public motives through the dispersion of interest into minute portions. The Romans were practically so successful a people because they retained the "heroic" temper for a longer time; not sharpening their wits too much by maritime commerce like the Carthaginians, and not made fastidious by having passed too rapidly from a barbaric life to the subtleties of philosophy like the Greeks. With them the dispersion of public effort by reason of private interests was thus delayed. What is called the "wisdom of the ancients" was the effect of the heroism, not the heroism the effect of the wisdom. They let themselves be guided with just steps by divine Providence, which in its dealings with the human race is entirely occupied in preserving it.

Thus Vico, while tracing a certain course of the nations which may be regarded as progressive since it ends in relative humanity and rationality, did not recognise any final order as the goal of nature or as fixed by divine decree. It might have seemed easy for him to imagine, after Plato, a State combining philosophic wisdom (the reality of that which was only imaginary in the first age) with nobility of temper and with social justice; and near the end he expressly discusses this;[1] but he always reasons as if he thought that these qualities, at their height, could not be combined in any one political system, but that, in the conditions of human nature, the periods of their relative predominance must be separated in time, the most admired virtues of one age being in general incompatible with the manners of another. Wisdom may seem to be treated as exceptional when he says that in all orders the mind must rule the body; but he means, not an all-comprehensive philosophic thought, a "recondite wisdom" such as would be that of Plato's higher order of guardians, but the practical wisdom appropriate to each period. Thus the immanent order of the world is for him, as we shall see, made actual in a series of recurrences (*corsi e ricorsi*) by which the different possibilities all get their turn.

[1] Cf. iii. 1036–1037.

As he says in dealing with the "fundamental history of Roman law", the nature of the law is determined by the order of the State at the time. Governments must be conformable to the nature of the governed. The rigours, solemnities, scruples, subtleties of words, and finally the secrecy of the Roman laws at the early stage, have been quite wrongly ascribed to imposture on the part of the nobility. They were the natural results of early modes of thought and feeling. With the popular republics, and afterwards the monarchies, the secrecy of early law disappeared. Only the "reason of State" in the special sense, understood by few, was by its eternal property reserved as a secret within cabinets.[1]

Distinguishing between the "three species of judgments" in the three ages, Vico remarks that at first all judgments were regarded as judgments of the gods; and so, in public harangues, the gods were attested as if they were near at hand and could hear. As an example, he cites from Tacitus the oration of a German chieftain,[2] in which he finds a vivid illustration of his own view that highly poetic feeling is associated with barbarism. Sublimity of language was born of the sublimity of the heart. With barbarism is united true grandeur and the true sublime. There is no hope of this, he repeats, either from the subtleties of philosophy or the polish of the arts.

To the notion of the "divine judgment" he traces the origin of duels; so characteristic, as he finds later, of the "second barbarism" among the European nations. In his effort to trace them in the "first barbarism" of Greece and Rome, he may be thought for once to stretch a point for the sake of the parallelism. This is not usual with him. He has no disposition to ignore the differences, but regards the second barbarism as more inhuman than the first precisely because there was more in it of reflectiveness.[3] This he might very well have brought out in the case of the duel; for the single combats of early antiquity were not the same in conception as the "judgments of God" in the Middle Ages, to which Vico, in agreement with the general view, traces the duel; and they soon became

[1] iii. 825. [2] iii. 829–830. [3] Cf. iii. 1046.

obsolete, leaving no relics in historic antiquity such as long infested modern times and have not even yet entirely disappeared. The cases he puts forward are: from Greek antiquity, the duel of Paris and Menelaus; and, from Roman antiquity, the combat between the Horatii and the Curiatii. In such armed judgments, he says, right was estimated by the fortune of the victory. They were not introduced "for want of proof", but "for want of judiciary laws".[1] In a time of undeveloped reason, they put a term to strife that might have gone on for ever, and were the providential means of preserving the human race.

Vico's next point is that the "divine judgments" of the first age of the nations ran down afterwards to a kind of *religio verborum*, seen in its most degenerate form in the Third Punic War—a deliberate act of ruthless oppression planned by the Romans in such a manner as to prevent its being said that they had literally broken their word. But also there have been cases in which leniency has been obtained from the victor by complying with the literal meaning of an oppressive command while evading what was intended. All these things, however, the "divine judgment", the duel, and the punctilio of formulae, belong to the provisional stages before the "immutable law of rational humanity, which is the true and proper nature of man",[2] comes at last to be understood.

Thus arrive in succession the three ages marked by their three different characters: (1) the religious times under "divine" governments; (2) the punctilious times, as of Achilles, and, in the "returned barbarism", of the duellists; (3) the civil, or modest, or human times. This last age begins, in the Roman jurisprudence, from the time of popular liberty. Under the monarchy it is stripped of some surviving fictions by which its character was disguised. In the course described, the Romans agree with all the other nations in the world: the modification in the last period has been wrongly explained

[1] iii. 838.

[2] iii. 851: "la ragione benigna, estimata da essa uguale utilità delle cause, che propiamente *fas naturae* dee dirsi, diritto immutabile dell' umanità ragionevole, ch' è la vera e propia natura dell' uomo".

by "some erudite interpreters" as due to the influence of philosophy.

Here in one instance it has come to be generally acknowledged that the view of "the learned" to which Vico raised objection was right; that, as Mr Benn has put it, "his insulating method did not allow him to recognise the inestimable debt of later Roman law to Greek philosophy".[1] In compensation, he has brought out in a most original way the influence exercised on philosophy by law and politics. As was slightly indicated above, he traces the whole development of logic and metaphysics in the post-Socratic schools of Greece to the practice of public deliberation in the Athenian Assembly and law-courts. From observing that the citizens of Athens made laws by coming to agreement in an idea of equal utility common to all, Socrates, he says, began the search for "intelligible kinds" or abstract universals, arrived at by induction, or collection of particulars having a certain uniformity among themselves.[2] Thus "from the popular republics issued laws, and from the laws philosophy". If Vico is somewhat inexact in detail in showing how, from this beginning, Plato and Aristotle found their way to a metaphysical philosophy, there is no doubt about the truth of his general view, that the direction of their thought to logic and morals and thence to metaphysics had its principal source in the dialectical method developed by the habit of public debate and turned most powerfully to account by Socrates for the examination of mind by itself.[3]

This, however, so far as it was a creative movement in philosophy, seems to have been a case of unique transition at Athens, as the earlier passage from rudiments of science to speculations about the nature of the whole was a case of unique transition in Ionia. Vico generalises too widely when he says that among the Romans, as among the Greeks, from the laws issued philosophy. In philosophy the Romans never

[1] *Mind*, N.S. xx. 442. [2] iii. 948.

[3] Cf. iii. 953: "Dallo che tutto si conchiude che dalla piazza d'Atene uscirono tali principii di metafisica, di logica, di morale".

claimed a higher rank than that of pupils; and their great merit was to have become willing pupils of the Greeks. In law their place is at the summit; and it is in dealing with the Roman law itself that Vico shows his deepest insight. For evidence about primitive law, he observes, where the Athenians had the mere legend of Draco, the Romans had definite documents. And, in the sense that he gives to the words, it is perfectly true that "the ancient Roman law was a serious poem, and the ancient jurisprudence a severe kind of poetry, within which are found the first outlines of legal metaphysic in the rough".[1] Ancient law is called by him a kind of poetry because its forms (its *actus legitimi*) are traceable to the "poetic thought" of early religion, and because its working out was effected by a system of fictions. By this general view he was able to make evident the essentially archaic and genuinely Roman character of the Twelve Tables.[2] The story of their being brought from Athens, and of their introduction as a complete code by particular legislators, he thoroughly refuted. In the fragments preserved, with their stratification, he finds abundant evidence for the native continuity of Roman legal institutions from the "heroic" to the "human" times.

In the archaisms of the Twelve Tables he naturally sees the characteristics of the aristocratic republics as conceived by him generally. The terribly severe punishments coming down from the "divine" or religious times, and the conservatism in guarding property, distinctions of order in the State, and the old forms of the laws, belong, in his view, to the "heroic" stage of political development. The necessity of such institutions, as part of the providential order of humanity, lies in the danger that, without them, the race should fall back into the semi-bestial vagabondage, with absence of private property and of fixed marriages, from which it has painfully emerged. Such severe guardianship of existing laws, however, is merely one stage. Political aristocracy gives place to democracy, and

[1] iii. 932.

[2] He notes particularly how often the number twelve recurs in mythical stories: cf. iii. 1075, 1141.

thence arises a new kind of monarchy. In democratic republics, and increasingly in civil monarchies, more and more exceptions are recognised by which laws are multiplied and the old rigour of literal interpretation disappears: "so docile are human minds, under the humane governments, to the recognition of natural equity".[1]

Though not conceiving a commonwealth mixed of the three forms traditionally enumerated (monarchy, aristocracy, democracy) to be capable of permanence, he nevertheless makes the historical observation that a democratic state may long retain an aristocratical government. And here he comes to the tangible ground for his law, formulated as universal, of transition to monarchy. When, in democratic republics aristocratically governed, the chiefs started factions in their personal interests, and the free peoples, for the sake of private utilities, let themselves be seduced by leaders to subject their public liberty to the ambition of these, seditions and civil wars brought on the monarchical form.[2] The comment made in an editorial note is here exactly to the point; that the statement of an apparent general law is in reality a statement of the empirical causes that brought about the fall of the Roman Republic.

With Vico's "eternal natural royal law,[3] by which the nations come to rest under monarchies", may be compared Hegel's dictum that the Oriental world recognised the freedom only of one, and that is despotism;[4] the Greek and Roman world recognised the freedom of some, and that is aristocracy or democracy; the modern world recognises the freedom of all, and that is monarchy. I cannot help thinking that Vico's position, apart from his Roman studies, was more influenced than he knew by Hobbes, whom he always treats as in error about the original foundations of society, but whose "mag-

[1] iii. 895. [2] iii. 903.

[3] This is formulated by him as a law in the scientific sense; in contrast with the imaginary "royal law" of the later jurists, by which the Roman people was said to have made over to Augustus the supreme power inherent in itself.

[4] τὰ βαρβάρων γὰρ δοῦλα πάντα πλὴν ἑνός. Eur. *Hel.* 276.

nanimous effort" he praises with his usual generosity to those whom he singles out as opponents.[1] For Hobbes, in his rational as distinguished from historical argument, gives the preference to monarchy, like Vico, on the ground that it allows the maximum of liberty and equality compatible with the egoism of ordinary human nature.

To point out that European civilisation has not actually fixed itself in the type of monarchy that he had in mind, namely, the Continental absolutism of his time, with its ideal of the benevolent and enlightened despot, would not be a refutation of Vico; for, while he thinks that the typical course of nations was completely realised by the Romans, and will be again if all the factors recur, he allows that it may be, and has been, prevented from repeating itself by various incidents in the histories of other peoples. And no political thinker ever kept himself clearer of prophecy. The criticism that might fairly be made is that European monarchy, if we take this to descend from the rule of the Caesars, would never have existed, in what Vico regards as its typical form, simply as a result of internal development in the ancient republics. For its ultimate structure the model set up by the monarchies of the East was decisive; and a new religion, claiming an Eastern origin, supplied the sanction under which it was to control the West for the longest time. To develop this would take us too far from exposition of Vico; but it may be indicated as one example of the difference that would be made in his doctrine by fuller recognition of contacts between varying types of political and social order.

THE RECURRENCES

In the exposition so far, it has only been occasionally necessary to mention statements of Vico concerning what he calls

[1] Grotius, whom (often grouped in a triad with Selden and Puffendorf) he also regards as having fallen into many errors, he speaks of as one of the four authors who had the largest share in forming his own mind; the others being Plato, Bacon, and Tacitus. (Cf. Croce, *op. cit.* p. 76.)

the "returned barbarism" of the Middle Age.[1] His general view of that period, summarised in the last book of the *Scienza Nuova,* must now be set forth with the aid of passages in the earlier books not hitherto much dwelt on.

Lest it should be supposed that he regarded the whole period between classical antiquity and the Renaissance with the ignorant contempt which its lovers in the nineteenth century were apt to ascribe to those who continued to hold that it represents on the whole a descent of the general European mind to a lower level than that which it had attained before and was to attain again, his special appreciation of some features of the intermediate age must be expressly pointed out. He finds it peculiarly rich in new inventions. The great inventions that have enriched human life, he repeats in many contexts, have been apt to come in the times bordering on barbarism, before there was philosophy with its method and system.[2] The later Middle Ages, close as they were to the "new barbarism", had indeed the subtlest metaphysical discussion in the form of scholasticism; but, side by side with this and yet totally uninfluenced by it, the most wonderful inventions and discoveries were being made in the human arts and sciences. These were made in an irregular way by relatively untrained minds.[3] The effort of genius from which they sprang Vico compares to that of ancient Athens in its time of splendour; when, as he says, it was creative by the *via unitiva* before Aristotle came with his syllogism and the Stoics with more subtleties;[4] after which the things really productive for the human race ceased for a time.

The fundamental question, however, for Vico, in terms of his own science, is not about such efflorescences, but about a certain co-ordination of social features in the ages as compared with one another. Applying this test of comparison, he finds that the collapse of the Roman Empire meant that the "human" age at last attained had to give way to new ages,

[1] The name of "middle age", Croce tells us (*op. cit.* p. 223), had appeared in Vico's time, though it is not used by him.

[2] Cf. ii. 633–634, 710. [3] ii. 349. [4] ii. 358.

"divine" and "heroic", as he calls them in his terminology, marked by a slow return from a "second barbarism" to the new human age of the modern world. And he clearly sees that the first ages after the collapse were very dark, and that emergence from them took a very long time.

His notion of a recurrence in human affairs is therefore essentially inductive. His theory is no mere revival or survival of the ancient doctrine of cycles such as we meet with at the Renaissance. Least of all does it resemble the Stoic dogma that the course of the universe is everlastingly repeated in all its details in a series of "great years". And there is no suggestion whatever of the Stoic cataclysm as an event in the future. Our world, as far as Vico speculates, is to go on. It may be, as Croce says,[1] that to those who have been accustomed to the idea of a continuous progress of Humanity Vico's philosophy has in it something desolate and sad; yet a coming generation, born amid "riddles of death Thebes never knew", may perhaps find sufficient hope for its day in a conviction like that of Vico, that there is an inner law which will at least preserve the race from perishing, as it was preserved during "those iron times", "in all those unhappy centuries",[2] of the "returned barbarism".

The course of events from the break-up of the Roman dominion he finds to be divisible, as has been said, into three ages having names in common with the corresponding three ages of antiquity, though never precisely agreeing with them. His comparison between the "divine" ages of the first and the second barbarism is relatively slight. Such features are noted as appropriation of sacerdotal titles by the kings, but not the new feature of the conflict of kings with the priesthood. In Vico's time, the Christian theocratic idea had been so far subordinated by the new monarchies, Catholic as well as Protestant, that it did not obtrude itself on a secluded philosopher. Aspirations towards a theocratic revival were reserved for the counter-revolution and Catholic reaction of the

[1] *Op. cit.* pp. 137–138.
[2] iii. 968–969.

nineteenth century. In the meantime, the Neapolitan thinker saw in the religion of the Middle Ages only the more obvious features in which it agreed with the public religions of antiquity. He compares, for example, the "devotion" of hostile cities by the Romans, to the end of taking over the gods and auspices of the vanquished, with the carrying off of the relics of saints by the *barbari ultimi* when they captured a city. The careful concealment of such relics by the cities that possessed them reminds him of the concealment of the name of Rome as a means of warding off the use of prayer or magical arts by enemy States. All this, however, was mere harmless "paganism", of which he could see examples in the life around him. It remained for Comte, among Vico's philosophical successors, to grasp the idea of the separated "spiritual power" which reached its consummation in the twelfth and thirteenth centuries, and then was slowly undermined by the kings and their lawyers; till, by the sixteenth century, even before the religious uprising, the political type of European society had been again reversed, and "civility" placed on the whole above religious interests.

Where Vico penetrates deepest is in his clear understanding of the new "heroic age" brought on by the incursions of the barbarians. This age of the West, now called distinctively "dark" because of the all-but-complete break in European culture, he finds to be the true analogue of the Homeric age of Greece. For the beginnings of the new heroic society we are to study the manners of the ancient Germans as described by Tacitus. The romantic gallantry of the later "sophisticated" mediaeval poetry is not to be looked for either in the new (northern) heroic age or in Homer.[1] In the whole of the *Iliad*, Achilles shows no trace of amorous passion for Briseis, though he has quarrelled with Agamemnon for depriving him of her; and Menelaus, in all the long war, gives not the least sign of jealous anger against Paris, who has robbed him of

[1] For an exact account of this distinction, which newer literary studies have brought more definitely into view, see W. P. Ker's *Epic and Romance*.

Helen, though it is for her sake that he has set all Greece in motion against Troy.[1]

Vico's editor has noted that he exaggerates the discontinuity of the dark ages with antiquity in accepting the legendary story that the Roman law was completely lost for a time and was only brought to light by an accident.[2] The philosopher seems, however, for the Latin countries at least, to have given an approximately true description of the state of language. There was a time when no one wrote the languages that were popularly spoken: so far as records were preserved, it was in a barbarous Latin only understood by an ecclesiastical nobility. Between hostile tribes that did not understand one another's languages, there was a return to a kind of hieroglyphic interchange by emblems of military chiefs marking out and guarding domains.

We have met already with the view taken about the duel. Though condemned by the canon law, Vico says when he comes to its mediaeval origins, it began as the return to a kind of "divine judgment". In a general way, this means for him, as we have seen, that force was identified with right. To be a corsair, he observes, became again honourable, as it was in the first heroic age.[3] Reductions of prisoners of war to slavery, especially between peoples of rival religions (Turks and Christians), took place as in the heroic age of antiquity. Both barbarisms had their mitigations in the refuge offered by sanctuaries.

Fundamentally characteristic of all heroic ages is the "feudal system" in a generalised sense; the "eternal principle of fiefs", as Vico calls it; meaning by "eternal" that it uniformly recurs when certain conditions of society recur. Thus the barbarian conquests brought back an order like that of remote antiquity after an interval of a thousand years; the relation of lord to vassal being essentially that of patron to client. In the oaths taken by subjects to their superior, and in the protection that

[1] ii. 644. So far as Achilles is concerned, this is inconsistent with what he says himself (*Il.* ix. 343): ἐκ θυμοῦ φίλεον, δουρικτητήν περ ἐοῦσαν.

[2] iii. 895–896.

[3] Cf. ii. 570–572.

the powerful owe to the weak, he says in one place,[1] consists the whole essence of feudalism. As in the first barbarism, so in the second, military, judicial and economic relationships were correlated on this basis.

The "Salic law", he holds, was common to the two barbarisms.[2] The later Roman jurists, who took the succession of females, when it was not denied, to be included in the succession of males, were interpreting early law by the more developed ideas of equity that had come to be accepted in their own age.

The inductive character of Vico's thought comes out especially in his account of the political transition from the "second barbarism" to modern times. We have seen what importance he assigns to democracy in the ancient transition. If he had reasoned in terms of a willed schematism, he might easily have found a basis for a symmetrical deduction of the corresponding modern development. Indeed, his editor is a little surprised that he did not treat the course of those Italian cities that passed through democracy to despotism as normal, and so confirm his general law of succession.[3] Evidently, however, he saw that city republics since the dissolution of the Roman Empire were local anomalies; that substitution of the nation for the city as political unit was henceforth inevitable. The characteristic movement from mediaeval to modern times was for him the foundation of the great national monarchies; the French monarchy being taken as the norm. In general terms, the "heroic monarchy" of the barbarian invaders is the starting-point, and the "civil monarchies" of Continental Europe in the eighteenth century are the culmination. An aristocracy of feudal chiefs with a titular monarch at their head has given place to the absolutism of the "enlightened sovereign", as in the case of the transition from the heroic age of antiquity to the imperial monarchy of Rome, but without the intermediate phase of the democratic republic. The system of fiefs has been subordinated; but within its "eternal nature", as recurring under the definable

[1] ii. 530. [2] iii. 874, 881. [3] iii. 982–983.

social conditions realised when Rome had ceased to impose order from the centre, are found the origins of the new kingdoms of Europe.[1]

This, of course, means that there was in his view of European history on the large scale what has turned out to be an important omission. The English development by which all royal attempts at absolutism had been curbed and the heroic kingship brought to its term in a constitutional as distinguished from a despotic monarchy, was quite unknown to him; and he did not perceive, as some, beginning with Leibniz, did, the precursory signs that heralded the French Revolution. He mentions, indeed, the anomalies that he knows, and he does not fail to recognise alternation between monarchy and democratic republic as possible phases in a total process;[2] just as, in one or two places, he recognises the possibility of a future community of nations ordered by law; but the suggestions are very slight, and form no part of his systematic theory. What impressed him was that over the whole earth a few great monarchies ruled, and seemed destined to rule, the world of peoples. On these he has some interesting discursive remarks. If, he says, some are still barbarous, the cause is in their remaining founded on the "vulgar wisdom of fantastical and fierce religions", along with unpropitious circumstances of climate.[3] Here he seems to recognise a retarding influence of religion on manners in later periods; and it is worth while to set the observation side by side with passages[4] in which he declares that the fierceness of early manners was tempered by the fearfulness and cruelty of religion. The Russians and Abyssinians he is obliged to treat, though Christians, as semi-barbarous. On the other hand, he finds considerable elements of humane culture in the Japanese, the Chinese and the Indians. The Japanese he compares to the Romans in the time of the Punic Wars, and he remarks on the strong infusion of

[1] iii. 1018: "dentro la natura eterna de' feudi ritruovarsi l' origini de' nuovi reami d' Europa".

[2] i. 39; iii. 1019.

[3] iii. 1023.

[4] *E.g.*, iii. 834–835.

aristocracy in their manners. In China he notes the mild religion and the literary cultivation.

The one certainty for him is the all but impossibility of restoring, and the difficulty of preserving, anything of the nature of an aristocratic republic, when once the recognition of the equality of human beings as such has been attained. Witness, he says, the failure of the attempt of Dion (though of the royal house) after the expulsion of Dionysius II from Syracuse, and the fate of the Pythagoreans of Magna Graecia; and, in modern times, the concessions to the multitude that have to be made by the few aristocratic republics that remain.[1]

What has been set forth, he declares with a noble consciousness of the value of his work, is the ideal history of the eternal laws in accordance with which all nations rise, advance, attain a determinate state, decline and fall; and if (which is certainly false) in the eternity of time infinite worlds were born, this ideal history would apply to the infinite worlds. Hence he could not do less than give to his work the invidious title of *New Science*; for that would have been to defraud it too unjustly of its right and reason as a science perfect in its idea, concerned with a universal argument about the common nature of nations.[2]

In concluding, he expressly discusses Plato's "fourth species of republic", in which the best should be supreme lords; which would be the true natural aristocracy. But such a republic, he now points out, is actually realised, not indeed in any particular State, but in the whole course of history as he conceives it. Providence brought it into being from the first beginnings of the nations, ordering it so that the best for the needs of their own time should rule. Human history shows us "an eternal natural commonwealth, in each kind best, ordained by divine providence". There is, therefore, for Vico, no special rightfulness of any one kind of government in the succession. In all he finds defects, corrected by the next in the series. While he admires the heroic virtues of the aristocratic

[1] Venice is no doubt alluded to: see iii. 1021.
[2] iii. 1032.

age and the sublime poetry which it inherits from the primeval time, he acknowledges, and even insists upon, its harshness and oppressiveness. This, he finds, was corrected when the mass of the people saw through the claim of mere birth, which was all that remained of the old heroism, and, emulating the virtues of the nobles, claimed equality. Providence, however, did not permit the destruction of all difference, but caused wealth to be recognised as the sign of fitness to rule, since to acquire or retain it implies merits such as industry, thrift, and foresight. In the popular republics philosophy arose to form a new kind of heroism; that of virtuous actions not done as of old under the impressions of religions, but from the pure idea.[1] Thus, if Vico can be said to regard any type of State as the most rational, it is the "free popular republic" illumined by philosophical reflection. But he sees clearly certain dangers of this apparently most rational State. In its general maxims of equity, arrived at by means of ethical philosophy, it is more sympathetic, and it expresses itself in a corresponding kind of poetry; but, as compared with the old aristocratic order, its temper is less noble through the dispersion of private interests and the decline of public spirit. When wealth, going beyond the limit of forming an order of citizens that is respected, becomes a means to the excessive power of private persons, there follows the descent to the worst of tyrannies, which is anarchy. On the plutocracy that ends in anarchical dissolution, Vico has little to say; but he evidently regards it as the natural outcome of the admirations of the vulgar.[2] It marks for him the penultimate stage of the Roman Republic. The three remedies employed by Providence are, he goes on to say: (1) monarchy, (2) foreign conquest, (3) return to barbarism. Monarchy comes in, after the oppressions of the aristocratical governments have been overcome, because meanness of mind in later and smaller men leads to conflicts about material interests that have to be solved by making a single

[1] iii. 1043. This power of philosophy, however, Vico does not regard as directly popular. The popular power of philosophy, he says (iii. 1050), is only indirect, by stirring up an eloquence that can move the feelings of the multitude.

[2] Cf. iii. 883: "le ricchezze, le quali sole son ammirate dal volgo".

person supreme. Thus the ultimate monarchy, treated in general as the last result of political progress, becomes, when seen from another side, the first of a series of scourges. For we must remember that Vico had always in mind the Roman polity; and that he saw this, after the fall of the Republic, subjected in turn to all three; till at last the deepest stage of descent was reached in what he calls the new "divine age", when there was nothing but religion to control the "new barbarism". From this, however, a new ascent begins, and the philosopher can sum up with a kind of optimism. The world of nations is something greater than the particular States supposed to have been constructed by the will of legislators. "Men have themselves made this world of nations; but this world without doubt has issued from a mind often diverse, and at times quite contrary, and always superior to the particular ends that men have purposed to themselves; which particular ends, made means to serve wider ends, it has always employed to preserve the human generation on this earth."[1] The excesses of every order in the succession of human societies bring on the corrections that find their embodiment in the next order; and at length, after running to ultimate dispersion, the nations rise again like the phoenix. "That which did all this was mind, because men did it with intelligence; it was not fate, because they did it with choice; not chance, because the results of their always so acting are perpetually the same." In a later dialect, it was at once teleology and causation.

Thus the law of change in the order of human society is nothing inevitable apart from human action. The greatness of Rome, which Plutarch ascribed to Fortune, was founded on its science of jurisprudence.[2] And the distinctively human State, Vico always assumes, can have its life prolonged by the wisdom of men.[3] Although he does not think that the

[1] iii. 1048; cf. i. 184. [2] iii. 1130; cf. ii. 595, n. 2.

[3] The method of preserving States, whatever their origin, is by justice and clemency. "Ed in tutte queste origini si scuopre disegnata la pianta *eterna* delle repubbliche, sulla quale gli Stati quantunque acquistati

political form called by him the aristocratic republic can be indefinitely preserved, it is his maxim that in all kinds of State the intellect (but practical, not purely theoretical) should give the direction, and that the arts in which the body is employed should be subordinate.[1] For himself, he claims no position but that of a theorist. Incidentally he calls political doctrine the queen of all the practical sciences;[2] but he recoiled from practical application; suppressing some pages he had written on the subject as mere repetition of his theoretical view. Indeed nothing could have been more futile in his time and circumstances than to come forward as a prophet or reformer. Yet his work has not been without practical influence. It is a remarkable fact that that which the theorists of perpetual progress regard as reactionary in his doctrine was one of the influences that stimulated the new birth of modern Italy. For his treatment of the theocratic Middle Age as a reversion to barbarism promoted the return of youth to the ideals of Greece and Rome, which meant the building up of a new human order. As in the case of Leopardi's pessimism, to go back with longing to a remoter past was for the time the means of preparing the way for a nobler future.

con violenza e con frode, per durare, debbon fermarsi; come, allo 'ncontro, gli acquistati con queste origini virtuose, poscia, con la froda e con la forza, rovinano" (i. 29).

[1] ii. 564. It is an eternal property of commonwealths "che senza un ordine di sappienti gli Stati sembrano repubbliche in vista, ma sono corpi morti senz' anima".

[2] ii. 534.

CHAPTER VI

TRANSCENDENCE IN SPINOZA

ὁ νοῦς
τῶν κατθανόντων ζῇ μὲν οὔ, γνώμην δ' ἔχει
ἀθάνατον εἰς ἀθάνατον αἰθέρ' ἐμπεσών.
Eur. *Hel.* 1014–1016.

EVERY great philosophical system contains elements that point beyond it. This is true even of the system which is perhaps the most logically compact and rounded of all time; that of Spinoza's *Ethics*. The special doctrines I propose to deal with are transcendent both in this sense and in the more ordinary sense of the term, by which it is opposed to immanent. Spinoza's aim as regards the universe being evidently to explain it from within, the doctrines of the infinity of the attributes of God or Substance and of the eternity of the mind have always puzzled those commentators to whom his ultimate view presented itself as a naturalistic pantheism. And the perplexity has been greater precisely because they definitely belong to the reasoned system and cannot be understood as a residue of theological orthodoxy. In trying to understand them, I have been led to reconsider the sources of the system, especially in the light thrown by the contribution of Dr Carl Gebhardt to the first volume of the *Chronicon Spinozanum* (1921). To develop the conclusions at which I have arrived, a little recapitulation will be necessary.

The distinguishing character of Spinoza's philosophical doctrine among those of modern times is that it takes the universe for its object without presupposing any inherited system to which its theses have to be made conformable. It thus ranks with the systems of the Greek philosophers as no other does; for if a few modern thinkers have assented as little to positions imposed by authority, none have so combined their freedom with thoroughgoing logic and at the same time avoided giving incidental excuse for treating them as apologists for a traditional faith.

Nothing, however, is without its antecedents, and one important condition of this complete and conscious liberty of philosophising can be traced back through the Renaissance to the Middle Ages. More has been added and is still being added to the proof; but the foundation was laid in what will probably be the most enduring work of Renan, his *Averroès et l'Averroïsme*. It is largely in consequence of that outcome at once of unwearied labour and of penetrating insight that we can now appreciate at its true value the important part taken by the Moslem world in promoting the emancipation of the West and preparing the recovery of Europe from the age of returned barbarism, as Vico called it, to a renewed intellectual civilisation.

The Arabian philosophers whose studies of Aristotle seemed to the mediaeval mind to have culminated in the Great Commentary of Averroes, had, we must remember, both secular and religious contacts with Christendom. The religion of Islam under which they lived was one branch of the Judaeo-Christian tradition; and in knowledge of Greek philosophy, from translations into their own language, they had, to about the end of the twelfth century, the advantage over the Latin West. Through a complex process of mediation, they knew the points of view both of Eastern and Western Christians and of the Jews, who were frequently the translators from Arabic through Hebrew into Latin; the Arabic translations of Aristotle having first been made from the Greek through Syriac. In this cosmopolitan culture it was the Arabians who first struck out for philosophical freedom. This they did through a rapid comparison of the three book-religions called revealed with the philosophy of Aristotle. The religions, as they saw, agreed in a kind of ethical theism; teaching that there is one God, who created the world, rules it in accordance with moral law, and has delivered this law to mankind through a revealer. Receiving on the other hand the independent tradition of philosophy, transmitted to them through the latest Neo-Platonists, for whom Aristotle had become the master of the sciences, they found in the philosopher a theology with characters distinguishing it from all the religions. Aristotle's God was indeed one, as against polytheism, but he was not a creator or legislator; and the philosopher's ethics, dealing rationally with the ends of action, presented itself as something independent of command and obedience. Its culmination was a life resembling that of the Deity, in as much as it was a thinking on thought; but this divine life was evidently attainable only by a few, and by them not always. Perhaps from Aristotle's own phrase about the adaptation of some ideas transmitted through popular religion "to the persuasion of the multitude", they arrived at their own revolutionary idea for facing the intolerant theocracies which had since come into the world. Their effectively new thesis was a clear-cut rejection (stated in peculiar terms) of the claim of popular religion, even in the forms that were professedly the most purified from heathenism, to be a mode of truth in distinction from utility. Ostensibly they spoke of a "double truth", philosophical on the one side and theological on the other; but by theology (as contained in the religions) they meant simply the legislation, as they called it, useful for those who lived under it, of Moses, Christ or Mohammed as the case might be. Their own philosophical doctrine was not that of a moral God who had appointed rewards and punishments for obedience or disobedience to His law. For them, pure speculative reason was the highest, and they found it in their interpretation of Aristotle; but, while pursuing philosophic truth, they were ready to be conformists in religion. All the legislations, they said, were alike good for those who had been brought up under them, in so far as they contained ethical precepts similar to those of philosophy, though necessarily practised by the many as an affair of custom and obedience, not of insight.

Of course the official representatives of the revealed religions, when they had the power, could not allow the distinction between two kinds of truth, stated in this form. It was too obviously an evasion of their claims to rule in the names of their lawgivers. By the end of the twelfth century, the Mohammedan clergy, by bringing popular pressure to bear on the Caliphs who out of interest in culture had hitherto supported the philosophers, compelled the withdrawal of toleration. The martyrdom of the philosophers under Islam indeed did not go beyond exile; but their writings, so far as they were properly philosophical and in a religious sense free-thinking, and did not limit themselves to special sciences such as medicine or astronomy, passed into oblivion for their own world.

The torch, however, was handed on to the Christian West through translation into Latin not only of the Arabic versions of Aristotle but of the infidel commentators themselves; and, just when the Church had apparently extinguished the religious heresies of the twelfth century, its chiefs found themselves confronted with a much larger body of ancient thought than had been accessible since the closing of the schools at Athens and the overwhelming of the West by the barbarian invasions. Some credit must be allowed them for deciding to permit the new movement under limits and not simply to crush it out. The Averroist distinction of the double truth was of course officially condemned; but the phrase, as Renan has pointed out, served from the thirteenth to the seventeenth century as some protection for free thought; and the notion of the separation of theology and philosophy in the sense of the Averroists did not become obsolete until in modern times toleration of a variety of sects within the State had become a definite principle and policy. This policy itself could probably not have been formulated without the preparation for it in the thought of the Middle Ages and the Renaissance.

The claim to liberty of philosophising by Giordano Bruno and Spinoza is in fact more deep-going than the carefully guarded and limited permission to a few not too heterodox sects to exist, which was all that even the most liberal political legislation was able to carry through for a time. And the almost identical positions of Bruno and Spinoza on the relations between philosophy and theology came to them from Averroism. In positive doctrine, indeed, neither of them can be called an Averroist; for they did not hold the distinctive view of the Arabians put forth as an interpretation of Aristotle's utterances about the active and the potential intellect; though traces of it lingered on in both. The distinction, however, between philosophy and theology, evolved to defend one heterodoxy, was capable of being turned to the defence of heterodoxy in general; and it could not be more generalised than it was by Bruno first and then by Spinoza.

No doubt the *Tractatus Theologico-Politicus* is far more systematic than anything in its kind that had gone before; but in its fundamental distinction between the many who live by a law formulated in books or in the creeds of a Church and the few who live by insight, it does not deviate from the positions of the Arabians or of a thinker of the early Renaissance like Pomponazzi. Where it is modern is in its definite foundation of Biblical criticism and in its appeal to the State as distinguished from the representatives of theology. Even Bruno, for example, in the late sixteenth century, could still appeal for recognition of the liberty of philosophising to those whom he called the not less learned than religious theologians. He had received his answer from the theologians of the Holy Office. Spinoza, proceeding on this side from Hobbes, argued for the sole right of the civil power to determine what shall be taught or not be taught on religion, and went beyond Hobbes in explicitly declaring that the liberty of philosophising is not only advantageous to the commonwealth but is indispensable to its safety and welfare. Having made this perfectly clear, he was ready to show that the Scriptures, Hebrew and Christian, if rightly interpreted, and if things belonging merely to the time and the particular views of the writers are set aside, furnish a basis for an ethical theism which the State may adopt as official, leaving philosophers free to seek deeper insight than is possible for those who follow the moral law merely through obedience to legislators whether civil or religious. Of the freedom thus claimed he made the fullest use in the *Ethics*. The link, which at the same time indicates the contrast, between the two treatises, may be found in *Eth.* ii. Prop. 3, Schol.: "Nemo ea quae volo percipere recte poterit, nisi magnopere caveat, ne Dei potentiam cum humana regum potentia vel iure confundat." For popular religion, even when most purified, moral precepts are divine commands obeyed in view of rewards and punishments. For speculative philosophy, divine commands (if the expression may be used) and necessity of nature are one and the same; and the whole of nature cannot be interpreted as adapted to the purposes of man; whose utility is indeed the measure in determining rational precepts for his own conduct, but does not enable the mind to infer what are the laws of that Nature which is greater than man and includes him as a small part. Nature in this sense and God are identical; and, when we have attained this view, we shall no longer reproach even the weaknesses and absurdities of men, since now they are seen as no less illustrating the power of nature, if not of man, than the things which we admire and in the contemplation of which we take delight (*Eth.* iv. Prop. 57, Schol.).

But here another question arises. Is not the content of the great philosophical systems religious in its own manner? It has at least this in common with the religions, that it goes beyond facts and laws of phenomena to a view of the whole which is not verifiable in the terms of science and common sense. And in detail we find a doctrine like Spinoza's in some respects coincident with that of philosophers who took themselves to be orthodox theologians. One of the most audaciously naturalistic propositions in the *Ethics* (Part iv. Prop. 68), by which it is affirmed that for the free man, who has adequate ideas, the words "good" and "evil" would have no meaning, has been found to be taken over from Maimonides, who in the twelfth century set himself, with a full knowledge of what had been done by the Arabians, to rationalise Jewish orthodoxy on the basis of Platonic and Aristotelian philosophy. For, according to Maimonides, the story of man's innocence before the Fall signifies that the knowledge of good and evil is not a knowledge of the nature of things as they really are. Spinoza himself, it may be noted, does not disdain to continue the use of the story as symbol; adding to it an interpretation of redemption by the spirit of Christ as a setting free of men from the illusion signified by the Fall. And he could easily have found other precedents in ostensibly orthodox mediaeval thinkers, Jewish or Christian; who often in effect use the sacred stories as no more than images of truth. Even in the most modern times, we may add, no thinker can altogether dispense with myth and legend to give colour. For myth and legend are creations of the human mind; and logic does not create, as science does not complete its work without imaginative extension. Thus, all things considered, we need have no difficulty in admitting that the great philosophies and the great religions at their highest point have much in common. And in no philosopher is there less difficulty in finding the point of contact with religious minds than in Spinoza; whose end, above the moral virtues, is essentially that of the mystics—the contemplative life.

It seems to be now ascertained that the first definite affirmation that the theoretic life is the highest began in Greece with the philosophico-religious school of the Pythagoreans. This affirmation was accepted by Plato, though at the same time he argued that contemplative minds ought to be compelled by the State, in its own interests, to descend to the government of practical affairs. The most typical form, perhaps, was given to the doctrine by Aristotle, who thought that the supreme value of the State itself was in making possible this highest life. From Plato and Aristotle, with shades of difference, the general view passed on to Plotinus and his successors, and thence, after finding expression in the writings of mediaeval mystics, was taken over into Christian orthodoxy as wrought out dialectically by St Thomas Aquinas and embodied artistically in Dante's *Paradiso*. Now this strain of thought, through both Jewish and Christian sources, arrived at Spinoza in the text-books he read in his youth; as was shown by Freudenthal in his epoch-making essay, *Spinoza und die Scholastik.* (This appeared in 1887 in a collection of Philosophical Essays dedicated to Eduard Zeller: see the remarks of Dr Carl Gebhardt in his obituary notice of Jacob Freudenthal in the *Chronicon Spinozanum*, ii.) In view, therefore, of now demonstrated facts, the schematic construction by which Spinoza's system was treated as simply a necessary development from Descartes, to which the latter part of the *Ethics* might be regarded as an addendum, is completely exploded. The end at which he aimed had been fixed in his own mind before he came in contact with Descartes and modern science. Profoundly as his mature system was influenced by the mathematico-physical ideal of scientific knowledge set up by the great French thinker, the search for the method of discovering truth in the sciences, or the promotion of natural knowledge, was not his ultimate aim. He could honour not only Descartes but Bacon and English devotees of experiment like Boyle; but for him their distinctive work was only an aid to philosophic insight. His ultimate aim was nothing less than an intuition of absolute truth concerning the whole. Since this intuition, in his philosophy, carried with it emotional acquiescence, it may be said that for Spinoza, more than for any other modern, philosophy became a religion.

Usually he does not himself call it religion, but places it beyond "religion and piety" in the ordinary sense of the terms. For these are, in his view as in that of the Averroists, something practicable by mankind in general without speculative philosophy. (See *Eth.* v. Prop. 41.) The practical virtues associated with religion, he expressly says, retain all their value for the utility of life even if there is nothing beyond them. But for him, as for the mystics, there is something beyond.

It has been disputed whether Spinoza himself was a mystic. If the state of the mystic is a peculiar experience attained by shutting off all grades of articulate knowledge, he was not a mystic; for the highest grade of insight which he deems attainable includes a kind of knowledge. His mysticism, if it is to be called such, is the accompaniment of definite thought, and is nowhere said to be incommunicable. Yet its historical relation to what has always been regarded as typical mysticism is undeniable; and its relation to the similar, but not identical, culminating point of the philosophy of Bruno confirms the derivation. Bruno, too, has the "intellectual love", though in him it takes the form rather of infinite aspiration (as he himself calls it) than of acquiescence in insight attained. By Bruno also it is not identified with moral virtue, and not brought under the head of religion, which he, too, associates with practice. These resemblances, both in language and in thought, there does not seem to be any sufficient reason for attributing to a direct influence of Bruno on Spinoza. They are perfectly explicable by common sources. Ultimately the spring of the conception of intellectual love in all its forms was Neo-Platonism. Bruno knew the sources in the actual works of the Neo-Platonists; reading Plotinus no doubt in the Latin translation of Marsilio Ficino, which appeared long before the Greek text was printed. (In 1580, when it appeared, Bruno had left Italy and was on his travels.) In common with Spinoza, he was familiar with the intermediate phases. Both philosophers had read the Cabbalists. Above all, there can be no doubt that both had read the *Dialoghi d'Amore* of Leone Ebreo. The excerpts given by Dr Carl Gebhardt (*Chronicon Spinozanum*, i) entirely confirm the inference drawn in the brief study of B. Zimmels (*Leo Hebraeus, ein jüdischer Philosoph der Renaissance*, 1886; see *Mind*, O.S. xi. 593). The phrases indicating both the ultimate sources of Leo himself and his influence as a precursor can be given in small compass. But first, it seems worth while to mention a few cases of coincidence which may warn us against rash inferences of direct borrowing. The real evidence of relationship will then seem all the more conclusive.

If we did not know that Bruno (as also Spinoza) cannot have read John Scotus Erigena, whose works were condemned to the flames by Pope Honorius III in 1225 and had passed out of sight till 1681, the case for direct influence would be very strong. For Erigena and Bruno quote the same lines of Virgil, and the same verse of the same psalm, to exactly the same philosophic purpose; namely, to enforce their own positions as regards the immanence of the world-spirit and the coincidence of contraries. Again, in the time of Shelley, Bruno's works were inaccessible except in a few scattered copies, and it is unlikely that the poet had met with any of them; yet the well-known metaphors in which the moth and the flame represent the lover and the beloved, and Actaeon and his hounds figure intellectual love, are conspicuous in the *Eroici Furori*. The hounds of Actaeon, in Bruno as in Shelley, are interpreted as his own thoughts, of which he is at once the father and the prey. Thus, in even so remarkable a coincidence between Bruno and Spinoza as the following, I do not think we need see anything more than coincidence. The love of divine things, Bruno finds (*Eroici Furori*, Part i. Dial. 5, 13), is not without affliction in desire, any more than the physical love described by the Epicurean poet (*i.e.*, Lucretius); and hence perhaps the wise Hebrew said that he that increaseth knowledge increaseth sorrow. Similarly Spinoza, quoting the same saying from *Ecclesiastes* (*Eth.* iv. Prop. 17, Schol.), uses it to illustrate the weakness of human nature, with which true knowledge has to struggle and by which it may be overpowered. Not, he adds (as Bruno does also), that folly is better than wisdom.

The case for the influence of Neo-Platonism is of a different kind. There are certain crystallised expressions that sum up the whole conception of intellectual love in the same pantheistic sense; and these we find emerging and re-emerging from late antiquity to the Renaissance. We also know in a general way the literary continuity (sometimes along side-paths) of the philosophy of the Middle Ages and the Renaissance with the last phase of Greek philosophy. Now the final expression, *amor intellectualis*, fixed by Spinoza, is evidently the νοῦς ἐρῶν of Plotinus. Leone Ebreo, whose dates are given as approximately 1460–1463 to 1520–1535, had no doubt read the Latin translation of the *Enneads* by Marsilio Ficino, which appeared in 1492. In him we find *amore intellettivo* and *amore intellettuale.* Of these Bruno took over the former and Spinoza the latter. Again, when Leo says: "il primo amore si è di Dio a sè stesso", and, with more circumstance, "in lui l' amante, e l' amato, e il medesimo amore è tutto una cosa" (Excerpts 119, 120), this corresponds to the words of Plotinus (*Enn.* vi. 8, 15): *καὶ ἐράσμιον καὶ ἔρως ὁ αὐτὸς καὶ αὑτοῦ ἔρως.* The position of Leo that the intellectual love is not a natural passion but an intellectual action, is of course that of Spinoza; and to this there is a corresponding expression in Proclus: *ὁ μὲν θεῖος ἔρως ἐνέργειά ἐστιν* (*Comm. in Alcib. I*). In the intermediate period we find a most decisive witness to the identity of the tradition in John Scotus Erigena: *Caritas in omnibus Deum, id est, se ipsam, diligit* (*De Praedestinatione*, iii. 6). By this the saying of Plotinus given above is linked in the long historical series (though Erigena did not know Plotinus directly and Spinoza did not know Erigena) with the well-known proposition of Spinoza (*Eth.* v. Prop. 35) that "God loves himself with an infinite intellectual love". Such coincidences are evidently not merely incidental, but point to definite origins; though of course the juxtaposition would be most misleading if we did not bear in mind that inherited philosophical expressions, when worked into the tissue of a doctrine, belong anew to each great thinker as his own.

This is illustrated by the very different developments in the *Eroici Furori* and in the Fifth Part of the *Ethics.* In Bruno they take a poetic form comparable to that of the *Vita Nuova,* which was undoubtedly his literary model. For Dante, indeed, there is a personal object of devotion, at least imaginary, while Bruno avowedly uses the imagery of lovers (and occasionally actual love-poems of his elder Neapolitan contemporary Tansillo, who is an interlocutor in the Dialogues) to communicate the idea of aspiration to intellectual beauty and ultimate truth. This is in complete contrast to Spinoza, who, with all his underlying depth of emotion, nevertheless reduces everything to the rigour of quasi-geometrical demonstration. Moreover, as has been hinted, there is a difference in the type of intellectual love described; which in Spinoza may be said to reach the phase of beatitude, or acquiescence in the knowledge of its object, while in Bruno it remains an infinite pursuit of the infinite. For in the rare cases where he speaks of the desire as achieved, it seems to end in martyrdom (of which he had a strange prevision) or in an absorption of sense and imagination "like a drop of water or a breath in the immensity of the sea or of the spacious air" (Part ii. Dial. 1, 12). This, however, is not strict doctrine. For Bruno, as for Neo-Platonism, there is in reality neither emergence from a ground nor re-absorption into it. And here, as we shall see later, Spinoza is at one with Bruno and the Neo-Platonists. By Bruno and Spinoza alike, the intellectual love is formally distinguished from religion; though with Bruno it seems occasionally to pass into religion in his own sense of a kind of ethical Stoicism. Incidentally he vindicates Epicureanism as having essentially the same end. Epicurus did not teach what the vulgar suppose, but held that the perfection of virtue is to attain impassibility, or even actual beatitude, in endurance (Part i. Dial. 5, 9). Moral virtue and divine or heroic love, according to Bruno's interpretation of Epicurus, are imperfect unless a feeling of happiness has been joined to them which no evil is able to take away. "That beauty, goodness and truth which is the fountain of all other truth, goodness, beauty" (Part ii. Dial. 1, 9) is to be so pursued that the mind, knowing the vicissitudes of mortal things, shall feel for them neither love nor hate (Part ii. Dial. 1, 4). This has an obvious affinity with some expressions of Spinoza; and in Spinoza also, though, as has been said, the intellectual love of God is usually distinguished from religion, there are passages where an approximation may be observed; as for example in *Eth.* iv. Prop. 37, Schol. 1: *quicquid cupimus et agimus, cuius causa sumus, quatenus Dei habemus ideam, sive quatenus Deum cognoscimus, ad religionem refero.*

Philosophically, Bruno's theory of the individual mind or soul in which the intellectual love comes to consciousness is less determinate than Spinoza's. There is indeed for him one certainty. Soul or form is as much substance as body or matter, and substance is imperishable. He quotes with conviction the lines of Ovid's *Metamorphoses* in which the poet affirms the intangibility of the soul by the accidents of death and dissolution: *morte carent animae.* But, for the rest, he does not definitely choose any one expression of his conviction. He can admit the general human mind of the Averroists as one term in a hierarchy; but he does not therefore deny the permanence of the individual soul as such. This he usually seems to imagine as thrown after death into the hazards of metempsychosis and forgetting its past life; yet, near the end of the Dialogues, he introduces an argument for a disembodied condition of the soul, or at least for an immortality more strictly personal, from its aspiration to a vision which it does not now possess, but which may be achieved "in a more excellent state" (Part ii. Dial. 4). When he says that the human intellect has infinite potency because it is eternal (Part i. Dial. 5, 12), he means the individual human mind and not the mind of the race.

In the case of Spinoza's eternity of the mind, whatever may be the obscurity of the conception otherwise, no doubt ought to be felt that what is meant is the individual mind. Of the general, or common, human mind of the Averroists there are indeed one or two reminiscences which I had overlooked till they were pointed out. With *Eth.* ii. Axiom 1, may be compared the more explicit statement in *Eth.* i. Prop. 17, Schol.: *Si unius existentia pereat, non ideo alterius peribit; sed si unius essentia destrui posset et fieri falsa, destrueretur etiam alterius essentia.* Yet he classes the notion of "man" as universal among ideas in the highest degree confused (*Eth.* ii. Prop. 40, Schol. 1); and, in the definitive doctrine of the Fifth Part, the *mens* which is eternal is the mind correlated with a particular body, and therefore unquestionably an individual mind.

The doctrine as it is set forth cannot by any means be modernised into Comte's "subjective immortality", or later theories, on the lines of this, which are sometimes described by the phrase "conservation of values". According to this type of theory, an achievement of one mind is preserved in the memory of others and then stored up in the social tradition, and so becomes part of a common treasury of thoughts and records of deeds done for humanity. Thus, in terms of Comte's doctrine, a mind that has disappeared objectively (that is to say, from the sum of things actually in the world) lives on subjectively in other minds after the physical death of the individual. Now there is no doubt that such a process does go on socially; and there is a recognition of it in the *Ethics* as rightly a source of mental satisfaction. Like Hobbes, Spinoza did not regard fame as illusory. *Gloria*, he says (*Eth.* iv. Prop. 58), *rationi non repugnat sed ab ea oriri potest.* To take pleasure in reputation, that is to say, can have a good sense when distinguished from "vainglory". In its good sense *gloria* is defined as "joy accompanied by the idea of some action of ours which we imagine that others praise" (*Eth.* iii. Affect. def. 30). Thus the element of satisfaction in the conviction of a thinker that his thought will be recognised as serviceable to the human race would not have been disdained by the philosopher who was himself one of the very small number of illustrious minds that we might suppose to have perhaps got beyond Milton's "last infirmity". This, however, was certainly not what Spinoza meant by the eternity of the mind. For eternity, as he understands it, is something beyond time, even when time is conceived as an illimitable future; which, in the case of human fame, it cannot be, as Cicero, who was as little as any man of letters indifferent to reputation with posterity, had shown in the *Somnium Scipionis*—a relic of antiquity probably well known to Spinoza.

The doctrine of the eternity of the mind, as developed in the Fifth Part of the *Ethics*, when reduced to the minimum of significance, may be stated thus. Every human mind is the correlate, in the attribute of Thought, of the body, or mode of Extension, of which that mind is the "idea". The existence of the body under certain conditions of time and space implies an essence not thus conditioned. Now this means that it is eternally true that if such and such a body exists, or has existed, or will exist, there is a necessary determination that it should be such and such. (How the body can remain the same while undergoing physical changes is explained in the Lemmas after Prop. 13 of Part ii.) When the mind, or mode of Thought correlated with that body, understands, not by mere experience nor even by reasoning, but by the intuition which finally emerges from reasoning and which is the third kind of knowledge, the eternal necessity that that body should be what it is in essence, there is a knowledge for that mind which is timeless and known as timeless. This eternal truth, known as eternal, is the essence of the individual mind. The insight being *sub specie aeternitatis*, there can be no question either of its coming to exist in time or ceasing to exist. The popular dictrine of the immortality of the soul, Spinoza expressly says, is not, as commonly held—that is, as referring to perpetual duration of an existence in time—philosophically true, but it contains a divination of the truth. In terms that are more Neo-Platonic than his own, but are not inconsistent with his fundamental thought, all have in themselves this eternal essence, but few make use of it. In his own words at the close of the *Ethics*: *Omnia praeclara tam difficilia, quam rara sunt.*

This is the minimum; but various things that Spinoza says show that the meaning, for himself, amounted to more than the minimum. For example: "The human mind cannot be absolutely destroyed with the body, but something of it remains, which is eternal" (*Eth.* v. Prop. 23). The mind is subject to passive affections, as distinguished from the intellectual love which is an action, only while the body endures (*Eth.* v. Prop. 34). There is nothing in nature which can take away the intellectual love (*Eth.* v. Prop. 37); whereas, when man is considered as a part of nature, the causes outside him far surpass in power the causes within him (*Eth.* iv. Prop. 3; cf. Appendix, cap. 32). Considered as a mode of thinking, as distinguished from imagining—that is, apart from the body, through which images arise—the human mind (by which is meant each individual human mind) is an eternal mode of the infinite intellect of God (*Eth.* v. Prop. 40, Schol.).

Knowledge of this eternity, with acquiescence in the knowledge, we are told, is attainable, and when it is attained the greater and better part of the mind does not perish with the body (*Eth.* v. Prop. 38; cf. Prop. 40, Coroll.). It is to this part that the *amor Dei intellectualis* belongs, and this love is eternal (*Eth.* v. Prop. 33), being a part of the infinite intellectual love with which God loves himself (*Eth.* v. Prop. 36).

Since acquiescence in the knowledge is beatitude, it follows that Spinoza had arrived at the conviction that in some sense the individual human mind may attain conscious eternal beatitude. It is clear, however, that in his view only few minds attain it; and there has always remained the difficulty that not all the subtleties of the exposition seem to make it quite compatible with the strict parallelism of the attributes of Thought and Extension.

It is not merely in the Fifth Part that the divergence appears. Turning back to Part ii, we find a similar difficulty arising within the complex doctrine of the *idea mentis* or *idea ideae* (Props. 20, 21). There is an idea of the mind, as the mind is the idea of the body; and this, we learn, is introspective knowledge, knowing that one knows (Prop. 21, Schol.). And, although it is said that "the idea of the mind and the mind itself are one and the same thing, conceived under one and the same attribute, namely, Thought"; or, as it is explained, if we know, we also know that we know; it is not made evident how there can be anything in the attribute of Extension to correspond to this duplication and reduplication in introspective knowledge. Body, Proclus said, cannot turn back upon itself, the whole to the whole; and Spinoza does not try to prove that it can. His own thought, finally expressed, is, as we have seen, that the best part of the human mind is transcendent to the human body. And in all this, it must be repeated (as others have said before), there is no accommodation to popular beliefs. So severe is the philosophical attitude that it seems almost incongruous to mention the absence of all play of fancy regarding the mind as manifested in time; though, in strict theory, this need not have been excluded; for it does not seem to follow, from the positive part of the doctrine, that each individual mind has only one embodied existence in the course of everlasting time. All that can be said is that eternal essence, in Spinoza's sense, does not necessarily involve more than one temporal embodiment. But this it undoubtedly involves, since there cannot be an essence without something of which it is the essence (*Eth.* ii. def. 2); and, since each thing is one, conceived under the two attributes, how is it permissible, within the doctrine, to set one of the two aspects free, as it were, from its concomitant? Was not Leibniz, having borrowed the parallelism from Spinoza, more logical in asserting successive re-embodiments of the minds or souls which he supposes to go on? Spinoza understood by the essence of the human body, not a particular collocation of particles, but a certain mode of order continuous amid the flux of its parts. Why should this mode not be repeated in new collocations corresponding to new temporal manifestations of the eternal mode that is the mind?

This is arguable; but to follow it out would be to depart from Spinoza's system. Within that system, it seems to me that we have come upon a difficulty not wholly soluble in its own terms, but profoundly suggestive in relation to the future of philosophy. Careful students of the *Ethics* have pointed out that it does not begin, like Descartes' *Principia,* with even a slight outline of theory of knowledge, but plunges directly into what we call, in the opposite use of the term to Spinoza's, an objective deduction of the order of the universe from the nature of Reality. Now the predominant movement of distinctively modern philosophy from Descartes to Kant has been in theory of knowledge. Descartes began by inquiring what is left if we set ourselves to doubt everything. His answer was that primary certainty is on the side of what we now call subjective thought. He was, however, too eager to proceed to the task of constituting scientific knowledge to delay long over what Aristotle had called first philosophy; and the importance of Descartes' influence on Spinoza consisted mainly in furnishing a model and a basis for the sure knowledge of nature in mathematical physics. Locke turned back to preliminary questions about the power of the mind to know; and the succession was continued through Leibniz (in the *Nouveaux Essais*) on the one side, and on the other side through Berkeley and Hume, to Kant's three *Critiques.* Hence it is not surprising that the later world, going back to the *Ethics* for inspiration on ultimate questions about the universe, should, in the light of analysis carried on for more than a century, find clefts in such a pre-eminently synthetic construction. The remarkable thing rather is that Spinoza himself, following out his direct synthetic method in the rigorous manner of a schoolman, should in the course of his demonstrations raise the subtlest questions as to what we now call the relation between subject and object; which were really easier to state in the syllogistic method of the schoolmen themselves than by the quasi-geometrical method first adopted by him as a means of expounding not his own philosophy but the philosophy of Descartes.

To understand the position more fully, we must turn to the other element of transcendence in Spinoza's system. The two elements are in reality closely connected; for the eternity of the mind reveals in the case of the microcosm precisely what the infinite attributes reveal in the case of the macrocosm; namely, that Spinoza's ultimate doctrine leans by its intrinsic nature to the idealistic as distinguished from the naturalistic side.

His naturalism has indeed been thought to be the completest possible; and it is true that his originality as compared with his ancient and mediaeval precursors nowhere comes out more distinctly than in his grasp of the mechanicist view of nature as prefigured by one side of Descartes' system. Here he made an immense advance on Descartes himself; for the parallelism of the attributes of Thought and Extension is not Descartes' own doctrine, though it was suggested by it. Descartes held that there are two substances, extended substance and thinking substance, which must be conceived as different in kind and yet as interacting. Both were created by divine volition and cannot continue without it. They are therefore not substances in the sense in which we say that God is Substance. Within the Cartesian school the nature of the interaction between the two substances, and even its possibility, raised endless problems. These Spinoza seemed to have effectively got rid of at a stroke by recognising only one Substance, which is God, and putting in place of extended things and thinking things the conception of these as modes of the two attributes of Extension and Thought. Each thing in nature can be regarded as a single thing with two sides; at once an extended thing marked off from other portions of Extension, and a thinking thing because every portion of Extension has a portion of Thought correlated with it. Between the modes of one attribute and the modes of the other there is no interaction. Everything that appears to us as body is in its degree animated (*Eth.* ii. Prop. 13, Schol.); and the causal series on the side of the animation of the universe is as unbroken as the mathematico-mechanical sequence that might be traced out by a completed physical science on the side of body.

In dismissing interaction, it may be incidentally observed, Spinoza got rid of a serious psychological error of the Cartesian system. He denies, and gives conclusive reasons for denying, the antithesis of Descartes between will which is infinite and intellect which is finite (*Eth.* ii. Prop. 49, Schol.). Any kind of infinity that may be ascribed to the will can be affirmed also of intellect if intellect is taken in the widest sense. Here there is a coincidence with Bruno, who asserted the infinity of both intellect and will. "Non è terminato (he says in the *Argument* prefixed to the *Eroici Furori*) l' atto de la volontà circa il bene, come è infinito et interminabile l' atto de la cognizione circa il vero."

So impressively was the doctrine of parallelism stated that in the nineteenth century it almost, but not quite, became scientific orthodoxy. Its fascination was in an apparent clearness for which physical science has less care since, for mathematicians, algebraical symbolism has tended to efface geometrical intuition. At present the whole question is again highly controversial; and it is interesting to note that from within Spinoza's system there arose certain puzzles which he could not solve to the complete satisfaction of sympathetic students in his own time.

The great difficulty with which he was confronted did not arise within each attribute, but in the relation of Thought first to Extension and then to the infinite attributes; which include Thought and Extension as the two known to us. That there should be more attributes than those that we know (whatever those may be) was a deduction from the notion of Substance if it was allowed to have attributes. For God as Substance, it was affirmed in the inherited philosophical theology, is infinite, and this infinity is absolute. The conception of absolute infinity, then, being applied to any question raised about the attributes, there seemed to be no reason for stopping short at any finite number (*Eth.* i. Prop. 10, Schol.). Of necessity the progression had been the same for the Greek as for the Hebrew monotheistic idea when it passed over into pantheism. It is by exactly the same type of reasoning that Melissus, in the Eleatic school, and Spinoza, proceeding from Scholasticism and Descartes, prove the mutual implication of unity and infinity in that which is ultimately real. The only difference between *Eth.* i. Prop. 8 and Melissus, Fr. 6, is that Spinoza proves the infinity of Substance from its unity and Melissus the unity of Being, or that which is, from its infinity: εἰ γὰρ εἴη, ἓν εἴη ἄν· εἰ γὰρ δύο εἴη, οὐκ ἂν δύναιτο ἄπειρα εἶναι, ἀλλ' ἔχοι ἂν πείρατα πρὸς ἄλληλα. Now these are equally in both cases propositions about Deity stated in technical language. Poetically, but probably on the basis of some pre-existent philosophical theology, transcendence together with immanence had already been asserted by Aeschylus: "Zeus is all things and what is beyond them."

But can attributes not known to us have any meaning conceivable by us? This question was most acutely raised by Spinoza's friend and correspondent Tschirnhaus. The correspondence has been found rather tantalising; but I think there is, in the concluding fragment of a letter from Spinoza (Ep. 68, Bruder), not indeed a solution in terms of the system as it stands, but a clear indication of the predominantly idealistic character of the doctrine. For it appears from the letter that, when pressed, Spinoza was obliged to affirm that there is not simply an infinity of ideas corresponding to the infinity of the attribute of Extension, but that each of the other attributes must be conceived as having infinite "ideas or minds" of its own. Thus, if we follow the train of reasoning to its logical conclusion, we must suppose the attribute of Extension to be the basis of one phenomenal world, namely, our own world of ideas; while the attribute of Thought (or animation) contains also infinite other worlds of phenomena correlated with the other attributes; and so is infinitely infinite as contrasted with the simple infinity of each attribute other than Thought. Now mathematico-mechanical method is directly applicable only to Extension; hence the order of things which it presents to us seems to shrink into complete subordination to absolute or universal Thought, which is as boundless as the whole of Reality, since everything that exists, whether known or unknown to us, has necessarily its expression in some idea or mind.

This, as we know, did not become Spinoza's actual teaching. The structure of the *Ethics* was not modified by the criticism. And his conviction is fundamental that mathematical method gives an insight into reality which nothing else can give. Without it, truth would have remained for ever concealed from the human race, and the illusion of final causes would never have been seen through (cf. Appendix to Part i). Beyond the effort by which each individual thing strives to preserve its being (*suum esse conservare conatur*) there is nothing in the universe that can be called teleology; and this also, no doubt, according to Spinoza's general philosophy ought to be capable ultimately of resolution into mathematico-mechanical necessity. What his doctrine might have been if he had lived earlier or later than the seventeenth century we cannot tell. We can but say that his pantheism was, in its actual statement, neither that of a Platonist of the Renaissance nor of a modern Evolutionist. Its distinctive form is traceable directly to Descartes (*Principia Philosophiae*, iii. §§ 2, 3) who (in this agreeing with the non-mathematical Bacon) laid down the rule that we are not to presume to explain the unknown by imagined purposes of God. Descartes himself was decidedly a theist without any perceptible tinge of pantheism; but, while not denying final causes, he treats it as extremely improbable that all things in the universe were designed for the sake of man; and the imagination that they are thus designed became for Spinoza the very type of the delusion that had set the human mind for ages on the wrong track. Now we may protest that the mechanical model of explanation, when taken as absolute and applied to the cosmos, is shown by modern theory of knowledge to have no ultimate theoretical validity; and that the profoundly impressive passages in which Spinoza identifies universal necessity with mathematico-mechanical determination, like similar passages in Lucretius founded on the obsolete Epicurean physics, while they belong to the permanently great things in literature, are not verifiable science. Yet, when all has been said, there was in both cases an immense liberation. For the most stringent exclusion of all purpose from nature delivers the moralist most completely from what has been called the naturalistic fallacy. If ends in nature are denied, human life is left to be determined by the ideals of humanity. The precept "Follow nature", if this means the nature that is external to man, conceived not as fact or uniformity but as a power issuing commands, becomes, for any one who has really understood Spinoza, the fallacy of trying to turn "is" into "ought". For those who, starting with that effort to preserve themselves which is the basis of virtue, live according to reason, the ultimate end becomes the common good of mankind. As he shows by calm analysis of the affections, the *conatus* by which everyone aims at self-conservation is fulfilled not by hate and discord but by love and concord. And it is interesting to note that, in exemption from the fallacy of taking non-human nature for a preceptress (thus providing arguments for Edmund in *King Lear*, or for the actual Archelaus of Macedonia as viewed by his theoretical admirers in Plato's *Gorgias*), he is at one with his great pantheistic precursors, teleologists though they were in their manner. Perfection in his own kind is the aim of man for himself, but not to go beyond the kind (*Eth.* iv. Praefatio). This is also a thought of Nicholas of Cusa. Similarly Bruno says that to cease to be of its kind is for any being the thing most feared: as gods most fear to lose their identity as gods (*Giove sommamente teme di non esser Giove*), so the horse most fears to cease to be a horse (*Spaccio della Bestia Trionfante*, Dial. 1); a thought for which the reason, agreeing with that of Bruno, is given by Spinoza: *equus namque ex. gr. tam destruitur, si in hominem, quam si in insectum mutetur.* Suicide (as Schopenhauer also says) always proceeds from causes external to the self. Self-destruction can never be directly an end. As an event its occurrence can be explained: *At quod homo ex necessitate suae naturae conetur non existere vel in aliam formam mutari, tam est impossibile, quam quod ex nihilo aliquid fiat* (*Eth.* iv. Prop. 20, Schol.).

But this does not mean that in man any more than in nature all degrees of reality are equal. No one has more definitely insisted that to have more varied powers of perceiving, imagining and acting is to be higher in the scale of being. While "the highest good of those who follow virtue is common to all, and all can equally enjoy it" (*Eth.* iv. Prop. 36), there are many kinds of bodily and mental culture of which the attainment can be approved though they are not the highest. Spinoza would have agreed with Bruno, and on the same ground, that to arrive at a level is not the ideal of humanity. Since there are degrees in the mind, says Bruno (*Eroici Furori*, Part ii. Dial. 2), the order of things should not be so perverted "che al fine succeda certa neutralità, e bestiale equalità, quale si ritrova in certe deserte et inculte republiche". Though few live according to the dictate of reason, says Spinoza (*Eth.* iv. Prop. 35, Schol.), yet from the actual order of society, adapted to ordinary human nature, more advantages than evils result; so that human civilised life is to be preferred in every way to that of brutes. As indications for the conduct of the individual life, two sentences sum up his attitude. "Things are in so far good as they help man to enjoy the life of the mind, which is defined by intelligence" (*Eth.* iv. Appendix, cap. 5). "The things that happen to us in opposition to that which the consideration of our utility demands, we shall bear with equal mind, if we are conscious that we have performed what belongs to us (*si conscii simus nos functos nostro officio fuisse*) and that the power we possess could not have extended itself so far as to enable us to avoid them" (cap. 32). For, as Spinoza adds in Stoic vein, we are parts of the whole of nature and have to follow; and when our better part, which is intelligence, understands this, it will acquiesce and seek to persevere in its acquiescence.

INDEX OF NAMES

DATE

DEC 1 6 '75	
GAYLORD	